Modern Critical Interpretations

Modern Critical Interpretations

Toni Morrison's
The Bluest Eye

Edited and with an introduction by
Harold Bloom
Sterling Professor of the Humanities
Yale University

CHELSEA HOUSE PUBLISHERS
Philadelphia

Printed and bound in the United States of America

10 9 8 7 6 5 4 3

∞ The paper used in this publication meets the minimum
requirements of the American National Standard for
Permanence of Paper for Printed Library Materials,
Z39.48-1984

Library of Congress Cataloging-in-Publication Data

Toni Morrison's The Bluest Eye / edited and with an
introduction by Harold Bloom.
        p.   cm. — (Modern critical interpretations)
    Includes biographical references and index.
    ISBN 0-7910-5191-9 (hc)
    1. Morrison, Toni. —Bluest eye.   2. Afro-Americans
in literature.   3. Girls in literature.   4. Ohio—In
literature. I. Bloom, Harold.   II. Series.
PS3563.08749B55   1999
813'.54—dc21   98–53872
                                          CIP

Contributing Editor: Tenley Williams

Contents

Editor's Note

My Introduction is a brief tribute to the aesthetic universalism of *The Bluest Eye*, a narrative perpetually fresh and not freighted with ideologies.

I am grateful to Tenley Williams for assistance in editing this volume.

Keith E. Byerman begins the chronological sequence of criticism by observing that the grotesque in *The Bluest Eye* essentially is societal, after which Madonne M. Miner finds a tragic version of the myths of Philomela and of Persephone in the rape of Pecola. Tragedy is again invoked by Stephanie A. Demetrakopoulos, who finds *The Bluest Eye* to be a triumph of compassion.

Black childhood is stressed as a symbolic matrix by Karla F. C. Holloway, while Susan Willis passionately associates Morrison's magical realism with the goad presented to it by our racist society.

Michael Awkward convincingly delineates Morrison's agon with Ralph Ellison's great novel, *Invisible Man*, the unacknowledged precursor of *The Bluest Eye*, after which Donald B. Gibson argues that Morrison's first novel already protests against class, racial, and gender oppressions.

Linda Dittmar also imports Morrison's later ideologies into *The Bluest Eye*, despite the novel's eloquent skepticism, while Shelley Wong again sees the book as an indictment of our social and economic order, as does Dorethea Drummond Mbalia. This political emphasis is authorized by Morrison herself in her 1994 Afterword, and is adumbrated by Linden Peach.

Jan Furman, linking *The Bluest Eye* with *Sula*, interestingly surmises that Morrison broods on whether "economic and social gains are worth the sacrifice of community."

A wholly political reading returns with Laurie Vickroy, who blames colonialism, after which James A. Wren contributes a note on folk medicine in *The Bluest Eye*.

Leester Thomas emphasizes the novel's theme of being "homeless at home," after which John N. Duvall shrewdly follows Michael Awkward in uncovering Morrison's sly contest with Ralph Ellison.

Introduction

T*he Bluest Eye*, Morrison's first novel, was published when she was thirty-nine and is anything but novice work. Michael Wood, an authentic literary critic, made the best comment on this "lucid and eloquent" narrative that I have ever seen:

> Each member of the family interprets and acts out of his or her ugliness, but none of them understands that the all-knowing master is not God but only history and habit; the projection of their own numbed collusion with the mythology of beauty and ugliness that oppresses them beyond their already grim social oppression.

Morrison herself, in an Afterword of 1994, looked back across a quarter-century and emphasized her "reliance for full comprehension in codes embedded in black culture." A reader who is not black or female must do the best he can; like Michael Wood, I have found *The Bluest Eye* to be completely lucid since I first read it, back in 1970. Like *Sula* and *The Song of Solomon* after it, the book seems to me successful in universal terms, even if one shares neither Morrison's origins nor her ideologies. *Beloved*, Morrison's most famous romance narrative, seems to be to be problematic, though it has reached a vast audience. A generation or two will have to pass before a balanced judgment could be rendered upon *Beloved* or Morrison's later novels, *Jazz* and *Paradise*. But her early phase has many of the canonical qualifications of the traditional Western literary kind that she fiercely rejects as being irrelevant to her.

The essays I have reprinted in this volume are, almost all of them, ideological, and follow Morrison's lead in being the kind of appreciation that she wants. I add a brief appreciation here, in the full awareness that I am necessarily incorrect, since I am an outworn aesthete, and not a "cultural

1

critic." What I never forget about *The Bluest Eye* is its terrifying penultimate paragraph, where the narrator censures herself and her friends for turning away from Pecola because the child's madness, engendered by the trauma of being raped by her father, Cholly, "bored us in the end":

> Oh, some of us "loved" her. The Maginot Line. And Cholly loved her. I'm sure he did. He, at any rate, was the one who loved her enough to touch her, envelope her, give something of her filled the matrix of her agony with death. Love is never any better than the lover. Wicked people love wickedly, violent people love violently, weak people love weakly, stupid people love stupidly, but the love of a free man is never safe. There is no gift for the beloved. The lover alone possesses his gift of love. The loved one is shorn, neutralized, frozen in the glare of the lover's inward eye.

The unhappy wisdom of this is happily free of any cultural narcissism whatsoever. Class, race, even gender do not over-determine this bleakness. Morrison's heroic survivors in *Beloved* are intended to stand up both in and against their history. Perhaps they do, but the torments they have endured also are tendentiously elaborated, because the author has an ideological design upon us, her guilty readers, white and black, male and female. The narrator of *The Bluest Eye* persuades me, where the narration of *Beloved* does not. In D. H. Lawrence's terms, I trust both the tale and the teller in *The Bluest Eye*. In *Beloved*, I do not trust the tale.

KEITH E. BYERMAN

Intense Behaviors: The Use of the Grotesque in The Bluest Eye and Eva's Man

At the end of Toni Morrison's *The Bluest Eye*, the little black girl Pecola, a victim of incest, is pictured talking to herself in a mirror about her imaginary blue eyes. At the end of *Eva's Man*, by Gayl Jones, Eva is describing, in increasingly incomprehensible terms, her poisoning and castrating of the man with whom she lived. Both of these female characters are the central figures of the novels under discussion, and each is, in literary terms, a grotesque. But such figures are not being used by Morrison and Jones just to shock or entertain; rather, they use these bizarre characterizations to examine the even greater grotesqueries of American society. Pecola epitomizes the American obsession with whiteness, while Eva, in a slightly different way, exemplifies the society's fixation on sexual dominance. The novels develop, then, a grotesque within a grotesque and serve to show the particular appropriateness of the grotesque in black literature that is also social criticism.

The grotesque as a literary convention has two aspects that can be found in the fiction under discussion. Flannery O'Connor has described one of these by saying of grotesque characters: "They seem to carry an invisible burden; their fanaticism is a reproach, not merely an eccentricity." Frederick J. Hoffman, in discussing the Gothic and grotesque in Southern writing, comments that "one thing is expectedly true: in a society where intensities of behavior are frequent, the 'gothic' is a kind of norm. . . .

From *CLA Journal* 24, no. 4 (June 1982). © 1982 College Language Association. Reprinted by permission of the College Language Association.

There are frightening and often puzzling details, which the reader finds difficult to fit into context, so he concludes that they are 'grotesque' . . . ." As shall be seen, this social element is the most basic theme of the two novels. The supposed normalities of American life are shown to be absurd and ominous distortions.

The second aspect has to do with the reader's reactions to grotesque literature. The grotesque appeals to something in us that is pre-rational, that defies our intellectual categories. Unlike other writing that is concerned with the beautiful and the realistic, the grotesque is deliberately extravagant, distorted, violent, and ugly. We find it, nonetheless, strangely attractive as well as repulsive. Michael Steig has said that "the grotesque involves the arousing of anxiety by giving expression to infantile fears, fantasies and impulses . . . ."

Such a reaction must be created by Jones and Morrison because the social elements they are talking about are themselves pre-rational. It is assumed by these writers that the reader shares the attitudes toward sexuality and race that they are criticizing. The moral visions of the novels can only be understood if these exist. Therefore, the incest, narcissism, murder, and castration of the books reach beneath the usual level of reader response to give a particular kind of shock of recognition.

In *The Bluest Eye* and *Eva's Man*, then, the social manifestations of the grotesque described by O'Connor and Hoffman are combined with the psychological ones mentioned by Steig. Morrison describes a social situation so distorted by the myth of whiteness that it produces a child, Pecola, who is so obsessed by the blue-eyed beauty of Shirley Temple that she creates a self-contained reality that cannot be penetrated even by rape and incest. Jones shows us a society so fixated on the domination of women that Eva can liberate herself only by biting off the penis of her lover. We as readers are forced to consider not only the absurdity of idolizing a blue-eyed child and protecting the sexual vanity of a pre-adolescent boy, but also the horror when these absurdities lead to murder, incest, and schizophrenia.

The world of *The Bluest Eye* is clearly one that has a distorted sense of color. All the blacks in the book feel insecure and even inferior because of their skin tone. The narrator says of Pecola's family, the Breedloves:

> It was as though some mysterious all-knowing master had given each one a cloak of ugliness to wear, and they had each accepted it without question. The master had said, "You are ugly people." They had looked about themselves and saw nothing to contradict the statement; saw, in fact, support for it leaning at them from every billboard, every movie, every glance. "Yes," they had said.

"You are right." And they took the ugliness in their hands, threw it as a mantle over them, and went about the world with it.

The significant point here is that such a burden is accepted without direct coercion. There are few white characters in the novel to impose the view. The ideological hegemony of whiteness is simply too overwhelming to be successfully resisted. No alternative source of valuation is provided for these characters. As a case in point, the narrator Claudia serves as a contrast to the Breedloves and especially to Pecola. Though much less passive and more aware of her black identity, Claudia, too, must eventually accommodate herself to the dominant view. When little, she has the disturbing habit of tearing apart the white dolls she is given as gifts. "But the dismemberment of dolls was not the true horror. The truly horrifying thing was the transference of the same impulses to little white girls. . . . To discover what eluded me: the secret of the magic they weaved on others." The magical secret points us toward the nonrational basis of the social belief. Claudia's bizarre response seems an almost reasonable treatment of this complex of ritual and superstition. She seeks understanding where only unthinking faith is tolerated. She changes, however:

> When I learned how repulsive this disinterested violence was, that it was repulsive because it was disinterested, my shame floundered about for a refuge. The best hiding place was love. Thus the conversion from pristine sadism to fabricated hatred, to fraudulent love. It was a small step to Shirley Temple. I learned much later to worship her, just as I learned to delight in cleanliness, knowing even as I learned, that the change was adjustment without improvement.

Claudia, the strongest character in the book, cannot defy the myth and is even made to feel guilty for her childhood doubts. Knowing full well that the myth is a lie, she must nonetheless bow before its idol.

Pecola, in sharp contrast, never has any uncertainties about the gospel according to Shirley. She is portrayed throughout as a true believer who wants only to be like her idol. Every scene in which she appears is used to demonstrate her lack of self-esteem and her passiveness in the face of this American dream. Whites, lighter-skinned blacks, and dark-skinned blacks who redirect their self-hatred, all make her feel her unworthiness. She responds by seeking out a presumed medium who, she believes, can provide her with the emblem of whiteness, blue eyes. In her last scene, she sits in her room talking to an imaginary friend about the precise intensity of the blueness, about whether she, in truth, now has America's bluest eye.

But this rather pathetic obsession is made horrifying when we realize that, during this time, Pecola has conceived and miscarried a baby as a result of rape by her father. This reality is only on the fringes of her consciousness, and we must depend on Claudia and an omniscient narrator to provide us with the details.

What we learn is that the father himself has been victimized, in terms of sexuality, by the same whiteness that destroyed his daughter. Abandoned by his father and mother, Cholly has had no opportunity to develop any self-esteem. What little might have existed was destroyed when his first attempt at lovemaking was interrupted by white men who ridiculed him. This assault on his being saps him of his manhood, both physically and psychologically. He turns his anger against himself and the black girl with him since there is nothing he can do to the men who caused the trauma. Such a feeling of powerlessness only reinforces his self-hatred.

His rage eventually turns into alcoholism and repeated conflict with his wife, who seems to him, simply being his wife, to be a constant reminder of his ineffectiveness. He would love her, but because love imposes responsibility, he tries to hate her.

This same love-hate complex applies to his children. Moments before the incest, he sits watching Pecola:

> Guilt and impotence rose in a bilious dust. What could he do for her—ever? What give her? what say to her? What could a burned-out black man say to the hunched back of his eleven-year old daughter? If he looked into her face, he would see those haunted, loving eyes. The hauntedness would irritate him—the love would move him to fury. How dare she love him? Hadn't she any sense at all?

Somehow he wants her to be responsible for the misery of his life. He expects her to reinforce his self-hatred by despising him. The fact that she loves him only intensifies his despair. Such a reaction is to be expected from what we know of him. But what follows is not. In the midst of this emotional confusion, he sees Pecola make a slight gesture that reminds him of her mother in better days. A surge of tenderness causes him to move nearer his child. This protective gesture is then confused by his hatred, and he sexually assaults her. When she becomes pregnant, he abandons the family.

Pecola's reaction is to substitute the sweet world of Shirley Temple for her own bitter one. She escapes, but we as readers cannot. We are left in a state of the grotesque. On the one hand, we are repulsed by Cholly's action and sympathetic to his victim. On the other, we have been made to see that he is himself a victim of the society that condemns him. Because we have been introduced to his way of thinking and suffering, we verge on understanding his action and sharing his confusion. Both of these responses, repulsion against the action and attraction to the actor, are mutually necessary for the grotesque to work in this scene.

Similarly, Pecola leaves us with an ambiguous feeling. We are sorry for her victimization, but we know that she has entered a realm where her suffering will seldom come into her consciousness. That realm is, for us, both silly and pathetic. At a deeper level, Claudia has captured the impact of this particular grotesqueness by pointing out the Christ-like nature of her friend:

> All of us—all who knew her—felt so wholesome after we cleaned ourselves on her. We were so beautiful when we stood astride her ugliness. Her simplicity decorated us, her guilt sanctified us, her pain made us glow with health, her awkwardness made us think we had a sense of humor. Her inarticulateness made us believe we were eloquent. her poverty kept us generous. Even her waking dreams we used—to silence our own nightmares. And she let us, and thereby deserved our contempt. We honed our egos on her, padded our characters with her frailty, and yawned in the fantasy of our strength.

Pecola is a grotesque Messiah; she gives the world not grace but the illusion of relief from intolerable circumstances. She is sacrificed so that others may live with the perversions of society. She is a grotesque within a grotesque. She is unquestionably mad, but where in *The Bluest Eye* is there any sanity?

In *Eva's Man*, the madness of the central character is also readily apparent; but, significantly, the effect is to create an optimistic ending. Eva's act, though violent, is a way of resisting the oppression she has had to suffer. If Pecola is a suffering Christ, Eva is an avenging angel. Her crime is symbolic liberation from the particular grotesqueness of her society.

The burden of color in *The Bluest Eye* becomes the curse of sexuality in *Eva's Man*. Domination in this book is exercised by men, of whatever color. Women are the ones who are victimized. Virtually every woman in the novel suffers some attack on her integrity. Just as Pecola was educated in color inferiority, so Eva goes through a long training in sexual politics. Every aspect of her society—family, folklore, friendships, marriage—is presented as infused with sexuality. Eva can no more escape the omnipresent phallus than Pecola could the ubiquitous blue eyes.

The family in this case seems almost normal. The mother is concerned that her daughter learns proper social behavior, including the protection of her virtue. The father is a strong, authoritative figure who seems to deserve the respect he receives from Eva. But this situation is complicated by the presence of two other characters, Miss Billie and Tyrone. Miss Billie is the mother's closest friend, but her conversations are always related to the sexual aggressiveness of the men in the neighborhood. Thus the mother's teaching about chastity is complemented and contradicted by a sex education that demystifies and yet encourages sexuality. The primary lesson learned by Eva is that men are obsessed with sex.

Little in the book refutes this assertion. Tyrone is the mother's friend, though Eva, who narrates, can find no evidence of promiscuity. But Tyrone's attitude toward the child Eva is different. He finds her attractive, and despite her youth, repeatedly attempts to seduce her.

This activity ends only when the father discovers what he believes to be the unfaithfulness of his wife. What is taught to Eva, however, is not the expected lesson. He waits until he has occasion to return home early and finds the "lovers" together. He then quietly dismisses Tyrone and focuses his hostility on his wife. Eva describes the scene:

> Then it was like I could hear her clothes ripping. I don't know if the gentleness had been for me, or if it had been the kind of gentleness one gets before they let go. But now he was tearing that blouse off and those underthings. I didn't hear nothing from her the whole time. I didn't hear a thing from her.
>
> "Act like a whore, I'm gonna [f——] you like a whore. You act like a whore, I'm gonna [f——] you like a whore."
>
> He kept saying that over and over. I was so scared. I kept feeling that after he tore all her clothes off, and there wasn't anymore to tear, he'd start tearing her flesh.

What is important about his episode is not the obvious double standard, nor even the verbal and physical abuse; rather, it is the lesson taught Eva. It reinforces in a violent way what Miss Billie had said. The father, a figure of respect, becomes so obsessed that he punishes a woman Eva believes to be innocent instead of the man she knows from her own experience is guilty. To the extent she believes her father, she must feel that she, too, can never be innocent, since Tyrone found her attractive. To the extent that she disapproves of her father's action, she realizes that no man is to be trusted in sexual matters. It is little wonder that she does not tell her father of Tyrone's real offenses.

This process of education is strengthened by the folklore of the community. In the most prominent case, Miss Billie tells the story of the queen bee. The community holds her somehow responsible, even though she seems merely the victim of bad luck. When she falls in love again, she commits suicide rather than let another man die. Such a story only reinforces the view that women are by nature sinful, that they are responsible for the evil in the world. Original sin, in some cosmic way, has attached itself to the female gender. Eva is thus further encouraged to believe that a woman can never be innocent, even if she has done nothing.

This psychological training is complemented by her physical encounters with male companions. In addition to the trouble she has had with Tyrone, as a little girl she must deal with the sexually precocious Freddy. Although too young for intercourse, he is obsessed with the sexual act and substitutes a dirty popsicle stick for a penis when he play-acts a rape on Eva. When she tries to get advice about how to cope with his aggressions, Miss Billie only laughs and calls him a healthy young rooster. When another man later grabs for her crotch and she cuts his hand with a knife, she is the one put in jail for assault. Even the protection of her physical being is a matter of no consequence to her society. If she resists sexual encounters, then she is labeled silly or criminal. If she even appears to submit, then she will be labeled a whore.

She attempts to adapt herself to the distortions of her society despite her doubts. She marries James, a father figure, and moves with him to a new home. She becomes aware of his possible obsessiveness when he refuses to allow a telephone to be installed in the house, because, he says, he does not want her lovers calling. He reaches the high point of his madness when she repeats the mistake of her mother. A boy from the college she attends visits her one afternoon, and James comes home to find them talking. He then reenacts the violence of her father. Sending the boy away, he stares at her:

> He was just sitting there, real hard, and then he just reached over and grabbed my shoulder, got up and started slapping me. "You think you are a whore, I'll treat you like a whore. You think you a whore, I'll treat you like a whore."
>
> Naw, he didn't slap me, he pulled up my dress and got between my legs.
>
> "Think I can't do nothing. [f——] you like a damn whore."
> Naw, I'm not lying. He said, "Act like a whore, I'll [f——] you like a whore." *Naw, I'm not lying.*

This confrontation serves to convince Eva that her gender is indeed her destiny, that she cannot delude herself that she can be different from her mother. But she is in fact different from both her mother and the queen bee, both of whom resign themselves to their condition. Unlike Pecola, Eva cannot accept the myth of her society.

When she next encounters a man who would rob her of her humanity, she strikes out. Her relationship with Davis begins ambiguously. He initiates it with a comment that is a refrain in the book. When she asks why he is interested in her, he says that something in her eyes told him what she wanted. This reading of the eyes is a presumption of all the men that meet Eva. What is read, of course, is sexual desire. Davis is another obsessed man.

Despite this fact, she returns to the apartment with him, though she knows that she cannot give what he wants, since she is menstruating. Two things are clear at this point. One is that Eva differentiates between sexuality and sexual domination. She makes the point several times that she enjoys intercourse, and she only resists the assumption that women are nothing other than their sexual organs. The second point is that she is not deluded into thinking that Davis must be, finally, the "right man." The fact of her period makes it possible to test his perception of her.

He fails the test. Although he is kind and not initially insistent, he objectifies her to greater extent than any other man. He will not allow her to leave the room or to comb her hair. He loses patience and takes her despite her condition. He also remains indifferent to her sexual preferences and concerns himself only with demonstrating his prowess. He will not listen to her story, and at one point, he mistakenly calls her Eve rather than Eva.

She does not this time tolerate her own reification. She first poisons him, and then, when he is dead, she indulges in sexual play with the body which culminates in her biting off his penis. This scene is comparable in shock effect to the rape of Pecola. But Gayl Jones uses hers to suggest complex possibilities by attaching mythic associations to it. When Eva arrives, she is bleeding from her period. Later, she comments that she has a pain in her side. At one point, she says that she feels as though there were large rusty nails in her hands. This Christ imagery is completed when, after the murder, she pictures herself being told by a man that her breasts are loaves of bread. Furthermore, Davis's misnaming of her has a strange appro-priateness. At the moment of the castration, she relates her action to the biting of an apple. She is, in the light of these symbols, an Eve-Messiah who sacrifices another for both salvation and knowledge. She has gotten revenge for the death of the queen bee and the humiliation of her mother. But she has done this by symbolically liberating all women from the guilt attributed to them and by pointing to the true root of all evil.

She is mad, of course. And men put her in a prison for the criminally insane. Her incarceration replicates the confinement of her father's home,

James's home, and Davis's apartment, all of which were clearly institutions for the insane. But in this case there is a kind of freedom in knowing that her resistance has made it possible to escape men. Her liberation is epitomized in the sexual attentions she receives from Elvira, her cellmate. Eva has nightmares, and her crime and situation are abnormal by all conventional standards. But this abnormality only serves to intensify the awareness that the society she has offended is an even greater obscenity.

The Bluest Eye and *Eva's Man*, though very different, are alike in their use of the conventions of the grotesque. Each involves some sort of obscenity that shocks our sensibilities. The incest of Morrison's book is outdone by the necrophilia and castration of Jones's. Each gives us central characters who are shown to be insane. But each also goes further, for the real grotesqueness in both is revealed to be primarily in the fictional worlds of the books. And these worlds are our world. The two black female characters, in their suffering, act as vehicles for criticizing America's treatment of blacks and women. The grotesque is an especially appropriate form for this commentary because it takes what is considered normal and twists it so that it loses its familiar qualities and becomes alien to us as the observers. In the case of these two novels, the normalities of American life, sex, and race are exaggerated to reveal their basic destructive absurdity. The actions and mental states of the heroines are clearly a function of the distortions and perversions of their worlds. Eva and Pecola respond to their impossible situations in ways that are unacceptable, and each of them enters a kind of prison. But we as readers are made to understand that the real horrors are still loose in the world.

MADONNE M. MINER

Lady No Longer Sings the Blues:
Rape, Madness, and Silence in The Bluest Eye

Robert Stepto begins a recent interview with Toni Morrison by commenting on the "extraordinary sense of place" in her novels. He notes that she creates specific geographical landscapes with street addresses, dates, and other such details. His observations certainly hold true for Morrison's first novel, *The Bluest Eye*, set in a black neighborhood in Lorain, Ohio, in 1941. Reading *The Bluest Eye*, I feel as if I have been in the abandoned store on the southeast corner of Broadway and Thirty-fifth Street in Lorain where Pecola Breedlove lives, as if I have been over the territory traversed by the eleven-year-old black girl as she skips among tin cans, tires, and weeds.

Morrison's skill in creating this very specific place accounts, in part, for my sense of the strangely familiar, the uncanny, when I read her novel—but only in part. While reading, I am familiar not only with Pecola's neighborhood but also, in a more generalized way, with Pecola's story. The sequence of events in this story—a sequence of rape, madness, and silence—repeats a sequence I have read before. Originally manifest in mythic accounts of Philomela and Persephone, this sequence provides Morrison with an ancient archetype from which to structure her very contemporary account of a young black woman. In the pages which follow I want to explore intersections between these age-old myths and Morrison's ageless novel.

From *Conjuring: Black Women, Fiction, and Literary Tradition.* © 1985 Indiana University Press.

For an account of Philomela, we must turn to Ovid, who includes her story in his *Metamorphoses* (8 A.D.). According to the chronicler, this story begins with an act of separation: Procne leaves her much-loved sister, Philomela, to join her husband, Tereus, in Thrace. After several years, Procne convinces Tereus to make a trip to Athens and escort Philomela to Thrace for a visit. In Athens, Tereus barely manages to curb the lust he feels for Philomela. He caresses her with his eyes, watches possessively as she kisses her father good-bye, and uses each embrace, each kiss,

> . . . to spur his rage, and feed his fire;
> He wished himself her father—and yet no less
> Would lust look hideous in a father's dress.

Arriving in Thrace, Tereus drags Philomela into a dark wood and rapes her. The virgin calls out the names of father, sister, gods, but to no avail. Having indulged his lust, Tereus prepares to leave this "ringdove . . . with blood-stained plumes still fluttering" when she dares cry out against his sin:

> "I'll speak your deed, and cast all shame away.
>   . . .
> My voice shall reach the highest tract of air,
> And gods shall hear, if gods indeed are there."

Tereus cannot tolerate such sacrilege against his name, so he perpetrates yet another rape: with pincers he

> . . . gripped the tongue that cried his shame,
> that stammered to the end her father's name,
> That struggled still, and strangled utterance made,
> And cut it from the root with barbarous blade.

Deprived of speech and lodged in "walls of stone," Philomela weaves the tale of her plight into a piece of fabric, which she then sends to Procne. When Procne learns of her sister's grief and her husband's treachery, she determines upon a most hideous revenge; she slays the son she has had with Tereus and feeds his remains to the unsuspecting father. While Ovid's story ends with this feast, popular mythology adds yet another chapter, transforming Philomela into a nightingale, damned forever to chirp the name of her rapist: terue, tereu.

Obviously, male-violating-female functions as the core action within Philomela's story. Under different guises, this violation occurs several times: first, when Tereus ruptures the hymen of Philomela; second, when

Tereus ruptures the connecting tissue of Philomela's tongue, and, finally, when he enters her body yet again ("Thereafter, if the frightening tale be true,/On her maimed form he wreaked his lust anew"). With each act Tereus asserts his presence, his sensual realm, and denies the very existence of such a realm (encompassing not only sensuality, but the senses themselves) to Philomela. As if to reinforce the violation, Tereus, following his act of rape, encloses Philomela in silence, in stone walls. He thereby forces her to assume externally imposed configurations instead of maintaining those natural to her.

If man-raping-woman functions as the most basic "mythemic act" in Philomela's story, the most basic mythemic *inter*-act involves not only this pair, but another: father and sister of the rape victim. When, for example, Ovid notes that Tereus, lusting for Philomela, "wished himself her father," and when the chronicler describes Philomela, in the midst of the rape, calling out her father's name (for help, of course, but for what else?) he sets the act of violence within a familial matrix. Thus, we cannot limit consideration of this act's motivations and ramifications to two individuals. Interestingly enough, however, just as the basic mythemic act (man raping woman) robs the woman of identity, so too the mythemic interact; dependent upon the familial roles for personal verification ("mother of," "sister of," "wife of") the female must fear a loss of identity as the family loses its boundaries—or, more accurately, as the male transgresses these boundaries.

Having noted the most important structural elements in Philomela's story, we cross an ocean, several centuries and countless historical, racial, and class lines before coming to the story of Pecola. Despite obvious contextual differences between the two stories, structural similarities abound. Individual mythemes from Philomela's story appear, without distortion, in that of Pecola. First, in various ways and at various costs, the female figure suffers violation: by Mr. Yacobowski, Junior, Bay Boy and friends, Cholly, Soaphead. Second, with this violation a man asserts his presence as "master," "man-in-control," or "god" at the expense of a young woman who exists only as someone to "impress upon." Third, following the violation/assertion, this woman suffers an enclosure or undesirable transformation; she cowers, shrinks, or resides behind walls of madness. Finally, the most characteristic example of violation/assertion/destruction occurs within the family matrix; Cholly Breedlove rapes his own daughter, violating a standard code of familial relations. We now might look more closely at individual instances of mythemes structuring the Pecola story.

An early, and paradigmatic, example of male transgression and subsequent female silence occurs in the "See the Cat" section. Junior, a tyrannical, unloving black boy, invites a rather credulous Pecola into his house, ostensibly to show her some kittens; like Philomela, Pecola has no idea of the dangers involved in trusting herself to a male guide. Once inside, engrossed in admiration of the furnishings, she forgets about Junior until he insists that she acknowledge him:

> She was deep in admiration of the flowers when Junior said, "Here!" Pecola turned. "Here is your kitten!" he screeched. And he threw a big black cat right in her face.

Pecola immediately responds to this unexpected penetration by sucking in her breath; metaphorically she draws herself inward. She then attempts to flee, but just as Tereus confines Philomela behind stone walls, Junior confines Pecola behind the wall of his will.

> Junior leaped in front of her. "You can't get out. You're my prisoner," he said. His eyes were merry nut hard. . . . He pushed her down, ran out the door that separated the rooms, and held it shut with his hands.

Male realms expand as those of the female suffer an almost fatal contraction.

Junior does not actually rape Pecola. Morrison, however, duplicates the dynamics of the scene between Junior and Pecola in a scene between Cholly and Pecola, where rape *does* occur. Eleven-year-old Pecola stands at the sink, scraping away at dirty dishes, when her father, drunk, staggers into the kitchen. Unlike Tereus and Junior, Cholly does not carry his victim into foreign territories; rather, Pecola's rape occurs within her own house, and this fact increases its raw horror (Morrison denies us the cover of metaphor and confronts us directly with a father's violation of his daughter). As Morrison explains, several factors motivate Cholly, but the two thoughts floating through his besotted brain immediately prior to his penetration of Pecola point, once more, to his desire for confirmation of his presence. First, a gesture of Pecola's, a scratching of the leg, reminds him of a similar gesture of Pauline's—or, more accurately, reminds him of *his own* response to this gesture. He repeats his response, catching Pecola's foot in his hand, nibbling in the flesh of her leg, just as he had done with Pauline, so many years before. Of consequence here is not Pecola's gesture, but Cholly's belief that he can regain an earlier perception of himself as young, carefree and whimsical by using this girl/woman as medium. When Pecola, however, unlike the laughing Pauline, remains stiff and silent, Cholly shifts to a second train of thought, a second stimulus to self-assertion: "The rigidness of her shocked body, the silence of her stunned throat, was better than Pauline's easy laughter had been. The confused mixture of his memories of Pauline and the doing of a wild and forbidden thing excited him, and a bolt ran down his genitals, giving it length." Thus, on a literal level, Cholly expands as Pecola contracts:

> The tightness of her vagina was more than he could bear. His soul seemed to slip down to his guts and fly out into her, and the gigantic thrust he made into her then provoked by the only sound she made—a hollow suck of air in the back of her throat. Like the rapid loss of air from a circus balloon.

As in the episode with Junior, Pecola sucks inward, but without positive effect; like a deflating circus balloon, she *loses* the benefits of lifegiving oxygen and the power of speech.

To enforce this silence, Cholly need not cut off Pecola's tongue or imprison her behind stone walls. The depresencing of Pecola Breedlove takes a different form from that of Philomela. Upon regaining consciousness following the rape, Pecola *is* able to speak; she tells Mrs. Breedlove what has happened. But as Mrs. Breedlove does not want to hear and does not want to believe, Pecola must recognize the futility of attempted communication. Thus when Cholly, like Tereus, rapes a second time, Pecola keeps the story to herself; in silence this eleven-year-old girl steps across commonly accepted borders of reason and speech to enter her own personal world of silence and madness. Pecola's "self" becomes so crazed, so fragmented, that it conducts conversations with itself—and with no one else:

> "How come you don't talk to anybody?"
> "I talk to you."
> "Besides me."
> "I don't like anybody besides you. . . ."
> "You don't talk to anybody. You don't go to school. And nobody talks to you."

Of course, when Pecola comments that her mirror image does not engage other people in conversation, she engages in self-commentary; "I" and "you" are one and the same. Tragically, even when combined, this "I" and "you" do not compose one whole being. Claudia's description of the mutilated Pecola leaves no doubt that she no longer exists as a reasonable human being; like Philomela-turned nightingale, the "little-girl-gone-to-woman" undergoes a transformation:

> The damage done was total. . . . Elbows bent, hands on shoulders, she flailed her arms like a bird in an eternal, grotesquely futile effort to fly. Beating the air, a winged but grounded bird, intent on the blue void it could not reach—could not even see— but which filled the valleys of the mind.

Silent, isolated, insane: Pecola cannot escape.

In depicting the effects of rape on one young woman, Morrison sets into motion a series of associations that take their cue from gender. Men, potential rapists, assume presence, language, and reason as their particular province. Women, potential victims, fall prey to absence, silence, and madness. An understanding of the powerful dynamics behind this allotment of presence/absence, language/silence, reason/madness along sexual lines contributes to an understanding of the painful truths contained in Philomela's story, in Pecola's story, and in the story of yet another rape victim: Persephone. While clearly related to the Philomela myth, that of Persephone differs in certain details which, when brought to *The Bluest Eye*, prompt an even richer reading of the novel. Before engaging in an application of Persephone's story to that of Pecola, however, we might look at three different renditions of the Persephone myth, each of which may advance our understanding of the way Persephone's and Pecola's stories intersect mythopoetically.

Homer sets a springtime mood of warmth, gaiety, youthfulness, and beauty as he begins his rendition of Persephone's story:

> Now I will sing/of golden-haired Demeter,
> the awe-inspiring goddess,
> and of her trim-ankled daughter,
> Persephone,
> who was frolicking in a grassy meadow.

When Pluto, god of the underworld, abducts the "trim-ankled" young woman (and surely it is not mere coincidence that Morrison specifies Pecola's ankles as a stimulant to Cholly's desire) this mood changes abruptly; in terror, the virgin shrieks for her father, Zeus. While noting that Persephone directs her shrieks to her father, Homer also comments on the virgin's hopes relative to her mother:

> Still *glimpsing* the earth,
> the brilliant sky,
> the billowing, fish-filled sea

and the rays of the sun,
Persephone vainly hoped to see her mother again.

Homer establishes a causal connection between rape and the loss of a particular *vision*. He further substantiates this connection in Demeter's response to
her daughter's rape, a punitive response which involves Demeter's changing
the world so that its occupants will no longer see fruits and flowers:

> She made that year
> most shocking and frightening
> for mortals who lived on the nourishing earth.
> The soil did not yield a single seed.
> Demeter kept them all underground.

The goddess imposes a sensual deprivation on mortals parallel to the sensual
deprivation suffered by her daughter (note that *The Bluest Eye* opens with a
statement of similar deprivation: "Quiet as it's kept, there were no marigolds
in the fall of 1941"). By the end of the hymn, Demeter and Pluto reach a
compromise; half of the year Persephone resides with her mother and the
flowers grow; during the other half, Persephone remains with Pluto and the
earth produces no fruits.

James Frazer, in *The Golden Bough*, relates another version of the
Persephone story. In substance, Frazer comes very close to Homer; in detail,
however, the two diverge, and Frazer's details reverberate in *The Bluest Eye*.
First, Frazer provides more specifics about Persephone's "frolic"; the young
woman gathers "roses and lilies, crocuses and violets, hyacinths and narcis-
suses in a lush meadow." Individual flowers in Frazer's catalog call forth associations of importance to *The Bluest Eye*: the virginal lily, bloody hyacinth
(taking its color from the slain youth, Hyacinth, beloved of Apollo) and
narcotic Narcissus (taking its name from the self-enclosed youth, Narcissus,
capable of seeing only himself). The mythic situation itself, flower picking,
finds an analog in the novel as Pecola, on her way to the candy store, peers
into the heads of yellow dandelions. Second, Frazer's more detailed description of Persephone's abduction and underworld residence might serve as
metaphoric description of Pecola's state of mind following her rape: "the
earth gaped and Pluto, Lord of the Dead, issuing from the *abyss*, carried her
off . . . to be his bride and queen in the *gloomy subterranean world*." Finally,
when Frazer concludes the story, he notes that although the "grim Lord of
the Dead" obeys Zeus's command to restore Persephone to Demeter, this
Lord first gives his mistress the seed of a pomegranate to eat, which ensures
that she will return to him. Tereus and Cholly also "give seeds" to women,

thereby ensuring that the women never will be able to reassume their previously experienced wholeness.

In a very recent reworking of the Persephone story, Philips Chesler focuses most intently on the fate of this myth's female characters. Because she places women's experiences at the center of her version, Chesler begins with a chapter of the story which does not appear in Homer and Frazer: Persephone menstruates. Further, Chesler specifies the nature of certain acts and relationships that her male counterparts choose to obscure; she identifies rape as rape, fathers as fathers:

> One morning Persephone menstruated. That afternoon, Demeter's daughters gathered flowers to celebrated the loveliness of the event. A chariot thundered, then clattered into their midst. It was Hades, the middle aged god of death, come to *rape* Persephone, come to carry her off to be his queen, to sit beside him in the realm of *non-being* below the earth, come to commit the first act of violence earth's children had ever known. Afterwards the three sisters agreed that he was old enough to be Persephone's *father.* Perhaps he was; who else could he be? There were no known male parents . . . and thus they discovered that in shame and sorrow childhood ends, and that nothing remains the same.

Morrison, like Chesler, pays attention to female rites of passage; she includes a description of Pecola's first menstruation, an experience which bonds Pecola to her adopted sisters, Claudia and Frieda. Also like Chesler, Morrison insists on the paternal identity of the rapist (Pecola need not shriek the name of her father as Philomela and Persephone do; father is right there) and emphasizes that the rape act brings one entire way of life to a close ("nothing remains the same"). This rapport between Chesler's Persephone and Morrison's Pecola surfaces in conclusions to the stories as well. Chesler writes:

> Persephone still had to visit her husband once each year (in winter, when no crops could grow), but her union with him remained a barren one. Persephone was childless. Neither husband nor child—no stranger would ever claim her as his own.

Pecola's fate runs along strikingly parallel lines. Despite the offerings and incantations of Claudia and Frieda, Pecola miscarries and remains childless.

Grown people turn away, children laugh, and no stranger attempts to share Pecola's world.

Structurally, the stories of Philomela, Persephone, and Pecola share the same blueprint: violated by a male relative, a young virgin suffers sensual loss of such an extreme that her very identity is called into question. In one brutally explicit scene Ovid conveys the terror of Philomela's sensual loss— Tereus severs his sister-in-law's tongue and deprives her of speech. As chroniclers of this same basic female experience, Homer, Frazer, and Chesler also must convey the terror of sensual loss. In their versions, however, sight rather than speech assumes priority, and they convey the terror of deprivation not in one explicit scene, but by depicting the ramifications of an altered vision. Of course, this particular emphasis encourages yet further consideration of the Persephone myth and Morrison's novel, the very title of which suggests an interest in the way vision structures our world. This interest, reflected in the novel's title, (what does it mean to see through "the bluest eye"?) and in sectional titles (how does one "see mother," "see father"?) springs naturally from Morrison's more fundamental interests: how does the world see a young black girl? how does a young black girl see a world? and finally, what are the correspondences between presence/absence, vision/nonvision, male/female?

As described by carious psychologists and psychoanalysts, the processes of identity construction and personal integration involve an extremely sensitive and constantly shifting balance between seeing and being seen—so that, for example, only after an infant sees itself reflected in the mother's eyes (that is, given a presence) can the infant, through its own eyes, bestow a presence on others. Throughout *The Bluest Eye*, Morrison provides several examples of the ways sex and race may prompt a dangerous distortion of this visual balance. An early instance of this distortion, and subsequent personal disintegration, occurs during an exchange between Pecola and Mr. Yacobowski, white male proprietor of a candy store on Garden Avenue. Pecola enjoys her walk to Mr. Yacobowski's store. Many times she has seen that crack in the walk, this clump of dandelions. Having seen them, she grants them a reality, a reality which redounds to include Pecola herself:

> These and other inanimate things she saw and experienced. They were real to her. She knew them. . . . She owned the crack . . . she owned the clump of dandelions. . . . And owning them made her part of the world, and the world part of her.

Such a happy rapport between viewer and vision is short-lived, however. When Pecola enters the candy store and comes under Mr.

Yacobowski's eyes, her existence, as well as the existence of her world, become matters of doubt. Mr. Yacobowski *does not see* her:

> Somewhere between the retina and object, between vision and view, his eyes draw back, hesitate, and hover. At some fixed point in time and space he senses that he need not waste the effort of a glance. He does not see her, because for him there is *nothing to see*. (my italics)

In effect, this scene parallels previously described rape scenes in the novel: male denies presence to female. Pecola cannot defend herself against this denial: "she looks up at him and sees the vacuum where curiosity ought to lodge. And something more. The total absence of human recognition—the glazed separateness." Nor can she defend her world; walking home, she rejects the dandelions she formerly has favored. They, like Pecola herself, certainly will not satisfy standards that the blue eyes of a Mr. Yacobowski may impose:

> Dandelions. A dart of affection leaps out from her to them. But they do not look at her and so not send love back. She thinks "They are ugly. They are weeds."

Before contact with this white male, Pecola creates belief in both a world and a self; following contact with Yacobowski, her conjuring powers impaired, she abandons the effort.

A second example of visual distortion finds Pecola face to face with Geraldine, one of those "brown girls from Mobile and Aiken" able to construct inviolable worlds by imposing strict boundaries between the acceptable and the unacceptable, the seen and the unseen. Unlike Mr. Yacobowski, Geraldine does *look* at Pecola, but, like Yacobowski, Geraldine does not *see* Pecola; she sees only a series of signs, a symbolic configuration. Thus, when Geraldine returns home and discovers a shrieking son, a frying feline on the radiator, and an unfamiliar black girl in her living room, she responds by distancing herself from Pecola. With no qualms whatsoever she relegates the young girl to the general category of "black female who is an embarrassment to us all", or, "black female whom we would prefer to keep out of sight":

> She looked at Pecola. Saw the dirty torn dress, the plaits sticking out of her head, hair matted where the plaits had come undone, the muddy wad of gum peeking out from between the cheap

soles, the soiled socks, one of which had been walked down to the
heel of the shoe. She saw the safety pin holding the hem of the
dress up. . . . She had seen this little girl all of her life.

Pecola, for Geraldine, serves as symbol of everything ugly, dirty, and
degrading. Physically as well as symbolically, Geraldine must negate Pecola,
must deny the ragged eleven-year-old access to her world. The woman who
does not sweat in her armpits or thighs, who smells of wood and vanilla says
to Pecola, *quietly* says to Pecola: "'Get out. . . . You nasty little black bitch.
Get out of my house!'" In other words, get out of my world, out of the vision
I construct before and about me. Pecola leaves. As she leaves, she hangs her
head, lowers her eyes; incapable of defending herself against visual distortion, Pecola attempts to deny vision altogether. But, even here, she fails: "she
could not hold it [her head] low enough to avoid seeing the snowflakes falling
and dying on the pavement." These snowflakes, falling and dying, suggest
the visual perimeters of Pecola's world. In an earlier comment, Morrison
generalizes as to the nature of these perimeters: "She would see only what
there was to see: the eyes of other people." As these eyes do not see her, or
see her only as a sign of something other, Pecola loses sight of herself.

Although Pecola's encounters with Mr. Yacobowski and Geraldine serve
as the most complete and sensitively drawn examples of visual imbalance
begun much earlier in Pecola's life—for that matter, begun even before Pecola
sees the light of day, while she is in Pauline's womb. During the nine months
of pregnancy, Pauline spends most afternoons at the movies, picking up an
education in white values of beauty and ugliness. Morrison describes this
education as yet another violation of male on female, white on black. There, in
a darkened theater, images come together, "all projected through the ray of
light from above and behind." This ray of light resembles a gigantic eyeball
(apologies to Emerson) which defines the boundaries of existence and which,
of necessity, projects a white male vision. Having absorbed these silver-screen
values, Pauline conjures up "a mind's eye view" of her soon-to-be-born child
more in keeping with a white fantasy than black reality. Upon birth, Pecola
gives lie to this view, and Pauline expresses her disappointment:

> So when I seed it, it was like looking at a picture of your mama
> when she was a girl. You know who she is, but she don't look the
> same. . . . Head full of pretty hair, but Lord she was ugly.

As various psychologists attest, the mother's gaze is of primary importance in
generating a child's sense of self. Tragically, Pauline looks at her infant
daughter and then looks away.

Morrison's novel contains repeated instances of Pecola's negation as other characters refuse to see her. *The Bluest Eye* also provides numerous instances of Pecola's desire to hide her own eyes, thereby refusing to acknowledge certain aspects of her world. Morrison articulates this desire for self-abnegation most explicitly in a postscript to her description of a typical fight between family members in the Breedlove home. Mrs. Breedlove hits Cholly with a dishpan, Cholly returns the blow with his fists, Sammy strikes at Cholly, while shouting "you naked fuck," and Pecola covers her head with a quilt. The quilt of course cannot completely block out this scene, so Pecola prays that God will make her disappear. Receiving no response from the man in the sky, she does her best on her own:

> She squeezed her eyes shut. Little parts of her body faded away. Now slowly, now with a rush. Slowly again. Her fingers went, one by one; then her arms disappeared all the way to the elbow. Her feet now. Yes, that was good. The legs all at once. It was hardest above the thighs. She had to be real still and pull. Her stomach would not go. But finally it, too, went away. Then her chest, her neck. The face was hard too. Almost done, almost. Only her tight, tight eyes were left. They were always left.
>
> Try as she might, she could never get her eyes to disappear. So what was the point? They were everything. Everything was there, in them.

These paragraphs forcefully convey Pecola's desire and her notion of how she might realize it. If Pecola were to *see* things differently, she might *be seen* differently; if her eyes were different, her world might be different too. As Morrison deals out one ugly jigsaw piece after another, as she fits the pieces together to construct Pecola's world, we come to understand the impulse behind Pecola's desire, as well as its ultimate futility. When the boys shout at her, "'Black e mo Black e mo Ya daddy sleeps nekked,'" Pecola drops her head and covers her eyes; when Maureen accuses her of having seen her father naked, Pecola maintains her innocence by disclaiming, "'I wouldn't even look at him, even if I did see him;'" when Maureen attacks her yet again Pecola tucks her head in "a funny, sad, helpless movement. A kind of hunching of the shoulders, pulling in of the neck, as though she wanted to cover the ears." By covering ears, eyes, and nose Pecola attempts to shut out the testimony of her senses. Reminded of her own ugliness or that of her world, she repeatedly resorts to an elemental self-denial.

Pecola quavers when Mr. Yacobowski and Geraldine refuse to acknowledge her. She shrinks in fear when Maureen and Bay Boy insist on acknowledging her ugliness. Quavering and shaking, Pecola does maintain a hold on her world and herself—until Cholly smashes her illusions about the possibility of unambivalent love in this world. Throughout the novel, Pecola ponders the nature of love, pursues it as a potentially miraculous phenomenon. On the evening of her first menstruation, for example, she asks, "How do you do that? I mean, how do you get somebody to love you.'" And, after a visit to Marie, Poland, and China, Pecola ponders, "What did love feel like? . . . How do grownups act when they love each other? Eat fish together?" When Cholly rapes his daughter, he commits a sacrilege—not only against Pecola, but against her vision of love and its potential. Following the rape, Pecola, an unattractive eleven-year-old black girl, knows that for her, even love is bound to be dirty, ugly, of a piece with the fabric of her world. Desperate, determined to unwind the threads that compose this fabric, Pecola falls back on an early notion: the world changes as the eyes which see it change. To effect this recreation, Pecola seeks out the only magician she knows, Soaphead Church, and presents him with the only plans she can conceive. She asks that he make her eyes different, make them blue—blue because in Pecola's experience only those with blue eyes receive love: Shirley Temple, Geraldine's cat, the Fisher girl.

In its emotional complications, Soaphead's response to Pecola's request resembles Cholly's response to Pecola's defeated stance; both men move through misdirected feelings of love, tenderness, and anger. Soaphead perceives Pecola's need and knows that he must direct the anger he feels not at her, but rather at the God who has encased her within black skin and behind brown eyes. But finally, when Soaphead decides to "look at that ugly black girl" and love her, he violates her integrity in much the same way Cholly violates her body when he forces open her thighs. Prompted by the desire to play God and to make this performance a convincing one, Soaphead casts Pecola in the role of believer. Thus, although he sees Pecola more accurately than other characters do, he subordinates his vision of her to his vision of self-as-God. He later boasts in his letter "To He Who Greatly Ennobled Human Nature by Creating It":

> I did what you did not, could not, would not do. I looked at
> that ugly little black girl, and I loved her. I played You. And it
> was a very good show!

Of course, the script for this show sends Pecola into realms of madness. Even Soaphead acknowledges that "No one else will see her blue eyes," but Soaphead justifies himself first on the grounds that "she will love happily ever after" and then, more honestly, on the grounds that "I, I have found it meet and right to do so." In other words, Soaphead's creation of false belief is not necessarily right for Pecola, but for himself. Morrison substantiates this assessment of Soaphead's creation a few pages later, when she portrays its effect on Pecola. Imprisoned now behind blue eyes, the schizophrenic little girl can talk only to herself. Obviously, this instance of male-female interaction parallels earlier scenes from the novel: "rape" occurs as Soaphead elevates himself at the expense of Pecola.

In *The Raw and the Cooked* Lévi-Strauss observes "There exists no veritable end or term to mythical analysis, no secret unity which could be grasped at the end of the work of decomposition. The themes duplicate themselves to infinity." Although the stories of Philomela, Persephone, and Pecola do not form a composite whole, each of them, with its varied and individual emphases, contributes to a much larger woman's myth, which tells of denial and disintegration, which unveils the oft-concealed connections between male reason, speech, presence and female madness, silence, absence. As a young black woman, Pecola assumes an especially poignant position in this growing complex of mythic representations; she is absent (and absenced) in relation to the norms of male culture and in relation to the norms of a white culture. Ultimately, I read Pecola's story as a tragic version of the myth; this twentieth-century black woman remains behind blue eyes, an inarticulate, arm-fluttering bird. But I cannot read *The Bluest Eye* as tragedy; Claudia, our sometimes-narrator, *speaks*, as does Morrison, our full-time novelist. Thus, although the novel documents the sacrifice of one black woman, it attests to the survival of two others—a survival akin to that of Philomela or Persephone—filled with hardship, but also with hope.

STEPHANIE A. DEMETRAKOPOULOS

Bleak Beginnings: The Bluest Eye

The Bluest Eye is in two ways Morrison's depression novel. First, it comes out of a spiritual loneliness when she was a divorced, single mother, with two preschool boys, and was trying to establish herself in the work world with little support system. In a film for the "Writer in America Series" she says that after her divorce "my spirit was hurt," and implies that writing the novel during the evenings after her children were in bed helped to heal her. She began the novel as a short story, writing her first words of fiction when her boys were barely toddlers, and she had to produce something to stay in a writers' group, apparently her only social outlet at that time. But the novel was actually completed later, finished during a time when she needed some release from the anxiety of being a Black editor in a predominantly white publishing house.

Secondly, Morrison places the novel in 1941 at the end of the Great Depression when life was hard for everyone, but even worse for Black people. It is one of the darkest works I have ever read, akin to the pessimistic naturalism of Theodore Dreiser's *Sister Carrie* or Emile Zola's *Germinal.* I say this for four reasons which will be developed at length: (1) Morrison's images of the earth herself as a barren or sterile mother; (2) her parallel images of society/culture as a stifling force with no help or compassion strong enough to redeem its members; (3) her development of feminine invisibility and mutilation as a paradigm for minimal human existence; and

From *New Dimensions of Spirituality: A Biracial and Bicultural Reading of the Novels of Toni Morrison.* © 1987 by Karla F. C. Holloway and Stephanie A. Demetrakopoulos. Reproduced with permission of Greenwood Publishing Group, Inc., Westport, CT.

(4) her use of closed form and its fatalistic implications in her philosophy.

The darkest and most permeating archetype of the novel is what I would name "Demeter Denied." And Morrison presses this on us unsparingly. An ancient Greek goddess, Demeter is in charge of the earth's fertility and its seasons; she is a major force of the Earth Mother, and her bond to her daughter Persephone symbolizes loving, cosmic on-goingness, a feminine ground of being. But the novel rejects the cyclicality of time as a healing force and rejects nature as a primal force that can nurture and rejuvenate. The chief narrator of the novel, Claudia, and her older sister Frieda plant marigold seeds the year that Pecola's father Cholly rapes and impregnates Pecola; shortly thereafter she miscarries and goes mad. Pecola is both the major protagonist and Morrison's symbol of utter human desolation. In the prologue, Claudia says that the earth, like Pecola, refused to grow the planted seeds; she closes the novel with the image of Pecola wandering, lost in madness at the edge of their town among refuse and sunflowers. Marigolds and sunflowers are gold, symbolic in alchemy of psychic and sacred wholeness. They are also flowers that image how the vegetative force of the earth quickens and rises towards the sun, following it with "trust," literally turning towards it. But the ungrown, sterile marigold seeds symbolize Morrison's sense of the earth as untrustworthy, contingent, penurious, grudging. In this novel there is no cosmic ground of being that mothers us all; time is linear and so much human and natural potential is irrevocably lost. The final vision of Pecola mad and lost amidst the garbage, yet juxtaposed to the sunflowers, is a metaphysically surreal jolt. Nature's lower life-forms (flowers) reemerge cyclically, but nature has no hierarchical values in her sustenance; she is amoral and cares not at all if higher developed creatures go mad or become altogether extinct.

Not only does Morrison reject the possibility of the earth's motherliness as a viable ground of being, she rejects the natural impulses of human beings themselves as forces to have faith in. By rejecting the seasons, the earth, human society, she exposes the romanticism of faith in these abstractions. The human body itself, and mother-daughter bonding, also are revealed as killers not healers. Since the mother-daughter dyad, as imaged in Demeter and Persephone/Kore, is so central to feminine identity, spirituality and affirmation, this resounding rejection is all the more powerful in a novel authored by a woman. Morrison's images of the human body are radically scatological. The novel opens with a story of Claudia vomiting in her bed. The childhood of Cholly, Pecola's father, features Aunt Jimmy's chamberpot reeking fumes out from under her bed into the whole house. Masculine libido deflects into child-molesting and incest. The seasons themselves are experienced by the children as different styles of whipping, and Pecola's family life (the ground of being, the mother-body of a child's existence) is defined by what degree of violence her parents daily mount against each other. Thus unpleasant truths about being embodied are forced on us repeatedly—truths we erase with technology and sanitation. What animal life we see is also far from the agents of the "Peaceable kingdom;" a malevolent local minister, Soaphead Church, manipulates Pecola into killing a sickly, diseased old dog who represents to him the horror of incarnation itself; a little boy from a structured, stifling home kills his mother's cat and blames Pecola.

Imagery of hope does exist within the family, but only in the most minimal form because the adults themselves are so overwhelmed with the struggle for survival. Claudia's mother, Mrs. MacTeer, scolds her children when they get sick, threatening to sap her energy so constantly depleted by the struggle for survival. But she does care for them, and part of Claudia's life urge is in the tactile memory of her mother's hand on her feverish forehead in the middle of the night—a loving mother's touch that belies the antagonistic, angry mother of the daytime. Claudia's father is silent, taciturn, but he is also the protective Vulcan, the keeper of the fires that warm his family. He is a fond father in his quiet way, smiling when the family boarder admired his daughters. But most important is his protectiveness, which shows how significant his girls' lives are to him. When the boarder sexually molests Frieda, Claudia's father goes into a rage and has to be stopped from killing him. So there is a backdrop of strong and caring but stressed adults in the sisters' childhood. There are also some adult examples of *joie de vivre* as embodied in the gossip of the mother and her friends and their laughter as they recount the foibles of their neighbors. Also, the mother does take in Pecola for a while, though she is understandably grudging about the expense. Nevertheless, Claudia's memories are mostly dark, and her sense of life as an adult telling the tale of Pecola is bitter, fraught with anguish. Claudia is a survivor in the same sense as the witness who tells Job what he has lost; she survives only to tell us what has been lost.

There is no affirmation of life through this survival. The life urge and spring reappear, but they are for Claudia unconnected with the ache of whipping, not the resurgence of beauty. And the meaning of Pecola is the symbolic reality that Claudia's reminiscences choose and brood over. But the only choice is between Claudia's crippled survival or "erasure." Not obliteration, not even the dignity of assassination, which Guitar threatens Milkman with in *Song of Solomon*—this is simple erasure: Pecola is erased as if she had never been. Her mother is an inverse Hestian force, spending all her energy on her employer's home and children and leaving her own home a cruel, bleak, and ugly place. Pecola's mother finds her too ugly to love; her schoolmates name her darker shade of skin as too ugly to accept. The only kindness

Pecola finds is the offhand acceptance from the three prostitutes, themselves outcasts who do not bother to intervene between Pecola and the destruction visited on her. Claudia's mother treats Pecola's first menstruation as something unsanitary that must be washed up after, although she does give the girls a quick hug when she finds out what is troubling them. Soaphead Church validates Pecola's wish for blue eyes, affirming the correctness of her rejection of her race.

Yet Morrison's imagery of Black invisibility is different from her depiction of the more universal female invisibility. Ralph Ellison's *Invisible Man* is the original and powerful introduction of the Black self concept into American consciousness. But his protagonist at least knows that he is invisible. He goes underground into his world of lights with self-knowledge that Pecola never approaches. I believe it would be difficult for most women of any background to come to the deep sense of separation and self that Ellison portrays. For Ellison, prestige and place are a priori rights women cannot assume as theirs. (Interestingly, there is only one very slight portrait of a woman in his novel.) Besides being cut off from self-knowledge because she is abused as a child, Pecola is also obstructed and deflected from higher consciousness of self because she is a female. Pecola, certainly, is expunged from human society even before she has awakened to a consciousness of self. Pecola stands for the triple indemnity of the female Black child: children Blacks, and females are devalued in American culture.

Several years ago I heard a woman at a conference suggest that the archetype underlying Pecola's erasure goes clear back to the ancient Greek myth of Procne and Philomela. There are various renditions of this myth, but basically it is a myth of the rape victim rendered voiceless by her attacker. Procne, the sister of Philomela, marries Tereus of Thrace and then sends him to fetch her sister who she misses. Tereus rapes Philomela in some versions; in others, he says Procne is dead and forces Philomela to marry him. He then cuts out her tongue so she cannot tell what happened; in some versions Philomela's arms are also cut off at the elbow so she cannot write his name. (Shakespeare's *Titus Andronicus* features this version.) Philomela's mutilations stand for, of course, the psychic state of a rape victim, who has traditionally been unable to tell of the crime committed against her. Perhaps the rapist was a relative, perhaps the victim would then be worth nothing on the "marriage market," perhaps she lived in a culture that stoned rape victims to death. Recent studies have shown the fear, the shrinking from all human contact, the passivity that rape victims feel; the armless Philomela stands for the castrated, ineffectual woman.

When one considers the chance of a woman undergoing rape even now, when it is no longer so socially accepted as male prerogative, the number of women psychologically crippled and brutalized for life in this secret way in the past must be very large indeed. When historians ask for the achievements of woman, this too must be considered as a force that silenced many, many women. Philomela, unlike Pecola, a grown woman, weaves a tapestry revealing her wrongs; sometimes she is transformed into a nightingale or a swallow that sings or can only twitter. So her human existence is finally canceled forever by the gods. Women forcibly regressed back into the biological matrix of life—this is the myth's image. The finally insane Pecola regresses to a vegetative state, becomes one with the sunflowers; the silenced proto-poet, she does not even twitter, but stands mute. Philomela's sister avenges her by killing Itys, the son of Procne and Tereus, and feeding him to Tereus for supper; Tereus is changed into a hawk. The hawk/nightingale imagery reflects, of course, the predator/prey motif.

In a way Claudia does do the sisterly act of avenging Pecola by telling what she can of the story; but Morrison must tell much of the background of Pecola's parents, Pauline and Cholly Breedlove, so the possibility of a bystander really being able to tell the whole story is implicitly obviated by the novel's shift in narrators. It is not possible for a tongueless victim—her human consciousness, indeed her consciousness of being human, erased before it even blooms—to tell her tale.

It seems to me that in all her novels Morrison tells stories that have not yet been told. This is the quintessential untold story, and it is a story that requires several points of view. There is Claudia's and the omniscient point of view, but finally Morrison gives us a stream of consciousness section that presents Pecola's version of what happened to her. This section is preceded by an adult conversation saying that Pecola's pregnancy is Pecola's fault, a classical blaming of the victim. We learn that Pecola's mother almost beat her to death when she found out that Pecola was pregnant; and the adults hope that baby won't be born because it will be "ugly" like Pecola. None of the bystanders can really see how Pecola perceives her life, not even the sympathetic Claudia. We must visit the immured insanity of Pecola's dialogue with her invisible friend, a dialogue that displaces her sense of blame onto a desire for blue eyes that would redeem all her "ugliness." This use of stream of consciousness and the closed form of the novel emphasize the Philomela archetype; Pecola truly cannot tell her story except as a writer like Morrison can imagine it. The closed form of the novel—the finished life stories of the protagonists, the Breedloves—symbolizes her characters' trapped, fixed lives.

Morrison shows us the love of order, the aesthetic response to it in Pauline, Pecola's mother; Chilly too had artistic potential as a musician. These seeds rot and fester in the lives of the parents; Pecola's brother leaves to rove the country as lost as his father before him. Everyone surrounding Pecola is finally as lost as she. The ungrown marigold seeds of the prologue reemerge in the final imagery of the sunflowers around the mad Pecola—this form insists that this female victim, with her poetic, inward nature, is lost, expunged forever, her voice and story lost. In this first novel, there is no room for epiphany, no possibility of reaching even for inner wholeness such as Nel has at the end of *Sula*. There is only recognition of loss, irrevocable loss.

Yet for me as a reader—though surely not for Morrison as she wrote this novel—there is a redemption in the fact that this story of incest has been told finally from a female point of view, told so well, and I believe, for the first time in human history in this depth and completeness. There is also an implicitly forgiving attitude in Morrison towards all her characters. We understand Cholly and Soaphead Church, and I find it impossible to hate them; their actions seem as inevitable as Pauline's. The book unfolds with all the necessity of any Greek tragedy, but only because the reader's compassion is aroused. No one is indicted for Pecola's destruction, but then in another way we all are. If no one is guilty, there is no scapegoat; the vision becomes more akin to the ancient Necessity, the bleak, irrevocable, futile-to-resist, faceless impingment of an inescapable destiny.

KARLA F. C. HOLLOWAY

The Language and Music of Survival

I thought of Shirley after I read this novel. Shirley was a childhood play-mate. Something brought her memory back to me . . . Shirley, with her linty braids, in her snotty, self-assured play, eating a piece of sugar bread, and me watching enviously as the crumbs from the sandwich mixed with the mucus above her upper lip.

Somehow, *The Bluest Eye* is a journey into Black memory, and as I remember Shirley I do not know whether she is the sisters Frieda and Claudia or Pecola—whether or not she is a child of hope or despair. Somehow though, it does not matter, because this is a novel in which I remember the scope and feel of my childhood. Yet this is a novel that is desolate. I do not think of my childhood in that way so where does this bitter stab of memory originate?

This, I believe, is a book in which the memories belong to Black readers. the funerals, the love, the helplessness and hopefulness—almost all of this book, except the rape of the ugly child Pecola, are identifiable Black events. Suddenly, the memories stop here, arrested by the horror of this incest-rape, and the impact of desolation hits in a cold, foreign way. As strongly as we Black women have participated with the story, the participation stops here. As strongly as we have felt our girlhood, our parenting, as strongly as we have remembered the slick nauseating feel of

From *New Dimensions of Spirituality: A Biracial and Bicultural Reading of the Novels of Toni Morrison.* © 1987 by Karla F. C. Holloway and Stephanie A. Demetrakopoulos. Reproduced with permission of Greenwood Publishing Group, Inc., Westport, CT.

Vaseline and Vicks sliding down our throats during some distant illness, as strongly as we have retained the preciousness of those brief, quick hugs and remembered, shuddering, the quick angry switches—it all stops with the rape of the ugly child Pecola.

But perhaps I need another beginning for discussing this story— something that will bring us closer to an understanding of the identity and the rejection, something that will explain Morrison's reminiscences on Black girlhood and something that will explain this rape of a child. I feel quite strongly that one way into the novel is to understand the impact of language. In *The Bluest Eye* there are numerous opportunities to sympathize with the characters and to understand their stories through their story telling as well as through the author's narration.

Within Black culture, the role of linguistic communication takes on a special, cultural identity. In African-American families, our special use of language is a way of retaining the ties between child and parent and between members of the same community, while distancing ourselves, at will, from a white community that does not share our values or our sense of identity. Our response to the indignities of racism has been to draw boundaries around our cultural identity that dare anyone's crossing. Language helps maintain this boundary. Whether we call it a dialect, Black English, Ebonics, or numerous other terms, the language of the Black community has African roots and maintains African identity in a world where identity is constantly threatened by cultural assimilation and dissemination.

In Claudia's opening reflection, as she tells about the marigolds in the fall of 1941, she mentions that she and her sister felt that planting the marigolds and then saying "the right words over them" would cause them to blossom, and that everything would be all right. "Everything" for these two children was overwhelming. They wanted to fix Pecola's ugliness, ensure the life of the child she carried, obliterate the gossip as well as their own ignorance and impotence. They needed magic words so that everything would be "all right." They must indeed be potent words. The sisters were to learn that year, about extremes—"innocence and faith," "lust and despair"—that were equally nonproductive. As Claudia continues this reflection, she says "there is nothing more to say," and we sense that she feels her language is finally an inadequate medium for carrying the truth and this story. I believe that when language within the Black community becomes an inadequate vessel for resolution or thoughtfulness, actual desolation is finally reached. As Claudia, Cholly and Mrs. Breedlove, and finally Pecola lose their verbal expression, they fall more deeply into a chasm of despair and face the fact that rescue is essentially unobtainable for any of them. But Claudia, who distances herself from the tragedy, regains her voice ("I talk about how I did not plant the seeds too deeply") and survives that year.

Claudia's discussion further reflects African values. She describes a conversation between her mother and one of her friends as a "gently wicked dance." This is an allusion that brings animation to the verbal symbol—that again invests it with a kind of mythology reminiscent of Africa. In Africa, many of the languages of the clans are oral, not written. In these types of languages, the capacity to express motion and feeling and symbolism, so often constrained by print in other languages, is therefore stronger, and closer to being itself. These are archaic languages in the sense that they create significance by bringing into consciousness and being heretofore unconscious. It is as if language is reaching back towards a reality that is only accessible through verbal symbolism—and whether or not the symbol is artistic (as in the gently wicked dance) or musical (the children listening to their mother's conversation listened for "truth in timbre"), the imagery of the linguistic medium carries the message for the culture, and is reliable, because it is drawn from archaism.

If we approach the story and the characters from this perspective, from the vantage point of seeing them through their language garments, and understand their development from these linguistic symbologies, a Black framework of comprehending the despair of the novel is gained.

This is a desolate novel. There is no mistaking the pitifulness and hopelessness of the story. If as we read we try to find solace in some imagined growth of Frieda and Claudia, then we are mistaken. If we want to decide that there is hope because these children do not meet Pecola's fate, then we approach the hopelessness of the social constructivist's criticism—the liberal's optimism that sees dandelions where the marigolds did not grow and misinterprets this as some sign of relief. Pecola thinks dandelions are pretty, but then trips in her thoughtful reflection, and decides, in anger, that "they are ugly." There is no relief of release in this novel. If we approach it truthfully, as the language compels us to do, we will understand that Morrison has written of desolation and decay, because this is where, as victims of our environments, we are left.

We are given the opportunity to compare mothers in this novel with the portraits of Mrs. Breedlove and Mrs. MacTeer. Claudia and Frieda's mother is the one to whom we listen in order to understand the impetus towards desolation, but also how to resist it. These signs toward salvation do not mean that her life is anywhere near ideal and easy. But the girls learn to listen to their mother's voice for signs of her temperament. And for a Black woman or a Black child, these signals that pass between them are all too familiar.

> If my mother was in a singing mood, it wasn't so bad. She would sing about hard times, bad times, and somebody-done-gone-and-left-me times. . . . Misery colored by the greens and blues in my mother's voice took all of the grief out of the words and left me with a conviction that pain was not only endurable, it was sweet.

Language becomes a means of catharsis and, following an ancient ritual from field days, song becomes a signal for many things inexpressible by action direct or indirect.

> My soul look back and wonder/How I got over . . . In Black America, the oral tradition has served as a fundamental vehicle for "gittin ovuh." That tradition preserves the Afro-American heritage and reflects the collective spirit of the race. Through song, story, folk sayings, and rich verbal interplay among everyday people, lessons and precepts about life and survival are handed down from generation to generation . . . the core strength of this tradition lies in its capacity to accommodate new situations and changing realities.

The girls learn from their mother, learn of their Blackness and their femaleness by listening to these sung messages and understanding better how to cope. Language is a powerful medium—it is stronger than a slap or a switch; it controls indirectly and from a distance. Listen as Claudia reflects that "my mother's fussing soliloquies always irritated and depressed us" and "if Mama was fussing . . . it was like somebody throwing stones . . ." The actual dialogues between mother and children, mother and Pecola, are not that eloquent or mellifluous—instead they reflect the ordinary. But it is not these dialogues that teach the girls about life, or cause them to question, or give them the seeds of reflective thought. It is the fussing soliloquies and the "songs my mother sang" that are instructive. And as Black women like me reflect on our childhoods, these songs, these soliloquies were part of our instruction too.

In contrast, Mrs. Breedlove has about lost her voice. A narrator, distant and uninvolved, takes over the telling of her story. There is no other alternative. Claudia cannot tell it. She is too young and her narration is restricted to reflection and commentary on the incidents that directly affect the sisters and their parenting. But we also know that Claudia cannot tell this story, and that no one *real* can tell it because one of the tragedies is that Mrs. Breedlove has lost her voice. We meet her slipping "noiselessly out of bed" and attempting to regain her control over her deteriorating and bleak life as she berates Cholly to get her some wood. But her tirade is met by silence and the narrator comments that "to deprive her of these [verbal] fights was to deprive her of all the zest and unreasonableness of life." Unlike Mrs. MacTeer, she could not, or did not know how to, take refuge in soliloquy or song. Bereft of this tradition, all her energy is spent trying to engage in a verbal battle one who would not give her fuel for the fire. Instead, she turns to Jesus and "discourses" with him about Cholly. But this dialogue is futile. We learn that Cholly pours out his "inarticulate fury" on his wife and that their fights were conducted with a "darkly brutal formalism" during which they did not "talk or groan or curse." Mrs. Breedlove's conversations with Jesus are an attempt at dealing with a consciousness over which she has little control. Jung characterizes this other consciousness as a "dangerous shadow and opponent who is involved as an invisible helper." The conflicting nature of this other (helper-opponent—Jesus-self) is indicative of its role. Jung suggests that recognition of the "shadow" is critical to its being a "helper." Mrs. MacTeer's talking to herself is such recognition. But Mrs. Breedlove's talk to Jesus is self-denial. She gains no strength by engaging an "other." In consequence, Pauline Breedlove loses the battles within her environment and Claudia and Frieda's mother endures.

These women's real strength lies in real speech: "All activities of men, and all the movements in nature, rest on the word, on the productive power of the word, and the awareness that the word alone alters the world . . ." *Nommo* ("word") in life-force and has sustained this powerfulness in African-American cultures. Its power can be destructive or sustaining—but its power seems to be held best by women who have remembered its creative potential.

Within this African perspective it is clear that the background of the Breedloves' anger is their inarticulateness, as well as the functional inarticulateness of the words they do exchange. Jesus can do little to give voice to Mrs. Breedlove's agony, and Cholly, knowing somehow instinctively that her strength would lie in an articulate and capable verbal battle, refuses to supply her ammunition. The only time when we learn the potential force and violence of Mrs. Breedlove's words is when they are directed towards Pecola. And we shudder at the intensity of the mother's reaction against her daughter, who has spilled blueberry pie on the floor of the white folks' kitchen where she works. It is a bitter confrontation, and if the words "the blacker the berry the sweeter the juice" do come to the reader's mind, we see the cruel twist of this metaphor as the mother's words are "hotter and darker than the smoking berries," causing the three girls to "back away in dread." Even more bitter is the narrator's final dialogue in this section, as the little white girl (the kind of girl Claudia would like to kill) gets the benefit of magically soothing language that should have been directed towards Pecola. Mrs. Breedlove (Polly) salves the quizzical uneasiness of the white child by saying "Hush. Don't worry none," in a whisper where the "honey in her words complemented the sundown spilling on the lake."

Claudia, who survives this story, has the attitude that enables her survival. Her anger is appropriately directed towards the whiteness of her adversary. She hates Shirley Temple, the white child in the kitchen, and all the things associated with her repression. Rather than embracing the enemy as does Pecola—she rejects it in a vitriolic (and I would argue "healthy") fashion. Morrison suggests that those children who are victims often embrace their captors (similar to the kidnapper-victim syndrome discussed in recent years). Pecola is possibly the most pitiful victim in all of Morrison's fiction. It is not hard to see why Mrs. Breedlove was misdirecting her concern and care. It is relatively easy to see the pattern of a woman who has fallen into a trap of protecting that which she is capable of protecting, that which she has some degree of control over, and that which she can claim proudly as her work—like the shiny kitchen floor. It is obvious that for her, loving Pecola, especially in her impoverished situation with a "no-'count" husband and a maladjusted son, is a risky proposition. Mrs. Breedlove's survival lies in distancing the possible from the impossible and in signing her allegiance to the possible. Do we fault her for her survival or do we fault a social structure that makes some mothers reject their own children or that makes them react to their children's illnesses with fear and anger? Serious illness presents both the possibility of death and mothers' impotence to shield their children from that possibility. So it is relatively easy to understand how Mrs. Breedlove becomes "Polly" in the white folks' house, and how she manages to be at least part of a person (even though her personhood is defined by her abuser) away from a family that calls for her to lose over and over again.

For Cholly, his doom of inarticulateness is easily traced. He is literally and essentially an abandoned child. Everything we learn about his background, every hurting and abusive gesture, every humiliation pushes him towards a strange and extreme sort of tragic hero-victim and carries our sympathy for this child to an incredible depth. As guileless readers we are easily led towards the shock of the scene where he rapes his ugly daughter. As we look backwards at Cholly's life, we identify quite easily with the pain of his childhood.

The incidents of Cholly's life, purposefully constructed out of ordinary Black experience, overwhelm us both in their quantity and ordinariness. His aunt's death is an event that seems a common Black family memory. Somebody has died from "food." In my own family, it was my Uncle Rufus's first wife, who was killed by "them greens." There are common memories of countless funerals where unmitigated grief is mitigated by the banquet that follows the burial. There is the almost enviable position of being "the bereaved" and comforted by ancient hands, or by unfamiliar hands; there are relatives who have your name, and your looks, though you didn't really know them before this. There are the cousins you meet on such occasions, and maybe fall in love with, and maybe experiment sexually with. But when Cholly and Darlene's sexual encounter turns into a humiliating and frightening experience through the perversity of the cruel and malicious white men who threaten them with guns (a symbolic signal to Cholly that male power does not belong to him), and when Cholly's reaction to this humiliation is virulent hatred for Darlene, instead of anger and hatred for the white men, we sense that something is wrong with this child and that his anger, although directed towards his survival, is dangerously regressive, a smouldering destructiveness aimed at himself and his own, both victims who cannot strike back:

> Sullen, irritable, he cultivated his hatred of Darlene. Never did he once consider directing his hatred toward the hunters. Such an emotion would have destroyed him. They were big, white armed men. He was small, black, helpless. His subconscious knew what his conscious mind did not guess—that hating them would have consumed him, burned him up like a piece of soft coal, leaving only flakes of ash and a question mark of smoke. He was, in time, to discover that hatred of white men—but not now. Not in impotence but later when the hatred could find sweet expression.

At this point, the subtle foreshadowing of Cholly's misdirection is paralleled in his wife's misdirected anger at her daughter and her friends while in the white folks' kitchen. Both suffer an indignity at not being able to protect, shelter, and care for those who, by rights of lineage and culture, are closest to them. Both manage this loss by actual avoiding even of an attempt at these responsibilities and projection of the onus of blame and impotence onto helpless others.

So this Black child runs away from home, finds, and is rejected by his father so devastatingly that he soils his pants in a final loss of control, and finally cries with a "longing that almost splits him open," relinquishing his final bits of selfhood on the banks of the Ocmulgee River.

Morrison notes that the "pieces of Cholly's life could become coherent only in the head of a musician." Her sense of this music's disconnectedness, not that of a symphonic unit, but a more fugal interweaving or a jazz counterpoint, is reminiscent of that musical release that saves Mrs. MacTeer. It is a way of expression that Cholly has lost, and Morrison's warning that Cholly was "dangerously free" is further foreshadowing that the emotions that govern and restrict, and the responsibilities that demand and freeze action are no longer a part of this man. Cholly never speaks again in this novel after the encounter with his father in the pool hall. He is rendered inarticulate because he cannot say whose child he is, and cannot claim the paternal-filial link that forced him to go to Macon in search of his father. From that point on, a narrator presents a third person perspective of Cholly's thoughts and feelings and becomes the musician intermeshing these pieces of Cholly's life and leading us to the point where we can bear to hear about the rape of his child.

Because of the intermeshing, Pecola's rape is not the only event of this novel; although by its emotional magnitude, it could have been. Instead what creates this story is the connection of misery that culminates in rape. What we remember is the generations-long symphony of sorrow that accompanies her tragedy. The "floodlight of drink" illumines this incident for the reader, and gives us an opportunity to participate in Cholly's muddled thinking—and his is the only perspective we are allowed. If we remember him feeling (again expressed narratively) hatred for "the one [his cousin, Darlene] . . . whom he had not been able to protect, to spare, to cover," then the sequence of his emotions when confronting his wife-like daughter at the kitchen sink ("revulsion, guilt, pity, then love") are not unanticipated. He was already voiceless, and his crawling and nibbling behavior and his tender and lustful feelings were all he had left. Because he has been rendered inarticulate, the force towards expressive action, an incoherent and blasphemous behavior, "speaks" for him. Unlike the control Mrs. MacTeer maintains because of her cathartic releases, what is left to Cholly is uncontrollable. (She at least knows what she releases, but he drown his consciousness in drink.) It is this rage that poor Pecola inherits, and it is this rage that rapes her. The result is that a child who had sought so desperately for acceptance and friendship and escape from the frightening scenes of her parent's battles is raped by this rage; what voice she had is ripped away from her in this tremendous and overwhelming act of paternal violence.

We've seen Pecola, up to this point, as others see her. We know nothing about her through her own voice—but we know that people see her as an ugly child and that this one label is the most significant aspect of her life. Pecola too sees herself as others have seen her, and for this reason thinks of herself as being ugly. It is important to admit that this is her reality. It is the overriding factor that pushes her fantasy of blue eyes from a Black girl's wish to have things white to a neurotic fantasy to make things right.

Between that story of Soaphead Church and the gift he gave to a pregnant child is the story of Claudia and Frieda learning a "secret, terrible story" from the only reliable source of information to their town—overheard conversations. All that Pecola could not feel, in her traumatized neurosis, was felt by these sisters—embarrassment, hurt and sorrow: "And I believe our sorrow was the more intense because nobody else seemed to share it. They were disgusted, amused, shocked, outraged or even excited by the story. . . . We looked for eyes creased with concern, but saw only veils."

The community's point of view towards Pecola is essential to an understanding of her plight. There's no good or easy or safe or accurate way of explaining the basis of the townsfolks' hateful accusations and behavior toward this child. It may be enough to say that she was the product of a family that was despised, and that they could not separate these feelings between parents and children. The town whores were the only ones who did not "despise" Pecola. Because of their isolation from the town's good Christian folk, their curious lack of antipathy for this universally rejected child was enough to condemn her in the eyes of anyone more upstanding than they. Pecola, who "looked and looked" at these women, was not even sure that they were real. So the release and escape that their life-style may have offered was unavailable to her. The truly ugly behavior of Maureen and Junior, two of Pecola's classmates, towards this pitiful child is the weight that destroys the potential for the friendship (of sorts) between the sisters and Pecola to balance her sorry existence. Although there may have been some refuge for her in the curious yet protective alliance between Frieda and Claudia in favor of this child, the rest of the real world's hatefulness and spite condemned her. The contrast between the life of the two sisters and Pecola's own was too stark, their lives too distant from her ugly reality.

Whatever the potential for salvation or the reasons for Pecola's insanity, we know she goes into it speechless. If language and speech do indeed offer retribution and salvation, then her silence is sufficient evidence to insure the hopelessness of this child. At the end of the novel Claudia and Frieda sign and say "magic" words and offer Pecola their linguistic magic. But Pecola's silence makes salvation unavailable to her and the sisters' incantations are powerless.

The only insight we have left of Pecola is her own, through the dialogue of her unconscious with itself. Earlier, I mentioned how the tapping into this unconscious self can be a form of endurance. Linguistic structuring of emotion, image, and thought became, for Mrs. MacTeer and her children magic words and song that brought grace. But because of the situation, because of her "ugliness," because of her dead baby, because of her yearning for blue eyes, this catharsis could not purge her; it remains locked inside her pitiful little body. We learn through this dialogue that Mrs. Breedlove does not speak to her daughter, that no one at school speaks to Pecola, and that the rape on the kitchen floor was not the only time Cholly violently molested his daughter. We learn that even this internal dialoguing of Pecola does not bring her solace, because she is afraid the eyes given her by Soaphead Church are not blue enough.

Morrison, or Claudia, comments almost at the very end of this novel that Pecola was "so sad to see." The elliptical relevance and significance of this assessment is all that is left of the story. Of course there is a tying off of loose ends. We learn that Cholly dies, that Mrs. Breedlove still does housework and that the guilt Claudia and Frieda feel at not being able to effect some magic for their friend causes them to avoid her—forever. They use her pain to assuage and measure their joy, and she becomes a necessary standard for the townsfolk and for the sisters, who have finally joined forces with the town, as we know is inevitable, because the strong and the survivors gain their strength from the weak and the pitiable.

Sky-blue eyes and sunflowers are images that mix air and light into Pecola's searchings through the earthen garbage. It is impossible not to see the collusion of these two images, earth and air, and their collapse into dust, an image that appropriately warns us that our protection from the extremes of innocence and lust, faith and despair, love and death, sanity and insanity, as well as earth and air, comes only because of our linguistic means of "rearranging lies and calling it truth and seeing in the new pattern, an old idea." Barfield suggests that meaning flows from this creative principle of rearrangement ". . . whether it lives on as given and remembered, or is re-introduced by the analogy-perceiving, metaphor-making imagination." The complexity and scope of Black language, the fundamental unity between spiritual and material aspects of existence, the harmony in nature and the universe and our given reality, Smitherman notes, assure us of the survival of our African communities. It is at once survival of a culture and survival of its language. Its evolution towards complexity gives it many ways to survive. So as we "rearrange" and make "new patterns" we are assuring a place for "old ideas."

I've grown past my childhood memory of Shirley and her sugar bread sandwiches and her brother June-bug and the parents that were inside of that house next door. And I am sure now that Shirley remembers me as snot-nosed and sooty too, if she remembers me at all. And perhaps Morrison is saying that the extremes of Black childhood memories etch themselves against the present, ensuring the survival of the past, clarifying Black adult living, and signaling our future. And perhaps Morrison is suggesting that when we take the time to reflect, we could all find some potential for more than we are, smoothed over by the passage of time and the inevitable crowding out of growth.

SUSAN WILLIS

Eruptions of Funk: Historicizing Toni Morrison

"I begin to feel those little bits of color floating up into me—deep in me.
That streak of green from the june-bug light, the purple from the berries
trickling along my thighs. Mama's lemonade yellow runs sweet in me. Then I
feel like I'm laughing between my legs, and the laughing gets all mixed up
with the colors, and I'm afraid I'll come, and afraid I won't. But I know I will.
And I do. And it be rainbow all inside."

This is the way Polly Breedlove in *The Bluest Eye* remembers the experience of orgasm—remembers it, because in the grim and shabby reality of
her present, orgasm (which we might take as a metaphor for any deeply
pleasurable experience) is no longer possible. Living in a storefront, her
husband fluctuating between brutality and apathy, her son estranged, her
daughter just plain scared, Polly has no language to describe the memory
of a past pleasure, except one drawn from her distant childhood.

The power of this passage is not just related to the fact that it evokes
the most intense female experience possible. Much of the impact is
produced by the way it describes. Morrison defamiliarizes the portrayal of
sensual experience. Adjectives become substantives, giving taste to color

From *Specifying: Black Women Writing the American Experience*. © 1987 Board of Regents of the
University of Wisconsin System.

45

and making it possible for colors to trickle and flow and, finally, to be internalized like the semen of an orgasmic epiphany.

As often happens in Morrison's writing, sexuality converges with history and functions as a register for the experience of change, i.e., historical transition. Polly's remembrance of childhood sensuality coincides with her girlhood in the rural South. Both are metaphorically condensed and juxtaposed with the alienation she experiences as a black emigrant and social lumpen in a Northern industrial city. The author's metaphoric language produces an estrangement of alienation. Although her metaphors are less bold in their form and content, they still achieve an effect very similar to that of the negritude poets. Indeed, the image of an internal rainbow evokes the poetics of surrealism, but in a language less disjunctive because prose reveals the historical and artistic process through which the image is produced.

When Polly Breedlove reminisces, her present collides with her past and spans her family's migration from the hills of Alabama to a small Kentucky town and her own subsequent journey as the wife of one of the many black men who, in the late thirties and early forties, sought factory jobs in the industrial North. The rural homeland is the source of the raw material of experience and praxis, which in the border-state small town is abstracted to colors, tastes, and tactile sensations. Ohio is, then, the site where images are produced out of the discontinuity between past and present.

Neither Morrison's use of metaphor, nor her general drive to return to origins is rooted in a nostalgia for the past. Rather, the metaphoric rendition of past experience represents a process for coming to grips with historical transition. Migration to the North signifies more than a confrontation with (and contamination by) the white world. It implies a transition in social class. Throughout Morrison's writing, the white world is equated with bourgeois class—its ideology and life-style. This is true of *Song of Solomon* in which Macon Dead's attitudes toward rents and property make him more "white" than "black." This is true of *Tar Baby* in which notions of bourgeois morality and attitudes concerning the proper education and role of women have created a contemporary "tar baby," a black woman in cultural limbo. And it is made drastically clear in *The Bluest Eye*, whose epigrammatic introduction and subsequent chapter headings are drawn from a white, middle-class "Dick-and-Jane" reader. In giving voice to the experience of growing up black in a society dominated by white, middle-class ideology, Morrison is writing against the privatized world of suburban house and nuclear family, whose social and psychological fragmentation does not need her authorial intervention, but is aptly portrayed in the language of the reader: "Here is the family. Mother, Father, Dick, and Jane live in the green-and-white house. They are very happy."

The problem at the center of Morrison's writing is how to maintain an Afro-American cultural heritage once the relationship to the black rural South has been stretched over distance and generations. Although a number of black Americans will criticize her problematizing of Afro-American culture, seeing in it a symptom of Morrison's own relationship to bourgeois society as a successful writer and editor, there are a number of social and historical factors that argue in support of her position. These include the dramatic social changes produced by recent wide-scale migration of industry to the South, which has transformed much of the rural population into wage laborers, the development, particularly in Northern cities, of a black bourgeoisie, and the coming into being, under late capitalism, of a full-blown consumer society capable of homogenizing society by recouping cultural difference. The temporal focus of each of Morrison's novels pinpoints strategic moments in black American history during which social and cultural forms underwent disruption and transformation. Both *The Bluest Eye* and *Sula* focus on the forties, a period of heavy black migration to the cities, when, particularly in the Midwest, black "neighborhoods" came into being as annexes of towns that had never before had a sizable black population. *Sula* expands the period of the forties by looking back to the First World War, when blacks as a social group were first incorporated into a modern capitalist system as soldiers, and it looks ahead to the sixties, when cultural identity seems to flatten out, and, as Helene Sabat observes, all young people tend to look like the "Deweys," the book's nameless and indistinguishable orphans. *Song of Solomon* focuses on the sixties, when neighborhoods are perceived from the outside and called ghettos, a time of urban black political activism and general countercultural awareness. And *Tar Baby*, Morrison's most recent book, is best characterized as a novel of the eighties, in which the route back to cultural origins is very long and tenuous, making many individuals cultural exiles.

With this as an outline of modern black history in the United States, Morrison develops the social and psychological aspects that characterize the lived experience of historical transition. For the black emigrant to the North, the first of these is alienation. As Morrison defines it, alienation is not simply the result of an individual's separation from his or her cultural center, although this is a contributory fact that reinforces the alienation produced by the transition to wage labor. For the black man incorporated into the wartime labor pool (as for many white Appalachians), selling one's labor for the creation of surplus value was only half of alienation, whose brutal second half was the grim reality of unemployment once war production was no longer necessary. The situation for the black woman was somewhat different. Usually employed as a maid and therefore only marginally incorporated as a wage laborer, her alienation was the result of striving to achieve the white bourgeois social model (in which she worked but did not live), which is itself produced by the system of wage labor under capitalism. As housemaid in a prosperous lakeshore home, Polly Breedlove lives a form of schizophrenia, in which her marginality is constantly confronted with a world of Hollywood movies, white sheets, and tender blond children. When at work or at the movies, she separates herself from her own kinky hair and decayed tooth. The tragedy of a woman's alienation is its effect on her role as mother. Her emotions split, Polly showers tenderness and love on her employer's child, and rains violence and disdain on her own.

Morrison's aim in writing is very often to disrupt alienation with what she calls eruptions of "funk." Dismayed by the tremendous influence of bourgeois society on young black women newly arrived from the deep South cities like "Meridan, Mobile, Aiken and Baton Rouge," Morrison describes the women's loss of spontaneity and sensuality. They learn "how to behave. The careful development of thrift, patience, high morals, and good manners. In short, how to get rid of the funkiness. The dreadful funkiness of passion, the funkiness of nature, the funkiness of the wide range of human emotions."

For Polly Breedlove, alienation is the inability to experience pleasure ever again—orgasm or otherwise—whereas for the "sugar-brown Mobile girls," whose husbands are more successful and therefore better assimilated into bourgeois society, alienation is the purposeful denial of pleasure. Once again Morrison translates the loss of history and culture into sexual terms and demonstrates the connection between bourgeois society and repression:

> He must enter her surreptitiously, lifting the hem of her night-gown only to her navel. He must rest his weight on his elbows when they make love, ostensibly to avoid hurting her breasts but actually to keep her from having to touch or feel too much of him.
>
> While he moves inside her, she will wonder why they didn't put the necessary but private parts of the body in some more convenient place—like the armpit, for example, or the palm of the hand. Someplace one could get to easily, and quickly, without undressing. She stiffens when she feels one of her paper curlers coming undone from the activity of love; imprints in her mind which one it is that is coming loose so she can quickly secure it once he is through. She hopes he will not sweat—the damp may get into her hair; and that she will remain dry between her legs— she hates the glucking sound they make when she is moist. When she senses some spasm about to grip him, she will make rapid

movements with her hips, press her fingernails into his back, suck
in her breath, and pretend she is having an orgasm.

At a sexual level, alienation is the denial of the body, produced when
sensuality is redefined as indecent. Sounds and tactile sensations that might
otherwise have precipitated or highlighted pleasure provoke annoyance or
disdain. Repression manifests itself in the fastidious attention given to
tomorrow's Caucasian-inspired coiffure and the decathexis of erogenous
stimulation. Although repression inhibits sexual pleasure, it does not liberate
a woman from sexuality. In faking an orgasm, the woman negates her pleasure for the sake of her husband's satisfaction, thus defining herself as a tool
of his sexual gratification.

To break through repressed female sexuality, Morrison contrasts images
of stifled womanhood with girlhood sensuality. In *The Bluest Eye*, the author's
childhood alter ego, Claudia, is fascinated by all bodily functions and the physical residues of living in the world. She rebels at being washed, finding her
scrubbed body obscene due to its "dreadful and humiliating absence of dirt."
Even vomit is interesting for its color and consistency as it "swaddles down the
pillow onto the sheet." In wondering how anything can be "so neat and nasty
at the same time," Claudia shows a resistance toward the overdetermination of
sensual experience, which, as Morrison sees it, is the first step toward repression. Openness to a full range of sensual experiences may be equated with
polymorphous sexuality, typified by the refusal of many young children to be
thought of as either a boy or a girl. As my own four-year-old daughter sees it
"Little girls grow up to be big boys," and because there is no firm distinction
between the sexes, her teddy bear is "both a boy and a girl." The refusal to
categorize sensual experience—and likewise sex—captures the essence of unre-
pressed childhood, which Morrison evokes as a mode of existence prior to the
individual's assimilation into bourgeois society.

The ultimate horror of bourgeois society against which Morrison
writes and the end result of both alienation and repression is reification.
None of Morrison's black characters actually accedes to the upper reaches of
bourgeois reification, but there are some who come close. They are saved
only because they remain marginal to the bourgeois class and are imperfectly
assimilated to bourgeois values. In *Song of Solomon*, Hagar offers a good
example. Rejected by her lover, she falls into a state of near-catatonia, oblivious to all around her. However, chancing to look in a mirror, she is horrified by her appearance and marvels that anyone could love a woman with her
looks. Thus roused from her withdrawal, Hagar embarks on a daylong shopping spree, driven by the desire to be the delightful image promised by her
brand-name purchases:

She bought a Playtex garter belt, I. Miller No Color hose, Fruit of the Loom panties, and two nylon slips—one white, one pink— one pair of Joyce Fancy Free and one of Con Brio ("Thank heaven for little Joyce heels"). . . .

The cosmetics department enfolded her in perfume, and she read hungrily the labels and the promise. Myurgia for primeval woman who creates for him a world of tender privacy where the only occupant is you, mixed with Nina Ricci's L'Air du temps. Yardley's Flair with Tuvaché's Nectaroma and D'Orsay's Intoxication.

Hagar's shopping spree culminates in a drenching downpour. Her shopping bags soaked, everything—her "Sunny Glow" and "fawn-trimmed-in-sea-foam shortie nightgown"—her wished-for identity and future—falls into the wet and muddy street. Returning home, Hagar collapses with fever and dies after days of delirium.

Hagar's hysteria and death mark the limits of her assimilation into bourgeois culture. Neither through withdrawal nor through commodity consumption can Hagar transform herself into an object. Her marginality, by reason of race and lumpen background, is the basis for her inalienable human dimension. As Morrison might have put it, she is simply too black, too human ever to become reified.

Reification, although never attained by any of Morrison's characters— not even those drawn from the white world—is, instead, embodied in a number of figural images from *The Bluest Eye*. These are celluloid images of Shirley Temple or her "cuute" face on a blue-and-white china cup, and the candy-wrapper images of Mary Jane. Most of all, reification is evident in the plastic smile and moronic blue eyes of a white Christmas baby doll. When Claudia destroys these—dismembering the doll and poking its eyes out—her rebellion is not just aimed at the idea of beauty incarnated in a white model. She is also striking out against the horrifying dehumanization that acceptance of the model implies—both for the black who wears it as a mask and for the white who creates commodified images of the self.

For Morrison, everything is historical; even objects are embedded in history and are bearers of the past. For those characters closest to the white bourgeois world, objects contain the residues of repressed and unrealized desires. For Ruth Foster in *Song of Solomon*, the daughter of the town's first black doctor and wife of the slumlord Macon Dead, a watermark on a table is the stubborn and ever-present reminder of her husband's remorseless rejection. The bowl of flowers around which their hatred crystallized is no longer present; only its sign remains, an opaque residue indelibly written into the table. If, for the bourgeois world, experience is capable of being abstracted to the level of sign, this is not the case for the world of the marginal characters. To cite another example from *Song of Solomon*, Pilate, Ruth Foster's sister-in-law and in every way her antithesis, enjoys a special relationship to all levels of natural experience—including a specific shade of blue sky. Now, color does not function as a sign in the way that the watermark on the table does. Although it bears a concrete relationship to a real object (the blue ribbons on Pilate's mother's hat), it is not an abstract relationship in the way that the watermark stands for the bowl of flowers. For Ruth Foster, the watermark is an "anchor" to the mental and sexual anguish imprisoned in the sign. In contrast, when Pilate points to a patch of sky and remarks that it is the same color as her mother's bonnet ribbons, she enables her nephew Milkman (Ruth Foster's overly sheltered son) to experience a unique moment of sensual perception. The experience is liberational because Pilate is not referring to a specific bonnet—or even to a specific mother; rather the color blue triggers the whole range of emotions associated with maternal love, which Pilate offers to anyone who will share the experience of color with her.

In contrast to the liberational aspect of *Song of Solomon*, Morrison's most recent novel, *Tar Baby*, registers a deep sense of pessimism. Here, cultural exiles—both white and black—come together on a Caribbean island where they live out their lives in a neatly compartmentalized bourgeois fashion: the candy magnate Valerian Street in his stereophonic-equipped greenhouse; his wife, cloistered in her bedroom; and the servants, Odine and Sydney, ensconced in their comfortable quarters. Daily life precludes "eruptions of funk," a lesson poignantly taught when Margaret Lenore discovers the bedraggled wild man, Son, in her closet. Although Son's appearance suggests Rastafarianism and outlawry, any shock value stirred by his discovery is canceled when he, too, proves to be just another exile. Except for one brief incident, when Odine kills a chicken and in plucking it recalls a moment from her distant past when she worked for a poultry butcher, there are no smells, tastes, or tactile experiences to summon up the past. Rather, there is a surfeit of foods whose only quality is the calories they contain.

In contrast with Morrison's earlier novels, the past in *Tar Baby* is never brought to metaphoric juxtaposition with the present. Rather, it is held separate and bracketed by dream. When Valerian Street, sipping a brandy in his greenhouse, lapses into daydream, his recollection of the past, which in essence contrasts entrepreneurial capitalism to modern corporate capitalism, does not intrude on his present retirement. The past is past, and the significant historical transition evoked is perceived as inaccessible and natural.

The past is made more remote when it informs a nighttime dream. This is the case for Sydney, who every night dreams of his boyhood in Baltimore. "It was a tiny dream he had each night that he would never recollect from morning to morning. So he never knew what it was exactly that refreshed him. For the black man who thinks of himself as a "Philadelphia Negro," the back streets of Baltimore are a social debit. His desire for assimilation to white bourgeois culture and the many years spent in service to the bourgeois class negate his ever experiencing the deep sensual and emotional pleasure that Pilate has whenever she beholds a blue sky or bites into a vine-ripened tomato.

With every dreamer dreaming a separate dream, there are no bridges to the past and no possibility of sharing an individual experience as part of a group's social history. Although a reminiscence like Pilate's recognition of the color blue can be communicated, a dream, as Son finds out, cannot be pressed into another dreamer's head. Son's dream of "yellow houses with white doors" and "fat black ladies in white dresses minding the pie table in church" is an image of wish fulfillment, rooted in private nostalgia. It bears no resemblance to his real past as we later come to understand it out of what the novel shows us of Eloe, Florida, where tough black women with little time for pie tables have built their own rough-hewn, unpainted homes.

For the "tar baby," Jadine, fashioned out of the rich white man's indulgence and the notions of culture most appealing to bourgeois America (European education and Paris "haute couture"), the past is irretrievable and no longer perceived as desirable. As the individual whose cultural exile is the most profound, Jadine is haunted by waking visions, born out of guilt and fear. In her most terrifying vision, a mob of black women—some familiar, some only known by their names—condemn Jadine for having abandoned the traditional maternal role of black women.

Whereas Jadine lives her separation from the past and rejection of traditional cultural roles with tormented uncertainty and frenzied activity, Milkman, in Morrison's previous novel, experiences his alienation from black culture as a hollow daily monotony. Jadine, whose desire to find self and be free leads to jet hops between Paris, the Caribbean, and New York, has not had the benefit of a powerful cultural mentor like Pilate, who awakens Milkman's desire to know his past. In contrast, all of Jadine's possible cultural heroes are bracketed by her rupture with the past and her class position. Jadine rejects family—her Aunt Odine, for her homey ways and maternal nature—and culture—the black islanders, so remote from Jadine's trajectory into the future that she never even bothers to learn their names.

Milkman, on the other hand, has been born and raised in the ghetto, albeit in the biggest house. He has never been to college, but he has had the benefit of teachers—both the street-wise Guitar and the folk-wise Pilate. If Milkman's present is a meaningless void of bourgeois alienation, the possibility of a past opens out to him like a great adventure. A quest for gold initiates Milkman's journey into the past—and into the self—but gold is not the novel's real object. Imagining that gold will free him from his father's domination and his family's emotional blackmail, Milkman comes to realize that only by knowing the past can he hope to have a future.

There is a sense of urgency in Morrison's writing, produced by the realization that a great deal is at stake. The novels may focus on individual characters like Milkman and Jadine, but the salvation of individuals is not the point. Rather, these individuals, struggling to reclaim or redefine themselves, are portrayed as epiphenomenal to community and culture, and it is the strength and continuity of the black cultural heritage as a whole that is at stake and being tested.

As Morrison sees it, the most serious threat to black culture is the obliterating influence of social change. The opening line from *Sula* might well have been the novel's conclusion, so complete is the destruction it records: "In that place, where they tore night shade and blackberry patches from their roots to make room for the Medallion City Golf Course, there was once a neighborhood." This is the community Morrison is writing to reclaim. Its history, terminated and dramatically obliterated, is condensed into a single sentence whose content spans from rural South to urban redevelopment. Here, as throughout Morrison's writing, natural imagery refers to the past, the rural South, the reservoir of culture that has been uprooted—like the blackberry bushes—to make way for modernization. In contrast, the future is perceived of as an amorphous, institutionalized power embodied in the notion of "Medallion City," which suggests neither nature nor a people. Joining the past to the future is the neighborhood, which occupies a very different temporal moment (which history has shown to be transitional), and defines a very different social mode, as distinct from its rural origins as it is from the amorphous urban future.

It is impossible to read Morrison's four novels without coming to see the neighborhood as a concept crucial to her understanding of history. The neighborhood defines a Northern social mode rather than a Southern one, for it describes the relationship of an economic satellite, contiguous to a larger metropolis rather than separate subsistence economics like the Southern rural towns of Shalimar and Eloe. It is a Midwestern phenomenon rather than a Northeastern big-city category, because it defines the birth of principally first-generation, Northern, working-class black communities. It is a mode of the forties rather than the sixties or the eighties, and it evokes the many locally specific black populations in the North before these became assimilated to a larger, more generalized, and less regionally specific sense of black culture that we today refer to as the "black community."

The fact that Milkman embarks on a quest for his past is itself symptomatic of the difference between the forties neighborhood and the sixties community. In contrast with Milkman, the black youth of the forties had no need to uncover and decipher the past simply because enough of it was still present, born on successive waves of Southern black immigrants. For Milkman the past is a riddle, a reality locked in the verses of a children's song (the "song of "Solomon") whose meaning is no longer explicit because time has separated the words from their historical content. Childhood and the way children perceive the world are again a figure for a mode of existence prior to the advent of capitalism and bourgeois society. And in *Song of Solomon*, it coincides with the function of song in all marginal cultures as the unwritten text of history and culture.

Milkman's quest is a journey through geographic space in which the juxtaposition of the city and the countryside represents the relationship of the present to the past. In tracing his roots from the Detroit ghetto, where he was familiar with Pilate's version of the Solomon song, to Danville, Pennsylvania, where his father grew up; and then to Shalimar, Virginia, where his grandfather was born and children still sing of Solomon, Milkman deciphers the twin texts of history: song and genealogy. In so doing, he reconstructs a dialectic of historical transition, in which the individual genealogy evokes the history of black migration and the chain of economic expropriation from hinterland to village, and village to metropolis. The end point of Milkman's journey is the starting point of his race's history in this country: slavery. The confrontation with the reality of slavery, coming at the end of Milkman's penetration into historical process, is liberational because slavery is not portrayed as the origin of history and culture. Instead, the novel opens out to Africa, the source, and takes flight on the wings of Milkman's great-grandfather, the original Solomon. With the myth of the "flying Africans" Morrison transforms the moment of coming to grips with slavery as an allegory of liberation.

The fact that geographic space functions for history is symptomatic of a time when a people's past no longer forms a continuity with the present. It is one of the features that differentiates literary modernism from realism, in which people's lives are portrayed as integral to the flow of history. Because the past is perceived as problematical and historical transition is represented by the relationship among countryside, village, and city, *Song of Solomon* is very similar to the great modernist novels of the Latin American "Boom" (the literary movement born with the Cuban Revolution and brought to an end with the assassination of Allende). In Morrison's *Song of Solomon*, as in the Peruvian Mario Vargas Llosa's *La Casa Verde*, the synchronic relationship defined in geographic space stands for a diachronic relationship. The most interesting feature about these modernist texts is that, in reading them, the reader, like Milkman, restores diachrony to the text and, in so doing, realizes the historical dialectic that the text presents as inaccessible.

Milkman's journey into the past takes him out of consumer society, where he, Christmas shopping in the Rexall store, practices the translation of human emotions into commodities, and thrusts him into the preindustrial world of Shalimar, where for the first time in his life Milkman sees women with "nothing in their hands." Stunned, Milkman realizes that he "had never in his life seen a woman on the street without a purse slung over her shoulder, pressed under her arm, or dangling from her clenched fingers." The vision of women walking empty-handed produces an estrangement of Milkman's normal view of women who, conditioned by a market economy, haul around purses like grotesque bodily appendages.

The descent into the past means stepping out of reified and fetishized relationships. Milkman's sensitivities are abruptly awakened when, trudging through the woods, he is scratched by branches, bruised by rocks, and soaked in a stream. As all of his commodified possessions fall away—his watch, his Florsheim shoes, and his three-piece suit—he comes to realize a full range of sensual perceptions (along with some human social practices—like sharing) he had never before experienced. Entering Solomon's General Store, Milkman is struck by its dramatic antithesis to the big-city department store, in which money (rather than need or use) mediates the exchange of human identities for brand names.

For Macon Dead, Milkman's father, all human relationships have become fetishized by their being made equivalent to money. His wife is an acquisition; his son, an investment in the future; and his renters, dollar signs in the bank. The human sentiments he experienced as a boy have given way to the emotional blackmail he wages as an adult. Driven by the desire to own property, the basis of bourgeois class politics, Macon Dead uses property, like a true capitalist, for further accumulation through the collection of rents. When Milkman, echoing his father's words, refers to money as "legal tender," he reveals how deeply fetishized and abstracted the concept of money itself has become. In this context, the search for gold takes on new meaning as a search for the only unfetishized form of value and, in an allegorical sense, as the retrieval of unfetishized human relationships.

However, Macon Dead is not so totally integrated into the bourgeois class that he cannot sense the impoverishment of his life—"his wife's narrow unyielding back; his daughters, boiled dry from years of yearning; his son, to whom he could speak only if his words held some command or criticism." A

phantom in search of some vision of human fulfillment, Macon wanders one
evening into the southside ghetto, his sister's neighborhood. There, drawn
by her singing, he pauses to peer in her window. In every way Pilate is her
brother's emotional and social antithesis. What Macon sees when he looks
into Pilate's house is a totally alternative life-style, whose dramatic opposition to the spiritual impoverishment of Macon's world gives rise to utopian
moment:

> . . . he crept up to the side window where the candlelight
> flickered lowest, and peeped in. Reba was cutting her toenails
> with a kitchen knife or a switchblade, her long neck bent almost
> to her knees. The girl, Hagar, was braiding her hair, while Pilate,
> whose face he could not see because her back was to the window,
> was stirring something in a pot. Wine pulp, perhaps. Macon
> knew it was not food she was stirring, for she and her daughters
> ate like children. Whatever they had a taste for. No meal was
> ever planned or balanced and served. Nor was there any gath-
> ering at the table. Pilate might bake hot bread and each one of
> them would eat it with butter whenever she felt like it. Or there
> might be grapes, left over from the winemaking, or peaches for
> days on end. If one of them bought a gallon of milk they drank it
> until it was gone. If another got a half bushel of tomatoes or a
> dozen ears of corn, they ate them until they were gone too. They
> ate what they had or came across or had a craving for. Profits
> from their wine-selling evaporated like sea water in a hot wind—
> going for junky jewelry for Hagar, Reba's gifts to men, and he
> didn't know what all.

In its journey back to rural origins, the novel demonstrates that
Pilate's household is not, as this passage tends to suggest, structured in
infantile desires and relationships, but that the world of childhood is rooted
in rural society, where reciprocity and the unmediated response to desire
determine social life. The utopian aspects of Pilate's household is not
contained within it, but generated out of its abrupt juxtaposition to the
bourgeois mode of her brother's household. In contrast to Macon's world,
which is based on accumulation, Pilate's household is devoted in true
potlatch fashion to nonaccumulation. With everyone working to separate
berries from thorns, winemaking is not a means for creating surplus value,
but a communal social activity whose natural raw material suggests, in
Morrison's symbolic register, another link to rural agricultural society. Reba,
who wins lotteries and department-store giveaways, enjoys a noncommodified

relationship to objects, in which value is defined not by an object's monetary equivalent but by the spontaneous way she comes to possess it and the pleasure it renders in the giving. Finally, Pilate's only pretense to property ownership is purely symbolic: a bag of bones, which turn out to be her father's, and rocks, a single one gathered from every state she has visited.

Throughout her writing Morrison defines and tests the limits of individual freedom. Unlike those characters who realize total freedom and, as a result, are incapable of living in society and maintaining human relationships, like Cholly Breedlove and Sula, Pilate lives an unencumbered life that is the basis for a social form of freedom, rich in human understanding and love, which is neither sexual nor familial. In the text, Pilate's freedom, which makes her different from everybody else, has a very curious explanation: namely, the lack of a navel.

Now, it would be wrong to simply see Pilate's lack of a navel as just one more example of the mutilated, deformed, and stigmatized characters who tend to crop up in Morrison's writing. And it would be equally wrong to dismiss these forms of physical difference as nothing more than the author's obsession with freaks of nature. Rather, as Morrison herself indicates, Pilate's lack is to be read in social terms. The lack of a navel, like the other versions of physical deformity, functions as a metaphor that allows the reader to perceive a unique personal relationship to society as a whole.

Born without a navel, Pilate is a product of an unnatural birth. In social terms, her father dead and having never known her mother, she is an orphan. Her smooth, unbroken abdominal skin causes her to be shunned by everyone who either befriends her or comes to be her lover. Consequently, she has "no people." Because no clan claims her, she is outside all the potentially limiting aspects of blood relationships and traditional forms of social behavior. Apparently without a past and a place, Pilate embodies the "mythic hero" first portrayed by Faulkner's Thomas Sutpen in *Absalom! Absalom!* The difference between Faulkner and Morrison, conditioned by the intervening years, which have brought black civil rights, countercultural politics, and the feminist perspective, is that, while Morrison invests her "mythic hero" with utopian aspirations, Faulkner does not. In making Sutpen and his "design" for plantation and progeny the epitome of Southern class society, Faulkner negates the utopian potential that his mythic outsider first represents in opposition to the stifled, small-town sensibilities of Jefferson, Mississippi.

Another dimension that Pilate's lack of a navel allows the reader to experience is the child's discovery of sexual difference. The metaphor of lack articulates the relationship between the advent of adult sexuality and the way it transforms the individual's relationship to others. As a child, having seen only her brother's and father's stomachs, Pilate imagines that navels, like

penises, are something men have and women lack. Later, when others point
to her lack as a form of freakishness, Pilate achieves adult sexuality only to
have it denied her. Deprived of sex because of her unique body and the
superstitious fear it creates, Pilate's lack becomes the basis for her liberation
from narrowly defined human relationships based on sexuality and the
expansion of her social world to one based on human sensitivity. This is very
different from the way Pilate's sister-in-law, Ruth Foster, lives her sexual
deprivation. Shunned by her husband, she turns inward to necrophiliac
fantasies of her father, a mildly obscene relationship with her son, and
masturbation. Ruth, like many of Morrison's female characters, is dependent
on a possessive and closed heterosexual relationship; she never comes to see
human relationships as anything but sexual. For her, the denial of sex simply
means a more narrowly defined sexuality and the closure of her social world.

The only aspect of Pilate's lack as a metaphor for social relationships
that is not explicit but does, nevertheless, inform Morrison's treatment of
Pilate is its function as a figure for the experience of racial otherness. This is
not the case for other instances of lack, which, like Pecola's lack of blue eyes
and Hagar's lack of copper-colored hair, capture the horror of seeing oneself
as "other" and inferior. Although Pilate, like many of Morrison's other characters, does undergo a moment of looking at (and into) the self, during which
she recognizes her lack (or difference) and, as a consequence, determines to
live her life according to a very different set of values, her moment of self-
recognition (unlike many of theirs) is not couched in racial terms. Because
lack in every other instance is a figure for the experience of race, it would
seem to be implicit—if not explicit—in the character of Pilate. There is just
no need for Pilate to affirm herself through race as the shell-shocked
Shadrack does in *Sula* when, amnesiac and terrified by his own body, he
glimpses the reflection of his face and sees in it the bold reality of his
"unequivocal" blackness. For Pilate, blackness is already unequivocal. And
pastlessness does not endanger identity, or separate her from society, as it
does for Shadrack. Rather, it liberates the self into society.

As a literary figure for examining the lived experience of social difference, and testing the human potential for liberation, lack has its opposite in a
full term: bodily stigma. In contrast to Pilate, who has no mark, Sula possesses
a striking birthmark above her eye. A patch of skin unlike that found on any
other human, Sula's birthmark is thought to represent a tadpole, a flower, or a
snake depending on the mood of the beholder. Stigma is the figural equivalent of Sula's role in the community. As a social pariah branded as different, she
is the freedom against which others define themselves.

Bodily deformity is another metaphor for the experience of social
difference. When Shadrack awakes in a hospital bed, he comes into a world

so totally fragmented and sundered that he is unsure where his own hands might be; after all, "anything could be anywhere." When he finally does behold his hands, he imagines that they are monstrously deformed—so terrifyingly that he cannot bear to look at them. Totally disoriented, his hands hidden behind his back, Shadrack is expelled from the hospital and pushed out into the world—a lone, cringing figure in an alien landscape.

For Morrison, the psychological, like the sensual and the sexual, is also historical. In a novel whose opening describes the leveling of a neighborhood and its transformation into the Medallion City Golf Course, Shadrack's experience of bodily fragmentation is the psychological equivalent of annihilating social upheaval, which he was subjected to as an army draftee (the army being the first of capitalism's modern industrial machines to incorporate black men). Shadrack's imagined physical deformity is a figure for the equally monstrous psychological and social transformations that capitalism in all its modes (slavery, the military, and wage labor) has inflicted on the minds and bodies of black people.

Shadrack's affirmation of self, arising out of the moment he sees his image reflected in a toilet bowl and beholds the solid and profound reality of his blackness, ranks as one of the most powerful literary statements of racial affirmation. Race is the wellspring of Shadrack's inalienable identity. Everything about him and within him may be subject to transformation, but his blackness is forever. This sense of continuity in the face of chaos lies at the heart of Shadrack's cryptic, one-word message to the child Sula: "'Always.'" It is the basis for both Shadrack's and Sula's reinsertion into society as representations of freedom. As both messiah and pariah, Shadrack is marginal, accepted by, but never assimilated into, the black community. He, like Sula and Morrison's other social pariah, Soaphead Church, provides a point of perspective in the community that is both inferior and exterior; he allows the community to define itself against as form of freedom, which being a social unit, it cannot attain. Morrison's characters demonstrate that the black community tolerates difference, whereas the white bourgeois world shuts difference out. She underscores the fact that for the white world, under capitalism, difference, because it articulates a form of freedom, is a threat and therefore must be institutionalized or jailed.

In *Tar Baby*, bodily deformity takes a very different form. Because this novel describes an already-sundered black community whose exiles have neither the wish nor the capacity to rediscover the source of black culture, freedom cannot be articulated (as it was in the previous novels) by an individual's moment of self-affirmation and reinsertion into society. Having no possible embodiment in the real world—not even as a pariah—freedom takes mythic form and defines the text's alternate, subterranean world, in which, in sharp contrast with the bourgeois world of manor houses and leisure, a centuries-old band of blind black horsemen rides the swamps.

Blindness is another way of giving metaphoric expression to social difference and freedom. It overlaps with the function of lack in that the lack of sight, which in bourgeois society is the basis for an individual's alienation, is in the mythic world the basis of the group's cohesion and absolute alternality. This is because blindness is not portrayed as an individual's affliction, but rather a communally shared way of being in the world. Once again, the figure of deformity evokes a historical reality. The myth of the blind horsemen has its roots in the many real maroon societies whose very existence depended on seclusion and invisibility. This is the social reality for which blindness is a metaphoric reversal.

A final metaphor for social otherness is self-mutilation. Unlike lack and deformity, self-mutilation represents the individual's direct confrontation with the oppressive social forces inherent in white domination. Because it functions as a literary figure, self-mutilation is portrayed in Morrison's writing as liberational and contrasts sharply with all the other forms of violence done to the self. For instance, when Polly Breedlove lashes out at her child Pecola, berating her and beating her for spilling a berry cobbler while at the same time comforting and cuddling the white child in her charge, she internalizes her hate for white society and deflects the spontaneous eruption of violence away from its real object and toward a piece of herself. Unlike Polly Breedlove's violence toward the self, which locks her in profound self-hatred, self-mutilation is portrayed as a confrontational tactic that catapults the individual out of an oppressive situation. Because it involves severing a part of the body, self-mutilation brings about the spontaneous redefinition of the individual, not as an alienated cripple—but as a new and whole person, occupying a radically different social space.

When, as an adolescent, Sula is confronted by a band of teenage Irish bullies, she draws a knife. Instead of threatening the boys with it or plunging it into one of them, she whacks off the tip of her own finger. Terrified, the boys run away. Sula's self-mutilation symbolizes castration and directly contests the white male sexual domination of black women that the taunting and threatening boys evoke. Her act, coupled with words of warning, "If I can do that to myself, what you suppose I'll do to you?" represents the refusal—no matter how high the cost—to accept and cower in the face of domination.

For its defiance of oppressive social norms as well as its symbolic nature, Sula's act of self-mutilation has its precedent in her grandmother's solution to a similar confrontation with a bourgeois-dominated society. Abandoned by her husband, with three small children and nothing but five eggs and three beets among them, Eva Peace takes a truly radical course of action that lifts her out of the expected role of an abandoned black mother circa 1921, who could do nothing more than live hand-to-mouth, and gives her a very different future. Leaving her children in the care of a neighbor, she sets out. "Eighteen months later she swept down from a wagon with two crutches, a new black pocketbook, and one leg." Eva never confirms neighborhood speculation that she allowed a train to sever her leg because the way in which she lost it is not important. The real issue is what her self-mutilation enables her to achieve. As the juxtaposition between Eva's "new black pocketbook" and "one leg" suggests, monthly insurance checks make it possible for her to build a new life. The construction of a rambling, many-roomed house for family and boarders gives physical evidence of Eva's confrontation with and manipulation of the written laws of white society, whose unwritten laws would have condemned her to a life of poverty.

Yet the most radical aspect of Eva's act is not the simple and direct contestation of capitalism that her self-mutilation represents but the subsequent lack that allows a wholly new social collective to come into being around her. If the loss of a limb means that Eva practically never leaves her room, it does not signify withdrawal. Instead, Eva is "sovereign" of an entire household, which includes three generations of Peace woman as its nucleus (Eva, Hannah, and Sula); their boarders (the young married couples and an alcoholic hillbilly); and their adopted outcasts (the three Deweys). For its fluid composition, openness to outsiders, and organization on a feminine principle, Eva's household represents a radical alternative to the bourgeois family model.

At one level, Morrison writes to awaken her reader's sensitivity, to shake up and disrupt the sensual numbing that accompanies social and psychological alienation. This is the function of her "eruptions of funk," which include metaphors drawn from past moments of sensual fulfillment as well as the use of lack, deformity, and self-mutilation as figures for liberation. At a deeper level, and as a consequence of these features, Morrison's writing often allows an alternative social world to come into being. When this happens, "otherness" no longer functions as an extension of domination (as it does when blackness is beheld from the point of view of racist bourgeois society, or when the crippled, blind, and deformed are compared to the terrorizing totality of a whole and therefore "perfect" body). Rather, the space created by otherness permits a reversal of domination and transforms what was once perceived from without as "other" into the explosive image of a utopian mode. Morrison's most radical "eruption of funk" is the vision of an alternative social world. It comes into view when Macon Dead peers into Pilate's window; when the child Nel, the product of her mother's stifled bourgeois morality, scratched at Sula's screen door; and when the intimidated and fearful Pecola visits her upstairs neighbors, the three prostitutes.

It is not gratuitous that in all these cases the definition of social utopia is based on a three-woman household. This does not imply a lesbian orientation, because in all cases the women are decidedly heterosexual. Rather, these are societies that do not permit heterosexuality as it articulates male domination to be the determining principle for the living and working relationships of the group, as it is in capitalist society.

Morrison's three-woman utopian households contrast dramatically with an earlier literary version that occurs, paradoxically again, in Faulkner's *Absalom! Absalom!* During the grinding culmination of the Civil War, the men all gone—siphoned off by the army, the economy reduced to bare subsistence, the novel brings together three women: Judith, Sutpen's daughter and heir; Clytie, Sutpen's black nonheir; and the young spinstress, Miss Rosa, Sutpen's nonbetrothed. Taking refuge in the shell of a once-prosperous manor house, they eke out their survival in a day-to-day basis:

> So we waited for him. We led the busy eventless lives of three nuns in a barren and poverty-stricken convent: the walls we had were safe, impervious enough, even if it did not matter to the walls whether we ate or not. And amicably, not as two white women and a negress, not as three negroes or three whites, not even as three women, but merely as three creatures who still possessed the need to eat but took no pleasure in it, the need to sleep but from it no joy in weariness or regeneration, and in whom sex was some forgotten atrophy like the rudimentary gills we call the tonsils or the still-opposable thumbs for old climbing.

In considering the catclysm of the Civil War and its destruction of traditional Southern society, Faulkner is led to imagine the basis for a potentially radical new form of social organization, based on subsistence rather than accumulation and women rather than men. However, the incipient possibility of social utopia dies stillborn, because the male principle and the system of patrimony have not been transformed or refuted, but merely displaced. Sutpen, even in his absence, is still the center of the household. Race, too, is not confronted or transcended. Rather, it, like sex, is simply dismissed. And with it go all vestiges of humanity.

The tremendous differences between Faulkner and Morrison, which include historical period, race, and sex, lie at the heart of their dramatically opposed images: the one dystopian; the other utopian. Rather than dwell on the social and historical factors that shape their fiction, I will emphasize the ways in which historical difference between the three women function to test the social dynamic within the group, and between it and society at large. Faulkner's retrenched espousal of the male-dominated social model and his tenacious refusal to imagine anything else condition his bleak vision of society. On the other hand, Morrison's projection of a social utopia arises from its confrontation with and reversal of the male-dominated bourgeois social model. Rather than systematically leveling social problems, Morrison foregrounds them. The utopian aspect of her vision is produced by the totality of its opposition to society at large—not by its individual members. This makes her portrayal very different from classical literary utopias, whose individuals are presented as perfect and harmonious models. None of Morrison's individual characters in any of her three utopias is perfect. Rather than supplying answers to social problems, they give rise to questions about social relationships and society as a whole. Thus Pilate demonstrates the insufficiency of the agrarian social mode to provide for its members once they are transplanted to urban consumer society. Her strength and resourcefulness cannot be passed on to her daughter and granddaughter because each is more distant from the rural society in which Pilate worked and grew up. Their experience of insufficiency leads to hollow consumption (Reba's of sex and Hagar's of commodities) and demonstrates the way consumer society penetrates and impoverishes human relationship.

When in *Tar Baby* "funk" erupts as myth, its potential for estranging fetishized relationships is minimized because of its distance from urban and suburban settings that condition the lives of more and more Americans, both black and white. Son's quest for the mythic community of blind maroon horsemen that ends *Tar Baby* may represent a dramatic departure from his previous endeavors, but it does not bring disruption into the heart of social practice, as occurs when the image of Pilate's household bursts upon Macon Dead's alienated and numbed sensibilities. Although *Song of Solomon* also had a mythic dimension, myth is integral to Milkman's concrete past, as he discovers by following his family's route back to slavery, whereas for Son, it represents a very distant cultural source not directly linked to his present.

"Funk" is really nothing more than the intrusion of the past into the present. It is most oppositional when it juxtaposes a not-so-distant social mode to those evolved under bourgeois society. Morrison's method might be thought of as a North American variant of the magical realism that we have come to associate with Gabriel García Marquez. If in his *One Hundred Years of Solitude* pleasurable delight is synonymous with barbed political criticism, this is because the text's metaphoric incidents and characters are created out of the juxtaposition of First and Third World realities. Just as domination and dependency create separation and inequality between North and South

America, so too do Marquez's metaphors represent the unresolved contradiction between two possible readings: the one mythic and pleasurable, the
other historical and critical. The same holds true for Morrison, only the
terms of her geographic and historical equation are bound up and framed by
the history of the United States. North/South, black/white, these are the
ingredients of Morrison's magical realism whose tension-fraught and unresolved juxtapositions articulate the continuation of domination in our society
and the persistence of racism, and at the same time provoke Morrison's
creative and critical imagination.

MICHAEL AWKWARD

"The Evil of Fulfillment":
Scapegoating and Narration in The Bluest Eye

I had found my tongue.

—Toni Morrison
The Bluest Eye

. . . all the voice in answer he could wake
Was but the mocking echo of his own.
                    *   *   *   *

He would cry out on life, that what it wants
Is not its own love back in copy speech,
But counter-love, original response.
And nothing ever came of what he cried . . .

—Robert Frost
"The Most of It"

. . . just as the male artist's struggle against his precursor takes the form of what
[Harold] Bloom calls revisionary swerves, flights, misreadings, so the female writer's
battle for self-creation involves her in a revisionary process. Her battle, however, is not
against her (male) precursor's reading of the world but against the reading of her.
                    —Sandra Gilbert and Susan Gubar,
                        The Madwoman in the Attic

In the previous chapter I attempted to chart Zora Neale Hurston's successful *denigration* of the novel. *Their Eyes Were Watching God* provides particularly compelling evidence in support of Hurston's claim that "everything that [the

From *Inspiriting Influence: Tradition, Revision, and Afro-American Women's Novels.* © 1989 by Michael Awkward.

Afro-American] touches is re-interpreted for his own use." Such reinterpretation of expressive forms requires, as I have argued, not only a sensitive exploration of the lives of black characters, but also an energetic revision of the Western forms themselves. Hurston's placement of her novel in the Afro-American expressive cultural tradition in general, and in the Afro-American literary tradition in particular, is signalled by that novel's employment (and successful resolution) of the Du Boisian concept of double consciousness in both its content and its narrative strategies.

In the present chapter, I shall focus on Toni Morrison's *The Bluest Eye*. Morrison's narrative stands as her initial attempt at generic *denigration*, as her first effort to create what elsewhere she has called "A genuine Black . . . Book." But while, as in the case of Hurston's text, it is possible to read in Morrison's novel clear signs of a merging of narrative voices, the narrative events of *The Bluest Eye*—and particularly Pecola's schizophrenic double voicedness exhibited when she believes she has been granted the "bluest eyes in the whole world"—portray double consciousness as a constant and, for Pecola at least, a permanently debilitating state.

The following discussion will attempt to account for the reasons *The Bluest Eye* can present merged Afro-American consciousness only in its strategies of narration. Before such accounting is possible, however, it is necessary first to discuss the specifics of Morrison's placement of herself within the Afro-American literary tradition. This placement, I will argue, evidences a self-conscious rejection of the models of such preeminent figures as James Baldwin and Ralph Ellison, and a clear exploration of the types of thematic and formal concerns found in Hurston.

I

In "Rootedness: The Ancestor as Foundation" Morrison insists that ancestors play an essential role in individual works in the Afro-American canon. She states:

> [I]t seems to me interesting to evaluate Black literature on what the writer does with the presence of the ancestor. Which is to say a grandfather as in Ralph Ellison, or a grandmother as in Toni Cade Bambara, or a healer as in Bambara or Henry Dumas. There is always an elder there. And these ancestors are not just parents, they are sort of timeless people whose relationships to the characters are benevolent, instructive and protective, an they provide a certain kind of wisdom.

Despite the apparent optimistic assurance of this statement, Morrison is well aware that "the presence of the ancestor" is not always viewed by the Afro-American writer as "benevolent, instructive and protective." Indeed, she argues—just a few sentences following the above declaration—that the works of Richard Wright and James Baldwin exhibit particularly identifiable problems with the ancestor. For Morrison, Wright's corpus suggests that he "had great difficulty with that ancestor," and Baldwin's that he was confounded and disturbed by the presence or absence of an ancestor. (Although Morrison does not specify which texts she has in mind, one assumes that she is referring to Wright's *Native Son I* and *Black Boy* and to Baldwin's *Go Tell It on the Mountain* and "Note on a Native Son.")

Morrison's singling out of Wright and Baldwin as figures in whose work ancestors represent troubling presences (or absences) is not, it seems to me, a random act. For in addition to both writers' *intra*textual struggles with ancestors, the Wright-Baldwin personal and literary relationship represents the most fabled *inter*textual association in Afro-American letters. Baldwin's attacks on his acknowledged precursor Wright offer intriguing Afro-American examples of what Harold Bloom has termed "the anxiety of influence." In "Alas, Poor Richard," for example—an unconscionably vicious final assault on the recently deceased precursor—Baldwin asserts that the harsh criticism of *Native Son* that occupies the final pages of his essay "Everybody's Protest Novel" represented his attempt to create canonical space for his own perceptions of Afro-American life. He states: "I had used [Wright's] work as a kind of spring-board into my own. His work was a roadblock into my road, the sphinx, really, whose riddles I had to answer before I could become myself."

Though it is certainly far from a sympathetic postmortem, "Alas, Poor Richard" does exhibit a great deal of sensitivity to the complex system of violent verbal revision that characterizes the Western (male) literary tradition. For Baldwin discusses not only his own problematic relationship to precursor Wright, but also his view that he will himself inevitably represent for a younger writer an ancestral roadblock which that younger writer will need to clear away in order to create canonical space for himself or herself. He admits to not looking forward to being himself thrust into the role of villainous ancestor that he fashioned so successfully for Wright: "I do not know how I will take it when my time [to be attacked as ancestral roadblock] comes."

With the publication in 1970 of *The Bluest Eye*, it becomes evident that Baldwin's "time" had indeed come, perhaps much more quickly than he had imagined. Morrison, of course, makes no overt attack on ancestral figures of the sort that occurs in Baldwin's "Many Thousands Gone" or, for that matter, Ralph Ellison's "The World and the Jug." But her first novel does contain clear evidence of her (sometimes subtle) refigurations of key elements of Baldwin's and Ellison's corpuses. Specifically, Morrison refigures Baldwin's discussion of Wright in "Many Thousands Gone" and the Trueblood episode of Ellison's *Invisible Man*. Only by understanding the nature of Morrison's disagreements with and formal revisions of Ellison and Baldwin can we fully comprehend her rejection of these strong male figures as literary ancestors.

II

The thrice-repeated primer that serves, in its varying degrees of decipherability, as part of *The Bluest Eye*'s prefatory material assumes a central position in the critical discourse surrounding Morrison's novel. In "Dick-and-Jane and the Shirley Sensibility in *The Bluest Eye*," for example, Phyllis Klotman argues that the various versions of the primer "are symbolic of the lifestyles that the author explores in the novel either directly or by implication." Klotman goes on to suggest her view of the specific referents of each version of the primer:

> The first [version] is clearly that of the alien white world. . . . The second is the lifestyle of the two black MacTeer children, Claudia and Frieda, shaped by poor but loving parents trying desparately to survive. . . . The Breedloves' lives. . . are like the third—the distorted run-on—version of "Dick and Jane."

Another reading that suggests that the primer offers an interpretive key to Morrison's text, Raymond Hedin's "The Structuring of Emotion in Black American Fiction," astutely discusses Morrison's manipulation of the contents of the primer. Hedin says:

> Morrison arranges the novel so that each of its sections provides a bitter gloss on key phrases from the novel's preface, a condensed version of the Dick and Jane reader. These phrases . . . describe the [American] culture ideal of the healthy, supportive, well-to-do family. The seven central elements of Jane's world—house, cat, Mother, father, dog, and friend—become, in turn, plot elements, but only after they are inverted to fit the realities of Pecola's world.

Hedin is correct in his suggestion that the body of *The Bluest Eye* represents an intentional inversion of the primer. Morrison's further manipulations of the primer are, indeed, even more striking. She employs the primer not only as prefatory material to the text proper, but also to introduce the chapters of *The Bluest Eye* that are recounted by the novel's omniscient narrative voice. The seven epigraphic sections are, as Hedin implies, thematically tied to the chapters which they directly precede. For example, the chapter which introduces the Breedlove family to the reader is prefaced by the primer's reference to Jane's "very happy" family: HEREISTHEFAMILYMOTHER FATHERDICKANDJANETHEYLIVEINTHEGREENANDWHITE HOUSETHEYAREVERYH

But the family presented in the subsequent pages of the novel is the very antithesis of the standardized, ideal (white) American family of the primer. The reader is informed, in fact, of the Breedloves' overwhelming unhappiness and self-hatred. The chapter discusses, among other things: the "calculated, uninspired, and deadly" fights of the Breedlove parents; the father Cholly's alcoholism and the mother Polly's perversely self-serving Christianity; the son Sammy's intense hatred of his father and the fact that he frequently runs away from home; and the daughter Pecola's tragic desire for blue eyes. The reader learns, in short, of the Breedloves' psychological and physical "unattractiveness," of the family's utter failure to conform to the standards by which the beauty and happiness of the primer family (and, by extension, American families in general) are measured.

But it is possible to make further claims for Morrison's employment of the primer as epigraph. In her systematic analysis of an inversive relationship between pretext (the primer) and text (her delineation of Afro-American life), the author dissects, *deconstructs*, if you will, the bourgeois myths of ideal family life. Through her deconstruction, she exposes each individual element of the myth as not only deceptively inaccurate in general, but also wholly inapplicable to Afro-American life. The emotional estrangement of the primer family members (an estrangement suggested by that family's inability to respond to the daughter Jane's desire for play) implies that theirs is solely a surface contentment. For despite Hedin's suggestion that this family is represented as "healthy" and "supportive," it appears to be made up of rigid, emotionless figures incapable of deep feeling.

Afro-American attempts to live in accord with these ultimately unhealthy standards occasion, as my subsequent discussion will demonstrate, not only an emotional barrenness similar to that of the primer family, but also intense feelings of failure and worthlessness such as those experienced by the Breedloves. By exhibiting that such negative feelings are direct functions of Afro-American adoptions of these myths, Morrison attempts to break the spell of the hypnotic propaganda of an overly materialistic America. She seeks, by means of her deconstruction, to mitigate the power of (American propagandistic) words and to make possible an emotion-privileging Afro-American environment. In her attempt to alter the reader's perception of what should be viewed as normative and healthy, Morrison's perspective is similar to that of her character Claudia when she discusses what would be for her an ideal Christmas. Claudia states:

> nobody ever asked me what I wanted for Christmas. . . . *I did not want to have anything to own, or to possess any object.* I wanted rather to *feel* something on Christmas day. The real question would have been, "Dear Claudia, what *experience would you like* on Christmas?" I could have spoken up, "I want to sit on the low stool in Big Mama's kitchen with my lap full of lilacs and listen to Big Papa play his violin for me alone." The lowness of the stool made for my body, the security and warmth of Big Mama's kitchen, the smell of the lilacs, the sound of the music, and, since it would be good to have all of my senses engaged, the taste of a peach, perhaps, afterwards. (my emphasis)

In privileging feelings and experience over ownership of objects, Claudia—and Morrison—rejects bourgeois standards of happiness. The false security of the "pretty," "green and white house" of the primer and its materialism are repudiated in favor of "experience"—the smell of lilacs, Big Papa's music, the genuine emotional security of Big Mama's kitchen.

Morrison's deconstruction of the primer and her exposure of an inversive relationship between pretext and text suggest that the author uses the primer consciously to trope certain conventions prominently found in eighteenth-, nineteenth-, and early twentieth-century Afro-American texts. The convention that Morrison revises here is that of the authenticating document, usually written by whites to confirm a genuine Black authorship of the subsequent text. The white voice of authority—a William Lloyd Garrison in the case of Frederick Douglass' *Narrative*, a William Dean Howell in the case of Paul Laurence Dunbar's *Lyrics of Lowly Life*—has traditionally authenticated the black voice in Afro-American literature.

Robert Stepto has suggested that such white pretextual authorization of the black voice has had a significant influence in shaping the Afro-American literary enterprise. Indeed, his study *From Behind the Veil* examines the various functions of strategies of authentication in selected (male-authored) Afro-American texts predicated on conscious revisions and refigurations of precursor texts. The increasing level of artistic sophistication Stepto observes in these narratives are, for him, a function of the

Afro-American writers' increasing ability to manipulate strategies and documents of authentication.

The Afro-American narrative moves, according to Stepto, from white authentication of blackness to, with the examples of Ralph Ellison and Richard Wright, black self-authentication. Morrison's manipulation of the pretextual material in *The Bluest Eye*'s prefatory primer signals, it seems to me, another step in the development of the Afro-American narrative as conceived by Stepto. Morrison returns to an earlier practice—of the white voice introducing the black text—to demonstrate, as I have suggested, her refusal to allow white standards to arbitrate the success or failure of the Afro-American experience. Her manipulation of the primer is meant to suggest, finally, the inappropriateness of the white voice's attempt to authorize or authenticate the Afro-American text or to dictate the contours of Afro-American art.

Morrison's attitudes about Afro-American expressive art differ significantly from those of Ralph Ellison. For unlike Ellison, Morrison appears to have little interest in comparisons of her work to that of white authors, and views such comparisons as "offensive" and "irrelevant." In Claudia Tate's *Black Women Writers at Work*, Morrison says "I find such criticism dishonest because it never goes into the work on its own terms. . . . [Such criticism] is merely trying to place the [Afro-American] book into an already established [read: white] literary tradition. In "Rootedness" Morrison offers, in direct contrast to Ellison (and Baldwin), what are the terms by which she believes her work should be judged:

> I don't like to find my books condemned as bad or praised as good, when that condemnation or that praise is based on criteria from other paradigms. I would much prefer that they were dismissed or embraced based on the success of their accomplishment within the culture out of which I write.

Morrison demands that her work be judged according to Afro-American expressive criteria.

Such comments from Morrison stand in direct contrast to statements by Ellison. In "The World and the Jug"—an essay whose expressed goal is a delineation of the fundamental difference of his fiction from that of Wright—Ellison refutes Irving Howe's claim that Wright is his literary ancestor. He states:

> . . . perhaps you will understand when I say he did not influence me if I point out that while one can do nothing about choosing one's "relatives," one can, as artist, choose one's "ancestors."

Wright was, in this sense, a "relative"; Hemingway an "ancestor."
Langston Hughes, whose work I knew in grade school and whom
I knew before I knew Wright, was a "relative"; Eliot, who I was
to meet only many years later, and Malraux and Dostoievsky and
Faulkner, were "ancestors". . .

Ellison denies an Afro-American literary family represented by Wright and
Hughes in favor of a (white) Western ancestry characterized by Hemingway
and Faulkner and predicated on what he considers to be the greater quality
of their achievements as artists. He insists, then, that a common (Afro-
American) culture background is not determinative of literary lineage.

Unlike Ellison, Morrison rejects a (white) Western ancestry in favor of
an (exclusively) Afro-American one. She strives to create not American or
Western, but an identifiably Afro-American (or Black) Art, works which are
identifiable as such because she "incorporate[s] into my fiction [elements]
that are directly and deliberately related to what I regard as the major characteristics of Black art." Just as she refuses to voice assent to critical assess-
ments of her work that judge it by (white) Western standards or compare it
to that of white authors, so, too, does Morrison reuse to allow the white voice
and perception of the primer to authorize or authenticate the supremely self-
conscious example of Black Art that is *The Bluest Eye*.

Such a rejection of white criteria of judgment of Afro-American art and
life is, unfortunately, not possible for the blacks who populate the pages of
Morrison's first novel. The differences between her views of Afro-American
art and those of Ellison (and Baldwin) are evident not only in statements such
as those cited above, but also in her depiction in *The Bluest Eye* of the dangers
inherent in Afro-American acceptance of white standards.

III

The black characters of *The Bluest Eye* appear to accept Western standards
of beauty, morality, and success despite (for the most part) being unable
themselves to achieve these standards. The first such apparent failure
chronicled in the text involves the MacTeer home's state of physical and
seeming emotional disrepair. In direct contrast to the primer house which
is "green and white," "has a red door" and "is very pretty" is the "old, cold,
and green" MacTeer house. The structure's physical disrepair is symbolized in its inability to protect its inhabitants from cold (and cold germ-
bearing) winds. Its apparent emotional impoverishment is exemplified for
the novels' first-person narrator by her mother's apparently insensitive reac-

tion to her daughter's contradiction of a cold and her resultant vomiting. Claudia says:

> My mother's voice drones on. She is not talking to me. She is talking to the puke, but she is calling it my name; Claudia. She wipes it up as best she can and puts a scratchy towel over the large wet place. I lie down again. The wags have fallen from the window crack, and the air is cold. I dare not call her back and am reluctant to leave my warmth. My mother's anger humiliates me; her words chafe my cheeks, and I am crying. . . . By and by I will not get sick; I will refuse to. But for now I am crying. I know I am making more snot, but I can't stop.

With a sufficient distance from this painful childhood experience, Claudia is able to see the inappropriateness of the images of cold and misery by which she characterizes her youth. As an adult she is able to see that her mother "is not angry at me, but at my sickness." Further, she is able to observe that in the anguish of her former pain was:

> a productive and fructifying pain. Love, thick and dark as Alaga syrup, eased up into that cracked window. I could smell it—taste it—sweet, musty, with an edge of wintergreen in its base—everywhere in that house. It stuck, along with my tongue, to the frosted windowpanes. It coated my chest, along with the salve, and when the flannel came undone in my sleep, the clear, sharp curves of the air outlined its presence on my mouth. And in the night, when my coughing was dry and tough, feet padded into the room, hands repinned the flannel, readjusted the quilt, and rested a moment on my forehead. So when I think of autumn, I think of somebody with hands who does not want to see me die.

This passage suggests Claudia's rejection of white evaluative standards vis-à-vis Afro-American life. Thus, her childhood, formerly conceived in a vocabulary of pain—her mother's droning voice, the scratchy wet towel, the coldness of the air—has been reconceptualized as filled with protective, "sweet," "thick and dark" love of a mother "who does not want to see me die." The passage recalls Nikki Giovanni's discussion in the poem "Nikki-Rosa" of "Black love" and the inability of white criteria to sense its contours:

childhood experiences are always a drag
if you're Black
you always remembering things like living in Woodlawn
with no inside toilet
and if you become famous or something
they never talk about how happy you were to have
your mother
all to yourself and
how good the water felt when you got your bath
from one of those
big tubs that folk in chicago barbeque in . . .

      *   *   *   *

And though you're poor it isn't poverty that concerns you
and though they fought a lot
it isn't your father's drinking that makes any difference
but only that everybody is together and you
and your sister have happy birthdays and very good
Christmases
and I really hope no white person ever has cause
to write about me because they never understand
Black love is Black wealth and they'll
probably talk about my hard childhood
and never understand that all the while I was quite happy.

Like Giovanni's persona, Claudia discovers that despite the difficulties of poverty in an opulent America, "all the while I was quite happy."

Such a rereading of her life evidences Claudia's ultimate achievements of an informed black perspective. But her achievement is not unproblematic, to be sure. Perhaps the most poignant (and certainly most "charged" in an intertextual sense) of the incidents that result in Claudia's ability to reread her own life is her attempt to understand the rationale for standards that insist on white physical superiority.

Claudia's efforts can profitably be viewed as tentative first steps toward initiation into the larger American society. Her search to comprehend the myth of white physical superiority while attempting, at the same time, to hold onto her views of her own people's beauty and cultural worth, exposes hers as a situation "betwixt and between" that the anthropologist Victor Turner has labeled liminality or marginality. In *Dramas, Fields,* and *Metaphors,* Turner discusses marginality in ways that help explain Afro-American double consciousness. Marginals, according to Turner:

are simultaneous members (by ascription, optation, self-definition, or achievement) of two or more groups whose social definitions and cultural norms are distinct from, and often even opposed to, one another. . . . What is interesting about such marginals is that they often look to their group of origin the so-called inferior group, for communitas, and to the more prestigious group in which they mainly live and in which they aspire to higher status as their structural reference group.

Certainly one way to conceive of the Afro-American's attempt to resolve double consciousness is as a struggle to be initiated into the larger American society. Such a struggle does not necessarily conclude in acceptance by that society (what Turner terms "aggregation"), to be sure. In other words, Afro-American double consciousness is not always resolved. As Turner insists, marginals—people situated betwixt and between antithetical, often antagonistic cultures—"have no cultural assurance of a final resolution of their ambiguity."

Social marginality (or double consciousness) can, then, be a permanent condition. To begin to resolve such ambiguity, Turner argues, it is necessary to seek both the origin and an understanding of the often self-aggrandizing myths of the "more prestigious group." The questing marginal must seek to understand the origins of myths, "how things came to be what they are." Consequently, adults' gifts of white dolls to Claudia are not, for the young girl and future narrator, pleasure-inducing toys but, rather, signs (in a semiotic sense) that she must learn to interpret correctly. Such interpretation requires mining the doll's surfaces (pink skin, blue eyes, blond hair)—a literal search for source(s):

I had only one desire: to dismember [the doll]. To see of what it was made, to discover the dearness, to find the beauty, the desirability that had escaped me, but apparently only me. Adults, older girls, shops, magazines, newspapers, window signs—all the world had agreed that a blue-eyed, yellow-haired, pink-skinned doll was what every girl child treasured. "Here," they said, "this is beautiful, and if you are in this day 'worthy' you may have it". . . . I could not love it. But I could examine it to see what it was that all the world said was lovable. Break off the tiny fingers, bend the flat feet, loosen the hair, twist the head around, and the thing made one sound—a sound they said was the sweet and plaintive cry "Mama," but which sounded to me like the bleat of a dying lamb, or, more precisely, our icebox door opening on rusty hinges in July.

One of this passage's dominant images—that of ritualistic sacrifice—fore-shadows Pecola's employment as scapegoat by *The Bluest Eye*'s black community. This passage also offers material which enables us to contrast Claudia's and Pecola's encounters with the myth of white superiority. Gifts of white dolls arouse in Claudia not affection—which would suggest acceptance of the myth—but, rather, a sadistic curiosity: she dissects white dolls and, later, trans-fers this urge to little white girls, in confrontation with images of beauty that imply that her own almost antithetical appearance is exceedingly unattractive.

Pecola, on the other hand, also faced with the pervasiveness of Western culture standards of beauty, accepts unquestioningly the myth's validity. Her family's perception of its physical appearance is represented by the omni-scient narrator as significantly different than that of other blacks who appear to accept Caucasian features as the norm:

> No one could have convinced them [the Breedloves] that they were not relentlessly and aggressively ugly. . . . You looked at them and wondered why they were so ugly; you looked closely and could not find the source. Then you realized that it was from conviction, their conviction. It was as though some mysterious all-knowing master had given each one a cloak of ugliness to wear, and they each accepted it without question. The master had said, "You are ugly people." They had looked about them-selves and saw nothing to contradict the statement; saw, in fact, support for it leaning at them from every billboard, every movie, every glance. "Yes," they had said. "You are right." And they took their ugliness in their hands, threw it as a mantle over them, and went about the world with it.

Jaqueline DeWeever has argued that *The Bluest Eye*'s obvious preoccu-pation with the often devastating effects of the pervasive Western standards of beauty on black Americans represents a foregrounding of a relatively minor scene in Ellison's *Invisible Man*. In the scene in question, Ellison's protagonist encounters a sign in a Harlem store window with the following inscription: "You too can be truly beautiful. Win greater happiness with whiter complexion. Be outstanding in your social set." It is certainly the case that *The Bluest Eye* manifests Morrison's revision of several aspects of Ellison's text—in particular, as I will later discuss in detail, the Trueblood episode in which the effects of incest are explored. But it seems to me fruitful to observe this thematic concern with comparisons of black and white phys-ical appearance in terms of the novel's female precursorial text, *Their Eyes Were Watching God*.

Morrison's discussion of an all-knowing master's decree that the Breedlove clan is ugly recalls most specifically not the invisible man's Harlem window shopping, but the infatuation of Hurston's Mrs. Turner with Caucasian features. Hurston says of the muck storekeeper:

> Mrs. Turner, like all other believers has built an altar to the unattainable—Caucasian characteristics for all. Her god would smite her, would hurl her from pinnacles and lose her in deserts. But she would not forsake his altars. . . . [She held] a belief that somehow she and others through worship could attain her paradise—a heaven of straight-haired, thin-lipped, high-nose boned white seraphs. The physical impossibilities in no way injured faith. That was the mystery and mysteries are the chores of gods.

Certainly Pecola's and Mrs. Turner's wishes are not exactly parallel, but they are unquestionably similar. Both believe that through energetic prayer their desires for the obliteration of the Negroid—in Pecola's case, her black eyes, in Mrs. Turner's, the Afro-American race altogether—can be achieved. Mrs. Turner, already possessing (she believes) the beauty that accompanies Caucasian features, prays that the rest of the blacks—whose pigmentation, immorality and lack of civility offend her—be whitened in a miraculous act of God. But Pecola, whose features—her "high cheek bones," "shapely lips," "insolent nostrils," and dark complexion—are undeniably black, desires from her god a seemingly much smaller miracle: to be given the bluest eyes in the world.

Just as fervently as Mrs. Turner prays for a wholesale black metamorphosis, so, too, does Pecola ask to be blessed with a symbol of beauty. Having been taught by school primers and Madison Avenue advertisers that beauty and happiness are possible only for whites, Pecola believes that the possession of the blue eyes of a white girl would significantly alter her desperately painful familial situation:

> It had occurred to Pecola some time ago that if her eyes, those eyes that held the pictures, and knew the sights—if those eyes of hers were different, that is to say, beautiful, she would be different. . . . If she looked different, beautiful, maybe Cholly would be different, and Mrs. Breedlove too. Maybe they'd say, "Why, looked at pretty-eyed Pecola. We mustn't do bad things in front of those pretty eyes". . . .
> Each night, without fail, she prayed for blue eyes. Fervently,

for a year she had prayed. Although somewhat discouraged, she was not without hope. To have something as wonderful as that happen would take a long, long time.

Like Mrs. Turner, Pecola realizes that patience is required if her dreams are to be realized.

In "Eruptions of Funk: Historicizing Toni Morrison," Susan Willis suggests that "[t]he problem at the center of Morrison's writing is how to maintain an Afro-American cultural heritage once the relationship to the black rural south has been stretched thin over distance and generations." If Willis is correct about the primary focus of Morrison's work, then surely Pecola's reaction seems to be the result of her spatial and psychological distance from Black cultural survival mechanisms that have served to preserve Afro-American racial pride. But Pecola's difficulties notwithstanding, *The Bluest Eye* does suggest that this legacy—however perverse its manifestations—is alive in other members of Pecola's community. For despite the apparent compliance signaled by its reaction to white standards, this community's reactions do evidence a (silent) rejection of white myths.

The survival of Afro-American mechanisms of self-preservation can be noted, for example, in Claudia's description of the outcome of her search for the source of white beauty. She says that the impulse to dismember white dolls gives way to "The truly horrifying thing":

> . . . the transference of the same impulses to little white girls. The indifference with which I could have axed them was shaken only by my desire to do so. To discover what eluded me: the secret of the magic they weaved on others. What made people look at them and say, "Awwww," but not for me? . . .
>
> If I pinched them [little white girls], their eyes—unlike the crazed glint of the baby doll's white eyes—would fold in pain and their cry would not be the sound of an icebox door, but a fascinating cry of pain.

Claudia's somewhat sadistic dismemberment of white dolls and her subsequent torture of white girls is meant to recall, it seems to me, Bigger Thomas' axed mutilation of the dead body of Mary Dalton (presented by Richard Wright as a symbol of young white female beauty) in *Native Son*. Morrison's refiguration of Wright's scene, as we shall see, is her means of adding her voice to the discourse surrounding Bigger's murder, the most renowned of which belongs to James Baldwin.

Claudia's impulses lend nominal weight to Baldwin's claim in "Many

Thousands Gone" that "no Negro living in America . . . has not . . . wanted
. . . to break the bodies of all white people and bring them low." But while
Baldwin suggests that such violent impulses are "urges of the cruelest
vengeance" and motivated by "unanswerable hatred," Claudia's acts, while
they are, in part, sadistic in nature (she apparently enjoys "the fascinating cry
of pain" of her victims), are motivated in the main by a need to locate the
source of a white physical superiority that is not immediately apparent to her.
Baldwin believes that, in general, the Afro-American refusal to give in to
such urges and "smash any white face he may encounter in a day" results
from a noble embrace of humanity. He states:

> the adjustment [from desiring to attack whites physically to
> attempting peaceful coexistence with them] must be made—
> rather, it must be attempted, the tension perpetually suspended—
> for without this he [the Afro-American] has surrendered his
> birthright as a man no less than his birthright as a black man.
> The entire universe is then peopled only with his enemies, who
> are not only white men armed with rope and rifle, but his own
> far-flung and contemptible kinsmen. Their blackness is his
> degradation and it is their stupid and passive endurance which
> makes his end inevitable.

For Baldwin, such "adjustment" allows the Afro-American to claim (or reclaim)
his humanity, a humanity which is, in Baldwin's words, "his birthright." This
adjustment not only permits the Afro-American to demystify and de-villainize
whites, but also to love his or her own people (a love of which, according to
Baldwin, Bigger Thomas is incapable).

Claudia's "adjustment," however, has significantly different causes and
consequences:

> When I learned how repulsive this disinterested violence [directed
> toward white girls] was, that it was repulsive because it was disin-
> terested, my shame floundered about for refuge. The best hiding
> place was love. Thus the conversion from pristine sadism, to fabri-
> cated hatred, to fraudulent love. It was a small step to Shirley
> Temple. I learned much later to worship her . . . , knowing, even as
> I learned, that the change was *adjustment without improvement*. (my
> emphasis)

Claudia's "conversion" is motivated not by an embrace of humanity but,
rather, by "shame." Apparently, the white-controlled societal forces that

promote a single standard of beauty for which Claudia is attempting to find a rationale provide no sufficient answers to the questing marginal's quandries about the origins of this standard. She learns only to feel ashamed of the curiosity that led to her "disinterested violence," and that her failure to accept without question the standards of white America is considered "repulsive."

Claudia terminates her search for the source of white myths and replaces the violent urges she had previously directed at whites with "fraudulent love." But the suppression of violent urges by Afro-Americans has significantly different implications for Morrison than for Baldwin. For Morrison, the Afro-American's humanity is not what is at stake, and "fraudulent love" of whites, the ultimate result of this rejection of violence, is not better or more authentically human. It is only different, only "adjustment" (an intentional repetition of Baldwin's terminology, it would appear) "without improvement."

The one feature that distinguishes Pecola (and her family) from the other Afro-Americans in the novel is the authenticity of her adoption of Western standards. The deeds of other characters—the adults' gifts of white dolls to black girls, "The eye slide of black women as [white girls] approached them on the street and the possessive gentleness of their touch as they handled them"—would appear to suggest an authentic love of whites and acceptance of white standards. But like Claudia's "fraudulent love," this apparent love is not real; rather, it is simply the response to "The Thing" that makes blacks feel guilt and shame about overt expression of Afro-American pride. In her provocative refiguration of Baldwin, Morrison implies that there is a wholesale Afro-American adoption of a self-protective mask. She suggests this further in her description of a group of boys who encircle Pecola and shout at her, "Black e mo. Black e mo. Yadaddsleepsnekked":

> They had extemporized a verse made up of two insults about matters over which the victim had no control: the color of her skin and speculations on the sleeping habits of an adult, wildly fitting in its incoherence. That they themselves were black, or that their own fathers had similarly relaxed habits was irrelevant. It was their contempt for their own blackness that gave the first insult its teeth. They seemed to have taken all of their *smoothly cultivated ignorance*, their *exquisitely learned self-hatred*, their *elaborately designed hopelessness* and sucked it all up into a fiery cone of scorn that had burned for ages in the hollows of their minds—cooled—and spilled over lips of outrage,

consuming whatever was in its path. They danced a macabre
ballet around the victim, whom, for their own sake, they were
prepared to sacrifice to the flaming pit. (my emphasis)

This passage vividly suggests the pattern of mask wearing that permeates
the Afro-American community depicted in *The Bluest Eye*. The existence
of such masking helps the reader to comprehend the devastating effects on
Pecola of the community's employment of her as scapegoat.

In her own view, as well as in that of the omniscient narrator,
Pecola's appearance is not what distinguishes her from her black peers.
Rather, she is held up as a figure of supreme ridicule strictly because, in
her detachment from her cultural heritage, she exists unprotected from
the disastrous effects of standards that she cannot achieve. She has not
properly learned the rules of black (urban) life, or, rather, she has learned
them too well. While other blacks pay *nominal* homage to the gods who
created the standards by which America measures beauty and worth, and
appear[,] as a consequence, to have "collected self-hatred by the heap,"
they actually maintain strong feelings of self-worth. They hide these feelings from gods who are interested only in surface—and not in spiritual—
devotion.

These people, in other words, represent a community that maintains, as does Janie in the face of Joe Starks' very similar tyranny in *Their
Eyes Were Watching God*, the Afro-American survival technique of self-
division. The community's worship at the altar of white beauty is only
gesture, only acts "smoothly cultivated" to fool the master, to appease the
gods. Because Pecola never learns of the potential benefits of masking and
self-division she represents a perfect target of scorn for the blacks who are
armed with this knowledge. These Afro-Americans, in fact, use Pecola as
ritual object in their ceremonies designed to exhibit to the master their
"rejection" of blackness.

The Bluest Eye, then, can be said to concentrate on the factors which
provoke Pecola's victimization in her own community. As we move
through the seasonally cyclical, inverted world that is represented in
Morrison's text, we see Pecola travel through various socioeconomic
sectors of the community and be abused by each in turn. Only by understanding the specific provocations for the sacrifice of Pecola Breedlove can
we comprehend the role of masking and double consciousness in the
tragedy of the novel. Such an understanding will enable us to grasp the
reasons that Morrison presents the (divided) Afro-American psyche as
unhealed in the text's narrative events.

IV

The passage that depicts the apparent self-hatred of the boys who surround and taunt Pecola precisely suggests her role as scapegoat, a role that several critics have discussed in explications of *The Bluest Eye*. The study most devoted to such a reading of Morrison's text is Chikwenye Ogunyemi's "Order and Disorder in Toni Morrison's *The Bluest Eye*." While it is laced with inanities and facile misreadings of the text, Ogunyemi's essay offers a sound analysis of the system of scapegoating operative in the novel. He states: "Running through the novel is the theme of the scapegoat: Geraldine's cat, Bob the dog, and Pecola are the scapegoats supposed to cleanse American society through their involvement in some violent rituals." He goes on to insist that the abuse heaped upon Pecola—from the circle of taunting boys to her father's molestation of her—can be characterized, in each instance, as a ritual of purgation. Such purgation, or cleansing of the spiritual self, is evident in Claudia's eloquent conclusion of the text:

> All of our waste . . . we dumped on her and . . . she absorbed. And all of our beauty, which was hers first and which she gave to us. All of us—all who knew her—felt so wholesome after we cleaned ourselves on her. We were so beautiful when we stood astride her ugliness. Her simplicity decorated us, her guilt sanctified us, her pain made us glow with health, her awkwardness made us think we had a sense of humor. . . . We honed our egos on her, padded our characters with her frailty, and yawned in the fantasy of our strength.

For my purposes here, a most helpful general discussion of the phenomenon of scapegoating which aids in the illumination of the motivations for such purgative abuse of Pecola is offered by Erich Neumann in *Depth Psychology and a New Ethic*. According to Neumann, scapegoating results from the necessity for the self and/or the community to rid itself of the "guilt-feeling" inherent in any individual or group failure to attain the "acknowledged values" of that group. This guilt feeling, or "shadow" as Neumann terms it, is discharged from the individual or communal self by means of:

> the phenomenon of the projection of the shadow which cannot be accepted as a negative part of one's own psyche and is there-fore . . . transferred to the outside world and is experienced as an

outside object. It is combated, punished, and exterminated as "the alien out there" instead of being dealt with as "one's own inner problem."

In combating the shadow that has been externalized and can, thus, be perceived as Other, the group is able to rid itself ceremonially of the evil that exists within both the individual member and the community at large. To be fully successful, such exorcism requires a visibly imperfect, shadow-consumed scapegoat:

> evil can only be made conscious by being solemnly paraded before the eyes of the populace and then ceremoniously destroyed. The effect of purification is achieved by the process of making evil conscious through making it visible and by liberating the unconscious from this content through projection. On this level, therefore, evil, though not recognised by the individual as his own, is nevertheless recognized as evil. To put it more accurately, evil is recognized as belonging to the collective structure of one's own tribe and is eliminated in a collective manner. . .

Neumann's observations apply to "mass" or general man who, in his estimation, "cannot . . . acknowledge . . . 'his own evil' at all, since consciousness is still too weakly developed to be able to deal with the resulting conflict. It is for this reason," according to Neumann, "that evil is invariably experienced by mass man as something alien, and the victims of shadow projection are therefore, always and everywhere, the aliens."

Neumann goes on to suggest that minorities and aliens typically provide the objects for "the projection of the shadow." This projection is, for Neumann, "symptomatic of a split in the structure of the collective psyche." The self is split, in other words, into the good, desirable, unshadowed ideal self and the evil, undesirable, shadowed black self. Neumann argues that this division is motivated by:

> unconscious feelings of guilt which arise, as a splitting phenomenon, from the formation of the shadow. It is our subliminal awareness that we are actually not good enough for the ideal values which have been set before us that results in the formation of the shadow; at the same time, however, it also leads to an unconscious feeling of guilt and to inner insecurity, since the shadow confutes the ego's pipedream that is identical with the ideal values.

Neumann's formulations of the scapegoat are richly suggestive in an analysis of both black-white relations and the difficulties inherent in an Afro-American sensibility that Du Bois characterizes as divided. For the Afro-American to split herself into shadow (evil, "black") and unshadowed (ideal, "American") selves, in a country which has traditionally viewed her as the (shadowed) personification of evil, is to invite such Afro-American self-contempt as is evident in *The Bluest Eye*. In circumstances where evil—which, for our purposes here, can be defined as a pronounced failure to achieve the ideal values and standards that have been set up by the tribe as exclusively desirable—must be eradicated from the community, that evil is often conceptualized both in the Euro-American psyche and in the divided Afro-American sensibility as the specifically and culturally black.

This eradication of black evil by whites is observable in such extreme instances as the lynching and mutilation of the genitals of black men under the guise of protecting white Southern womenhood. A milder (or, at least, less physically violent) intraracial form reveals itself in the passing for white of light-skinned blacks as depicted, for example, in James Weldon Johnson's *The Autobiography of an Ex-Coloured Man* and in Nella Larsen's *Passing*. In both cases blackness, as a valuable human condition, is denied and destroyed. *The Bluest Eye* offers less extreme (perhaps), but nonetheless cogent examples of this hopelessly futile effort on the part of Afro-Americans to exorcise what the divided psyche often holds as the evil of blackness. Morrison's novel also vividly suggests the resultant scapegoating that occurs as a function of what Neumann terms "the projection of the shadow."

Pecola's victimization at the hands of a circle of young black males, we see clear evidence of a projection of the shadow of evil upon her. These boys' insults are described as a function of their ability to disregard their similarity to their victim; the verse they compose to belittle her ("Black e mo. . . .Yadaddsleepsnekked") reflects their own skin color and, quite possibly, familial relations. Claudia tells the reader of the boys' "smoothly cultivated ignorance": "That they themselves were black, or that their own father had similarly relaxed habits was irrelevant." This ignorance renders them incapable of recognizing the irony implicit in their castigation of Pecola by means of a verse that, because it chronicles the allegedly depraved conditions of their own lives, is also self-discrediting. This irony is lost to the boys because of the success of their projection of the shadow of blackness onto Pecola.

This manner of projection is also observable in Pecola's encounter with Geraldine and her son Junior. Morrison tells the reader that the most treasured bit of education that Geraldine has received has been:

how to behave. The careful development of thrift, patience, high morals, and good manners. In short, *how to get rid of the funkiness*. The dreaded funkiness of passion, the funkiness of the wide range of human emotions.

Whenever it erupts, this Funk, they [black women like Geraldine] wipe it away; where it crusts, they dissolve it; wherever it drips, flowers, or clings, they find it and fight it until it dies. They fight this battle all the way to the grave. The laugh that is a little bit too loud; the enunciation a little too round; the gesture a little too generous. They hold their behind in for fear of a sway too free; when they wear lipstick, they never cover the entire mouth for fear of lips too thick, and they worry, worry, worry about the edges of their hair. (my emphasis)

As I have mentioned earlier, Susan Willis argues that alienation—both in terms of "an individual's separation from his or her cultural center" as well as in the form of a frowning upon the natural Afro-American characteristics of kinky hair and thick lips—typifies the lives of Morrison's characters. For example, Willis says of Pecola's mother, Polly Breedlove:

As a housemaid in a prosperous lakeshore home, Polly Breedlove lives a form a schizophrenia, where her marginality is constantly confronted with a world of Hollywood movies, white sheets and tender blond children. When at work or at the movies, she separates herself from her own kinky hair and decayed tooth. The tragedy of a woman's alienation is its effect on her role as mother. Her emotions split, she showers tenderness and love on her employer's child, and rains violence and disdain on her own.

Polly's self-division—characterized by Willis as "a form of schizophrenia" and as a "separat[ion from] herself"—is nowhere more poignantly exhibited than in the scene to which the critic alludes in which Pecola accidently spills a blueberry pie that her mother had made onto the newly cleaned floor of Polly's employer's kitchen. In the process, she frightens the young daughter of Polly's employer. Her mother's reaction indicates some of the consequences of her schizophrenia:

Most of the [pie] juice splashed on Pecola's legs, and the burn must have been painful, for she cried out and began hopping about just as Mrs. Breedlove entered with a tightly packed laundry bag. In one gallop she was on Pecola, and with the back of her hand knocked her to the floor. Pecola slid in the pie juice, one leg folded under her. Mrs. Breedlove yanked her up by the arm, slapped her again, and in a voice thin with anger, abused Pecola. . . .

"Crazy fool . . . my floor, mess . . . look what you . . . work . . . get on out . . . now that . . . crazy . . .my floor, my floor." Her words were hotter and darker than the smoking berries.

Polly's reactions evidence no interest whatsoever in her own child's welfare, not a bit of concern about the berry burns that caused her to cry out in pain. Instead, she strikes Pecola, and displays infinitely more anxiety about the condition of "my floor" than about her daughter.

Further, her subsequent gentle soothing of her employer's crying child and attention to her soiled dress contrast—painfully—to her further besoiling of Pecola's dress and refusal to offer her daughter any parental—or even human—compassion. Most telling of all the occurrences in this scene is the interchange between Mrs. Breedlove and the white girls after Pecola (and the MacTeer sisters) depart:

"Who were they, Polly?"
"Don't worry none, baby."
"You gonna make another pie?"
"'Course, I will."
"Who were they, Polly?"
"Hush. Don't worry none," she whispered, and the honey in her words complemented the sundown spilling on the lake.

In addition to the clear contrast between Polly's reaction to the white girl and her daughter—"the honey in her words" to the employer's daughter as opposed to the smoking berry heat of her abuse of Pecola—this scene presents the maid's refusal to share with the white girl Pecola's identity because of her shame at being identified with the clumsy, pathetic girl who knocks the blueberry pie onto the floor.

The projection of the shadow, and its resultant scapegoating, then, can lead to the sacrifice of the black offspring, to parental detachment from the child, and to complete adoption of white standards as suggested by the "whispered . . . honey in [the] words" of Polly to the Fisher girl. Such projection can also inspire, as in the example of Geraldine, a futile effort to erase the black self entirely.

Geraldine desires to repress and deny "the funk," to exhibit no characteristically or stereotypically Afro-American qualities such as thick lips, nappy edges, and "rounded enunciation." To get rid of funkiness is, for Geraldine, to get rid of blackness and, in an America where blackness is equated with evil, to embrace the ideal national virtues of "thrift, patience, high morals, and good manners." To turn again to Neumann's discussion of scapegoating, we can conceptualize Geraldine's efforts as an attempt to exorcise the shadow of her own blackness. This energetic attempt to eliminate the funk does not allow her the pleasure of loving either her husband, whose sexual advances are unsatisfying inconveniences, or her son, whose emotional needs she meets with an affectionless efficiency.

So when she encounters Pecola in her house—this little girl who represents for the entire community the literal embodiment of the shadow of blackness—and sees that the object of all her affection—her cat—is dead, Geraldine's reaction is one of a self-protective anger and horror. The text tells us:

> She looked at Pecola. Saw the dirty torn dress, the plaits sticking out on her head, hair matted where the plaits had come undone, the muddy shoes with the wad of gum peeping out from between the cheap soles, the soiled socks, one of which had been walked down into the heel of the shoe. . . . She had seen this little girl all of her life. . . . They [girls like Pecola] had stared at her with great uncomprehending eyes. Eyes that questioned nothing and asked everything. Unblinking and unabashed, they stared at her. The end of the world lay in their eyes, and the beginning, and all the waste in between. . . . Grass wouldn't grow where they lived. Flowers died. Shades fell down. . . . Like flies they hovered; like flies they settled. And this one had settled in her house.

For Geraldine, Pecola represents the repulsiveness of poverty, the vileness of blackness, the veritable eruption of funk. She equates Pecola with germ-infested pests, with flies that invade and soil carefully disinfected houses and elaborately prepared picnics. Pecola is everything that Geraldine is fighting to suppress. She is, for Geraldine, "funk," shadow, the blackness of blackness. When Geraldine tells Pecola to leave her house—"'Get out,' she said, her voice quiet. 'You nasty little black bitch. Get out of my house.'"—she is also, in effect, attempting to rid herself of her fears of her own evil, of her own unworthiness, of her own shadow of blackness.

Geraldine's efforts constitute, it seems to me, a splitting of herself into a good, moral, funkless self which she works diligently to maintain, and an evil, immoral, nappy-edged black self that she suppresses and attempts to expel. That this suppression and attempted exorcism of blackness render her incapable of enjoying life or of loving her family—or herself—seems to her a small price to pay for the warding off of the ignominy of an association with evil. Thus we see in Geraldine's characterization an example of defensive self-division similar to Janie's characterization an example of defensive self-division similar to Janie's during her marriage to Joe Starks in *Their Eyes Were Watching God*. But while Janie, as I argued in the previous chapter, divided herself into inside and outside in order to hold on to the natural and to the culturally black, Geraldine's self-division is caused by her attempt to expel her natural "funkiness" or blackness.

With the examples of Geraldine and Polly, it becomes clear that, as is the case with Hurston's novel, as exploration of Du Boisian double consciousness is at the center of the narrative events depicted in *The Bluest Eye*. But, as in Hurston's text, Morrison's exploration of the Du Boisian formulation does not reflect an uncategorial acceptance of the older writer's views of the Afro-American psyche. According to Du Bois, the Afro-American seeks to ease the pain of participation in antithetical cultures by means of conflation of blackness and Americanness. He speaks, as I have noted, of an Afro-American

> longing . . . to merge his double self into a better and truer self.
> In this merging he wishes neither of the older selves to be lost.
> He would not Africanize America. . . . He would not bleach his
> Negro soul in a flood of white Americanism.

Morrison presents evidence which disputes Du Bois' claims. Her characters' projections of the shadow of blackness, their unquestioning acceptance of American standards of beauty and morality, suggest that they have, indeed, bleached their black souls "in a flood of white Americanism." Theirs are not merged, but hopelessly divided selves, selves which attempt an erasure of blackness. In her exploration of divided and funk-rejected characters, Morrison both revises Du Bois and seems to refigure instances from Hurston's *Their Eyes Were Watching God*.

But while Geraldine's and Polly's shadow projections reflect suggestively the pattern of scapegoating in *The Bluest Eye*, they fail to attain the myriad symbolic implications of what must be considered the most deplorable and permanently damaging instance of scapegoating in the novel: Cholly's rape of his daughter Pecola. It is certainly possible to analyze Cholly Breedlove's incestuous act in ways that are similar to the above discussion of Geraldine and Polly: namely, as his attempt to relieve the persistent pain of the ignominy of his own sexual initiation by involving his daughter in an even more ignominious sexual act. But such an analysis, while it might prove useful to a further elaboration of scapegoating in *The Bluest Eye*, would fail to address what seems to me to be the intertextually charged nature of Morrison's depiction of incest. In particular, I believe that Morrison is consciously (and *critically*) revising the Ellisonian depiction of incest in the Trueblood episode of *Invisible Man*. Her revision of Ellison, as the following discussion will attempt to demonstrate, provides particularly compelling evidence to support feminist claims about the power of feminist literary and critical texts to alter substantively our readings of male canonical works.

V

The Breedlove family in Morrison's text possesses a parodic relation to Ellison's incestuous clan. The relation is initially suggested in the names of the respective families. Ellison's designation suggests that the sharecropper and his family are the true (genuine) "bloods" (an Afro-American vernacular term for culturally immersed blacks). The Breedloves' name, however, is bestowed with bitter irony; theirs is a self-hating family in which no love is bred. In both texts, the economically destitute families are forced to sleep in dangerously close(d) quarters. In *Invisible Man* cold winters—and a lack of money with which to buy fuel—force the nubile Matty Lou into bed between her still-procreative parents. In the case of *The Bluest Eye*, Pecola sleeps in the same room as her parents, a proximity which necessitates her hearing the "Choking sounds and silence" of their lovemaking.

Further, there are stark similarities between mother and daughter in both texts which contribute to the incestuous act. In Ellison's novel, as Houston Baker argues in "To Move Without Moving: Creativity and Commerce in Ralph Ellison's Trueblood Episode" (about which I will have more to say below), the daughter Matty Lou is her mother "Kate's double—a woman who looks just like her mother and who is fully grown and sexually mature." (On a night which Trueblood describes as "dark, plum black" such similarities would seem to have been a principle factor in the sharecropper's incestuous act.) And Cholly Breedlove's lust is awakened by Pecola's scratching of her leg in a manner that mirrored "what Pauline was doing the first time he saw her in Kentucky."

It is possible, with the above evidence in place, to begin to suggest the specifics of what seems to me to be Morrison's purposefully feminist revision. Read intertextually, *The Bluest Eye* provides—as I shall demonstrate below—an example par excellence of what the feminist critic Annette Kolodny has called "revisionary reading [that] open[s] new avenues for comprehending male texts." The Ellisonian conceptualization of incest differs markedly from what, through the example of Morrison's text, it seems to represent for the female imagination. The gender-determined differences between the presentations of incest can, I believe, be successfully accounted for if we turn briefly at this point to contemporary feminist discussions of female reading of male canonical works.

One of the contemporary feminist criticism's initial goals was the analysis of the implications for women readers of the overwhelmingly male authored and oriented Western literary and critical canons. Among the best early examples of feminist readings of male literary works is Judith Fetterley's landmark study, *The Resisting Reader*. In her introduction to this study, Fetterley asserts her belief that women have historically been taught to read like men. Prior to the recent burgeoning of feminist criticism, the reading of the canon's decidedly phallocentric works such as (to cite examples which Fetterley uses) Ernest Hemingway's *A Farewell to Arms* and F. Scott Fitzgerald's *The Great Gatsby* encourages women's agreement with the inscribed antifemale slant of the works. Having been taught to accept the phallocentric as indisputably universal, the woman reader unconsciously internalizes the often-misogynistic messages of male texts. She loses, as a result, any faith in the validity of her own perceptions of life and, according to Fetterley, accepts male (mis)representation of women without protest. In short, she learns to read like a man: "In such [male] fictions the female reader is co-opted into participation in an experience from which she is explicitly excluded; she is asked to identify with a selfhood that defines itself in opposition to her; she is required to identify against herself."

In the face of such derogative and self-negating instruction, a female must, in order to successfully participate as a woman in the reading experience, "become a resisting rather than an assenting reader and, by this refusal to assent, . . . begin the process of exorcising the male mind that has been implanted" in women. The removal of the male implant results, for Fetterley, in "the capacity for what Adrienne Rich describes as re-vision— 'the act of looking back, of seeing with fresh eyes, of entering an old text from a new critical direction.'" Feminist re-vision, according to Fetterley, offers the terms of a radically altered critical enterprise and the liberation of the critic: "books will . . . lose their power to bind us unknowingly to their designs."

Houston Baker's "To Move Without Moving" represents an excellent example in support of Fetterley's view of the (sometimes dangerously) persuasive powers of texts. For in this essay, the critical canon's most elaborate explication of the Trueblood episode of *Invisible Man*, we can observe the power of texts quite literally to bind even the most intellectually nimble readers/critics to their designs. Baker's unquestionably provocative recent study *Blues, Ideology, and Afro-American Literature* (in which the analysis of the Trueblood section appears) exhibits, particularly in a stunning reading of the economics of female slavery and the figuration of a community of female slaves in Linda Brent's *Incidents in the Life of a Slave Girl*, his awareness of the ways in which feminist theory can help illuminate literary texts. This sensitivity to feminist concerns is, unfortunately, missing from his readings of Ellison. Instead, Baker's essay mirrors the strategies by which Trueblood (and Trueblood's creator) validates male perceptions of incest while, at the same time, silencing the female voice or relegating it to the evaluative periphery.

Baker's begins his reading by citing Ellison's discussion in the essay "Richard Wright's Blues" of "The function, the psychology, of artistic selection." This function, according to the novelist, "is to eliminate from art form all those elements of experience which contain *no compelling significance.*" While Baker cites this statement by Ellison, for undoubtably significant reasons—to suggest, ultimately, an essential parallel between Ellison and his folk artist creation Trueblood—his choice provides a means to discuss the shortcomings of his own and Ellison's treatments of the subject of incest.

If it is accurate to perceive of the artistic process as an act of omission of insignificant life experiences, then it is equally true that the critical process consists, in part, of elimination from consideration those elements of the literary text that are without significant ideological or symbolic import. While I wish to avoid straying too far into issues of relativism that have been masterfully debated by others, Ellison's statements, situated as they are in Baker's essay, lead (I think necessarily) to an inquiry as to why neither Ellison's text nor Baker's critique of it treat the female perspective on and reaction to incest as containing any "compelling significance."

In the case of the novel, Trueblood's incestuous act is judged almost exclusively by men. This male judgment is offered by a cast which includes the black school administrators who wish to remove the sharecropper from the community and Trueblood's white protectors who pressure the administrators to allow the sharecropper to remain in his home and who "wanted to hear about the gal [Matty Lou] lots of times." They form, as it were, an exclusively male evaluative circle which views Trueblood's act as either shamefully repugnant (as in the case of the black college administrators and the black preacher) or meritoriously salacious (as in the case of the white protectors who provide Trueblood and his family with material goods).

Except for the mother Kate's memorably violent reaction to seeing her husband atop their daughter, the female perspective on Trueblood's act is effectively silenced and relegated to the periphery in the sharecropper's recounting of the story. Just as the Trueblood women run to the back of the cabin upon the approach of the car bearing Mr. Norton and the unnamed protagonist of *Invisible Man*, so, too do Matty Lou's and the town's doubtlessly unified female community's emotional responses to the incestuous act remain (conveniently, it would seem) out of the reader's sight. Never in Trueblood's rendering of the story are Matty Lou's feelings foregrounded or even actually shared with the reader. Further, Trueblood is well aware of the silent scorn that the women who help Kate attend to the unconscious Matty Lou bear for him. When he returns home after an exile precipitated, in his view, by the inability of others to distinguish between "blood-sin" and "dream-sin," he orders the scornful community of women that has formed in response to his "dirty lowdown wicked dog" act off of his property: "There's a heap of women here with Kate and I runs 'em out." Having effectively run out the openly critical female community and silenced, by means of his abominable act, his wife and daughter, Trueblood is able to interpret his act in an extremely self-serving way, untroubled by the radically incompatible perspectives of women. He can assert, for example, that the reason "Matty Lou won't look at me and won't speak a word to nobody" is that she is ashamed to be pregnant. And he can, despite his belief that he is a good family man, fail to see the bitter irony in his assessment of his family situation: "except that my wife an' daughter won't speak to me, I'm better off than I ever been before."

From a feminist perspective, Baker's reading of the Trueblood episode proves as problematic as the sharecropper's because he, too, relegates the woman's voice to the evaluative periphery and sketches his own circle of male to justify and validate the sharecropper's act. Through an imaginative employment of male voices of authority from Freud to Victor Turner and Clifford Geertz, Baker asserts that one of the dominant themes of *Invisible Man* is "black male sexuality." He speaks salutarily of the (re)productive energy of the black male phallus in Trueblood's tale: "The black phallus—in its creative, ambulant, generative power, even under conditions of castration—is like the cosmos itself, a self-sustaining and self-renewing source of life." It is in terms of Trueblood's phallic "generative power" that Baker discusses the symbolic import of the sharecropper's incestuous act:

> The cosmic force of the phallus thus becomes, in the ritual action
> of the Trueblood episode, symbolic of a type of royal paternity,
> an aristocratic procreativity turned inward to ensure the royalty
> (the "truth," "legitimacy" or "authenticity") of an enduring black
> line of descent. In his outgoing phallic energy, therefore, the
> sharecropper is . . . indeed, a "hard worker" who takes care of

"his family needs." . . . His family may, in a very real sense, be construed as the entire clan or "tribe" that comprises Afro-America.

Baker invokes an almost exclusively male chorus to support his reading of the Trueblood episode. He cites, for example, Geertz's discussion of the Balinese conception of "self-operating penises, ambulant genitals with a life of their own" in order to corroborate the sharecropper's statements which indicate the "natural unpredictability" of male arousal. He also cites Freud's speculations about incest which argue that prehistorical man "established a taboo on sexual intercourse with the women of their own clan" in order to "prevent discord among themselves and to ensure their newly achieved form of social organization." While statements from Geertz and Freud help Baker to substantiate points about the uncontrollability of phallic energy and about Trueblood's dream signalling a historical regression (points which support the sharecropper's claim that he cannot be blamed for his "dream-sin"), they fail, because they invoke worlds in which women are indisputably at the mercy of the phallic and legislative powers of men, to allow the critic to consider the response of the victim to her father's act.

And though Baker makes a valiant effort to endow the hastily considered Matty Lou with positive qualities, viewing her—along with her mother—as one of the "bearers of a new black life," she remains in the critic's interpretation of the episode—as she does in the sharecropper's narrative—simply an absence. While Baker's essay adds immeasurably to our understanding of Ellison's art and of the sharecropper as vernacular artist, it fails, unfortunately, to consider the subsequently silenced victim of Trueblood's unrestrained phallus. Only by failing to grapple seriously with the implications of Trueblood's representation of Matty Lou's state following the incestuous act—"Matty Lou won't look at me and won't speak a word to nobody"—can Baker conceive at the consequences of the taboo-breaking act as generally beneficial.

Unlike Baker's reading of the Trueblood episode of *Invisible Man* in which incest is conceptualized as material and tribal gain, Morrison's revision depicts it as painfully devastating loss. Actually, her reading of Ellison's text must be remarkably similar to Baker's, for in refiguring Trueblood in the character of Cholly Breedlove, she surrounds her creation with images consistent with the critic's conception of the Ellisonian character as majestic Afro-American vernacular artist free from social restraints. Morrison says of her character:

> Only a musician would sense, know, without even knowing that
> he knew, that Cholly was free. Dangerously free. Free to feel
> whatever he felt—fear, guilt, shame, love, grief, pity. Free to be
> tender or violent, to whistle or weep . . . He was free to live his
> fantasies, and free even to die, the how and the when of which
> held no interest for him . . .
>   It was in this godlike state that he met Pauline Williams.

Only an Afro-American artist with the blues sensibility that Baker argues
for Trueblood can organize and transform into meaningfully unified
expression the utter chaos of Cholly's life. But Morrison—the remarkably
skilled novelist who does transform Cholly's life into art—provides the
blues song that is *The Bluest Eye* with a decidedly feminist slant. For while
Ellison furnished his depiction of incest with a vocabulary of naturalism
and historical regression that permit it to be read in relation to undeniably
phallocentric sociocultural interpretations of human history, Morrison's
representation is rendered in what are, for a writer with Morrison's gift,
startlingly blunt terms.

      Trueblood's presence inside his sexually inexperienced daughter's
vagina is described in ways that suggest a significant symbolic import. The
sharecropper's dream of sexual contact with a white woman while in the
home of an affluent white man necessarily brings to mind images of lynching
and castration of Afro-American males by white men because of the threat of
black male sexuality. Consequently, Trueblood's actual presence inside his
daughter assumes less importance in the text than his dream encounter with
an unnamed white woman. Morrison, however, provides her depiction of
incest with no such historically symbolic significance:

> [Cholly's] mouth trembled at the firm sweetness of the flesh. He
> closed his eyes, letting his fingers dig into her waist. The rigid-
> ness of her shocked body, the silence of her stunned throat, was
> better than Pauline's easy laughter had been. The confused
> mixture of his memories of Pauline and the doing of a wild and
> forbidden thing excited him, and a bolt of desire ran down his
> genitals, giving it length, and softening the lips of his anus.
> Surrounding all of this lust was a border of politeness. He wanted
> to fuck her—tenderly. But the tenderness would not hold. The
> tightness of her vagina was more than he could bear. His soul
> seemed to slip down to his guts and fly out into her, and the
> gigantic thrust he made into her then provoked the only sound
> she made—a hollow suck of air in the back of her throat.

Cholly is far from the majestic figure that Baker argues for True-blood during his efforts to "move without movin" in his daughter's vagina. And though Morrison does endow the incestuous male figure with the capacity for sympathy—citing, for example, the "border of politeness" that accompanies his lust—Cholly's "wild," "confused" act lacks the inscribed symbolic weight of Trueblood's transgression. While the sharecropper's inability to withdraw from his daughter's vagina represents, according to Baker, Trueblood's "say[ing] a resounding 'no' to castratingly tight spots of his existence as a poor farmer in the undemocratic south," the tight sexual space represents for Cholly the forbidden area that must be forcibly entered and exited. The text of *The Bluest Eye* informs us: "Removing himself from her was so painful to him he cut it short and snatched his genitals out of the dry harbor of her vagina."

Morrison, finally, seems to be taking Ellison to task for the phallocentric nature of his representation of incest which marginalizes and renders as irrelevant the consequences of the act for the female victim. *The Bluest Eye* serves as a revisionary reading of the Trueblood episode of *Invisible Man*. Morrison writes her way into the Afro-American literary tradition by foregrounding the effects of incest for female victims in direct response to Ellison's refusal to consider them seriously. And so while the victims of incest in both novels ultimately occupy similarly silent, asocial positions in their respective communities, Morrison explicitly details Pecola's tragic and painful journey, while Ellison, in confining Matty Lou to the periphery, suggests that her perspective contains for him "no compelling significance."

Unlike Ellison, Zora Neale Hurston is immensely interested in exposing patriarchy's inherent oppressiveness. In the following discussion, I will offer an intertextual reading of *The Bluest Eye* and *Their Eyes Were Watching God* in order to suggest the ways in which Hurston's text can be seen as a direct, "benevolent" precursor to Morrison's first novel. Material for such a claim can be most clearly observed in a further analysis of Pecola and of the text's narrative strategies.

VI

One way to begin to analyze the intertextual relationship between Hurston's and Morrison's texts is to compare the titles of the novels. Henry Louis Gates, Jr. has suggested in "The Blackness of Blackness" that such an interpretive strategy leads to a full understanding of Ellison's signifying, in *Invisible Man*, on his precursor Wright. He asserts:

> [Ellison's] signifying . . . starts with the titles: Wright's *Native Son* and *Black Boy*, titles connoting race, self, and presence, Ellison tropes with *Invisible Man*, invisibility an ironic response, of absence, to the would-be presence of "blacks" and "natives," while "man" suggests a more mature and stronger status than either "son" or "boy."

It is similarly possible to chart a relationship between *The Bluest Eye* and *Their Eyes Were Watching God* by analyzing their respective titles. "Their eyes were watching God" connotes a communal observation of the wondrously curious acts of a god who is undeniably present in the world; "the bluest eye" implies loneliness (the single "eye"/I), blueness in the Afro-American vernacular sense, and implicitly suggests that solitude—distance from the tribe—is a function of aspirations for the non-black, for blue eyes. In other words, Pecola's (and, I would argue, Geraldine's and Polly's) status as "The bluest I" results from her adoption of white standards of perception. Hurston's title and text, then, suggest a common, culturally based method of (non-Western) perception of the world. Morrison's, on the other hand, imply solitude, distance from the group and, consequently, a means of viewing the world that is at odds with the Afro-American cultural heritage.

Morrison's apparent refigurations of Hurston's text are further observable in her various uses of nature in *The Bluest Eye*. Janie's fate is intricately bound to nature: the pear tree image dominates Hurston's novel. What is arguably the most important scene in the first half of the novel is Janie's education under the tutelage of a voice-capable nature which teaches her about natural marriage. Her improving self-image and defensive self-division are possible only when she rediscovers nature. Janie's remarkable harmony with nature stands in direct contrast to Pecola's natural discord. While the sexual awakening of Hurston's heroine occurs in the spring and corresponds with natural reproductive cycles, Pecola's sexual maturation, signaled by the commencement of her menstruation, occurs in the fall during a brief stay at the MacTeer household. The beginnings of both protagonists' physical maturity occasion inquiries about love and marriage. Janie's questions are answered by an instructive nature:

> She saw a dust-bearing bee sink into the sanctum of a bloom; the thousand sister-calyxes arch to meet the love embrace and the ecstatic shiver of the tree from root to tiniest branch creaming in every blossom and frothing with delight. So this was a marriage! She had been summoned to behold a revelation.

Pecola on the other hand, finds no answers in a family where love is not bred or in a northern city where she has little or no access to nature or to the wisdom of her culture. Just as Nanny reads signs of Janie's maturation into her kiss by Johnny Taylor, so too, do Frieda and Claudia view the menstruating Pecola as "grown-up-like." But this physical maturity is not accompanied by a fuller knowledge of the workings of her own body or of love and marriage, as Pecola's questions to her temporary bedmates suggest:

> After a long while [Pecola] spoke very softly. "Is it true that I can have a baby now?"
> "Sure," said Frieda drowsily. "Sure you can."
> "But . . . how?" Her voice was hollow with wonder.
> "Oh," said Frieda, "somebody has to love you."
> "Oh."
> There was a long pause in which Pecola and I thought this over. It would involve, I supposed, "my man," who, before leaving me, would love me. But there weren't any babies in the songs my mother sang. Maybe that's why the women were sad: the men left before they could make a baby.
> Then Pecola asked a question that had never entered my mind. "How do you do that? I mean, how do you get somebody to love you?" But Frieda was asleep. And I didn't know.

Answers to Pecola's quandries are unavailable. Having never felt the love of anyone, she has no idea how to "get somebody to love" her. When she ponders how romantic adult love might be manifested, the only example available is that of her bickering parents. She wonders if their relationship represents the norm:

> What did love feel like? she wondered. How do grown-ups act when they love each other? . . . Into her eyes came the picture of Cholly and Mrs. Breedlove in bed. He making sounds as though he were in pain, as though something had him by the throat and wouldn't let go. Terrible as his noises were, they were not nearly as bad as the no noise at all from her mother. It was as though she was not even there. Maybe that was love. Choking sounds and silence.

In contrast to Janie's instruction where she is able to observe the "love embrace" of elements of nature, Pecola has as her only example the "Choking sounds and silence" of her parents' sexual intercourse. Thus, while

Janie gains valuable information about marriage during the period of sexual awakening, Pecola acquires only misinformation: that love must necessarily be characterized solely by pain and absence. It is possible, then, to perceive of Pecola's fate—at least with respect to her sexual awakening—as directly contrasting that of Janie. Such contrast is further observable in a more elaborate discussion of the authors' presentation of nature in their respective texts.

Phyllis Klotman argues that "nature serves as the unifying element is the novel." It is true that, in terms of its strategies of narration, Morrison's text employs nature's seasons to provide *The Bluest Eye* with a sense of unity and wholeness. But nature here is represented as being at best indifferent to man. Claudia's first words in the novel suggest nature's apathy where humanity is concerned:

> Quiet as it's kept, there were no marigolds in the fall of 1941. We thought, at the time, that it was because Pecola was having her father's baby that the marigolds did not grow. A little examination and much less melancholy would have proved to us that our seeds were not the only ones that did not sprout; nobody's did. Not even the gardens fronting the lake showed marigolds that year. But so deeply concerned were we with the health and safe delivery of Pecola's baby we could think of nothing but our own magic: if we planted the seeds, and said the right words over them, they would blossom, and everything would be all right. . . . For years I thought my sister was right: it was my fault. I had planted them too far down in the earth. It never occurred to either of us that the earth itself might have been unyielding. . . . What is clear now is that of all that hope, fear, lust, love, and grief, nothing remains but Pecola and the unyielding earth.

Claudia's prefatory remarks imply an affinity between Pecola and the "unyielding earth," but it is one based on their common unpreparedness for reproduction. Nothing, not even the MacTeer girls' amateurish acts of conjuring, can encourage the barren earth to stimulate the growth of marigold seeds. The barren earth of Lorrain, Ohio, directly contrasts with the actively reproductive nature of the young Janie's backyard in which the protagonist of *Their Eyes Were Watching God* observes the potential of "ecstatic shiver[s]" in natural marriage.

Another contrast between the two novels is observable in Morrison's apparent revision of the optimism inherent in Tea Cake's final gift to Janie.

After she kills him self-defense, Janie finds among her third husband's belongings a package of seeds. She plans to plant these seeds outside her Eatonville home:

> The seeds reminded Janie of Tea Cake more than anything else because he was always planting things. She had noticed them on the kitchen shelf when she came home from the funeral and had put them in her breast pocket. Now that she was home, she meant to plant them for remembrance.

By planting the seeds, Janie will ensure that her memory of Tea Cake— whose given name, Verigible Woods, indicates his intense affinity with nature—will never die. In *Their Eyes Were Watching God*, the planting of seeds serves as a means of preserving life. Hurston's text ends with the suggestion that such preservation is indeed possible: "Tea Cake came prancing around her where she was and the song of the sigh flew out of the window and lit on the top of the pine trees. . . . Of course he wasn't dead. He could never be dead until she herself had finished feeling and thinking."

Morrison's text appears to revise Hurston's use of seeds, insisting that the natural world of the North has no ability (or desire) to save or preserve human life. The planting of seeds in *The Bluest Eye* serves to demonstrate not nature's harmony with humanity and the possibility of preserving (at least the memory of) life, but, rather, a barren earth's indifference to humanity's needs.

Nevertheless, as I have shown, Pecola is continually associated with domesticated animals who are themselves employed by members of *The Bluest Eye*'s black community as scapegoats. But, just as she is associated with nonhuman entities such as dogs, cats, and "the unyielding earth," she is also connected metaphorically to birds. For example, after her encirclement by the boys and Maureen Peal's unexpected attack, Claudia says of Pecola: "She seemed to fold into herself, like a pleated wing." This bird-like response to abuse calls Nanny's explanation to Janie of the diligence of her efforts to move from the white Washburn family's property and purchase her own home:

> Ah raked and scraped and bought dis lil piece uh land so you woudn't have to stay in de white folks' yard and *tuck yo' head* befo' other chillun at school. . . . *Ah don't want yo' feathers always crumpled by folks throwin' up things in yo' face.* (my emphasis)

Nanny's loving sacrifice is an effort to keep her granddaughter from suffering the ignominy of being perceived by the black community as a white folks' nigger, as an Afro-American who is influenced and controlled by a white perception of reality.

Pecola's tragic plight, on the other hand, stems primarily from her inability to achieve a positive reading of blackness in an urban setting dominated by pervasive white standards. Stuck in "de white folks' yard" of self-promotional propaganda, and unable to liberate herself from the oppressive influence of white American standards, Pecola cannot, unlike Milkman Dead in Morrison's *Song of Solomon*, "give up the shit that weighs [her] down" and "surrender . . . to the air." This pervasive whiteness, coupled with her victimization at the hands of self-protective Afro-Americans who view her as the shadow of blackness, causes her almost literally to transform into the type of victimized bird that Nanny's efforts save her granddaughter from becoming. As the narrator continues, Pecola is represented as a grotesque, flightless bird:

> The damage done [by the community's abuse] was total. She spent her days, her tendril, sap-green days, walking up and down, up and down, her head jerking to the beat of a drummer so distant only she could hear. Elbows bent, hands on shoulders, she flailed her arms like a bird in an eternal, grotesquely futile effort to fly. Beating the air, a winged but grounded bird, intent on the blue void it could not reach—could not even see—but which filled the valleys of the mind.

She remains tragically tied to white standards of beauty and is, even in her insanity, striving for "the blue void . . . [she] could not reach."

VII

The result of Pecola's victimization by her own community is a tragic schizophrenia, a psychotic double voicedness. This double voicedness results from her belief that she has been granted the beauty that she believes accompanies blue eyes. After her rape by her father and her encounter with the misanthropic Soaphead Church (which she believes concludes with her achievement of blue eyes), Pecola manufactures a friend in order to validate her newfound beauty.

Perhaps the greatest significance of Pecola's self-division to a discussion of the relation of Morrison's text to the Afro-American literary tradition is as a revision of Du Bois' conceptualization of the Afro-American psyche. For Pecola clearly loses the battle—as Du Bois conceives of it—to conflate

in her person blackness and Americanness. Her loss is reflected in her schizophrenic confirmation of the beauty of (unachieved) blue eyes and in her
total rejection of blackness. And so while Janie's divided consciousness healed
at the conclusion of *Their Eyes Were Watching God* to the point that she is
able to "pull . . . in her horizon . . . from around the waist of the world and
drape . . . it over her shoulder" as a symbol of her self-unity and unity with
the natural world, Pecola, burdened as she is with a permanently and debili-
tatingly dissociated sensibility, is depicted as involved in a futile effort to
achieve the unreachable, imperceptible "blue void."

Pecola's splitting into two voices corresponds directly to the two-
voiced narration of *The Bluest Eye*. The text of Morrison's novel has been
narrated by two distinct voices: by Claudia and by an omniscient presence.
For the greater part of the novel, these voices are in their focus and levels of
emotional involvement in the matters they relate unquestionably distinct
from one another. Claudia, who narrates the first chapter in each section of
the novel, relates matters about her own life and that of her family, as well as
information concerning Pecola about which she knows firsthand: her own
dismemberment of white dolls; Mr. Henry's fondling of her sister; Mrs.
Breedlove's abuse of her daughter in the Fisher home; and her sister's and her
own attempts to save Pecola's baby. On the other hand, the omniscient
narrator, whose voice controls the chapters that Claudia does not narrate,
conveys pertinent information about the histories of characters much older
than Claudia, as well as information about Pecola of which Claudia could not
possibly be aware: Cholly's reaction to the white hunters who discover him
and Darlene in the woods; Polly's fascination with the movies; Geraldine's
attempts to suppress the funkiness of passion; Cholly's motivation for raping
his daughter; and Pecola's schizophrenic discussion with herself.

But after the onset of Pecola's schizophrenic double-voicedness, the
distinctive narrative voices of *The Bluest Eye* apparently merge into a single
voice. Suddenly Claudia is privy to information which she clearly could have
learned only from the omniscient narrator. She plainly comprehends, for
example, the complex ritual of scapegoating in which the entire community
has involved Pecola:

> All of us . . . felt so wholesome after we cleaned ourselves on
> her. . . . Her inarticulateness made us believe we were eloquent.
> Her poverty kept us generous. Even her waking dreams we
> used—to silence our own nightmares. And she let us, and
> thereby deserved our contempt. We honed our eyes on her,
> padded our characters with her frailty, and yawned in the
> fantasy of our strength.

She is informed, further, of Pecola's desire for blue eyes—information that Pecola has shared only with God and with her imaginary friend—and of the Maginot Line's love for the abused protagonist. Claudia also knows the specifics of Cholly's incestuous act, and speaks of its motivation in the same terms as the omniscient narrator: as a function of his freedom.

> Cholly loved her [Pecola]. I'm sure he did. He, at any rate, was the only one who loved her enough to touch her, envelop her, give something of himself to her. But his touch was fatal, and the something he gave to her filled the matrix of her agony with death. Love is never any better than the lover. Wicked people love wickedly, violent people love violently, weak people love weakly, stupid people love stupidly, but the love of a free man is never safe. There is no gift for the beloved. The lover alone possesses his gift of love.

Not only then, does Claudia's voice occupy the position previously reserved for the omniscient narrator, it also evidences a scope and breadth of knowledge that had heretofore belonged only to that omniscient voice.

This merging of narrative voices recalls Janie's memorable phrase when she assigns to Phoeby the role of narrator of her story to the Eatonville community: "mah tongue is in mah friend's mouf." It does indeed appear that the scope of the omniscient narrator's knowledge has, in the concluding pages of *The Bluest Eye*, been imparted to Claudia, that the last paragraphs of the novel evidence the conflation of their voices, of their "tongues." But the situation of such a conflation of narrative voices suggests that this healing of double voicedness occurs as a direct function of Pecola's own schizophrenia. Just as the improved self-image of the community depicted in Morrison's text results from its sacrifice and projection of the shadow of blackness onto Pecola, so, too, it seems, can a healed narrative double voicedness be achieved only through the sacrifice of the female protagonist in the novel's narrative events. The sacrifice of Pecola—a young girl who measures her own worth in terms of idealized white standards of beauty and morality, and goes mad as a result—is, it would appear, necessary for the achievement of the Afro-American expressive ideal of merged consciousness, of unified voice.

Despite its undoubtedly tragic conclusion, *The Bluest Eye* can be said to serve as another illustration of the Afro-American enterprise devoted to the *denigration* of the genre of the novel. Morrison's successful *denigration* of the form is accomplished not simply in her employment of dual narrative voices, but, especially, in the ultimate merging of these voices in the conclusion of her text. And so while she can depict healed consciousness as a possibility for any of the characters of *The Bluest Eye* only through the example of Claudia (whose subsequent achieved black consciousness enables her to serve as a narrator of the novel), Morrison has, through her manipulation of the white voice of the primer, through her apparent revisions of precursor texts, and through her depiction of narrative voices as ultimately conjoined, added to the Afro-American literary canon another supreme example of a Genuine Black Book.

DONALD B. GIBSON

Text and Countertext in The Bluest Eye

I . . . have no hesitation in regarding the white race as superior to all others
in beauty. . . . Human groups are unequal in beauty; and this inequality is
rational, logical, permanent, and indestructible.
> —Count Joseph Arthur de Gobineau,
> *Essay on the Inequality of the Human Races*

Along with the idea of romantic love, she [Pauline] was introduced to
another—physical beauty. Probably the most destructive ideas in the history
of human thought. Both originated in envy, thrived in insecurity, and ended
in disillusion.
> —Toni Morrison, *The Bluest Eye*

Count Joseph Arthur de Gobineau, French diplomat, ethnologist, fiction
writer, bearer of the infamous reputation of "father of racism," and a corre-
spondent for sixteen years of Alexis de Tocqueville, wrote these words in the
early 1850s. Tocqueville, as might be expected, disagreed strongly with
Gobineau's authoritarian, anti-democratic stance and argued against the
whole of such racist and reactionary thinking. We might imagine further that
his counterarguments fell upon deaf ears because Gobineau's arguments
stem from very basic beliefs about human nature, the nature of the universe,

From *Toni Morrison: Critical Perspectives Past and Present.* © 1990 by Donald B. Gibson.

and ideas about social organization stemming from the nature of those beliefs. Gobineau's words contain implicitly the philosophical assumptions that beauty exists in and of itself, independent of human nature or character; and it forms some part of a larger structure of the universe. Gobineau's whole system of thought seems reactive against the tide of ideas that by his time had unseated the rationalism of the Enlightenment, ushered in the American and French revolutions, and paved the way for Darwin and other thinkers who believed the world to be in process rather than fixed within established, unchangeable limits. Toni Morrison did not need to have read Gobineau to react to him, for his legacy is not only in his text but in Western civilization's air. Her novel calls into question the mode of his thought and the whole authoritarian, politically reactionary system of beliefs about the nature of reality on which his and like thought is based.

Morrison's 1970 novel, for all its eloquence and beauty of expression, engages in sustained argument with modes of thought and belief explicitly stated in Gobineau's assertion above, but likewise, and perhaps more vividly presented in cultural icons portraying physical beauty: movies, billboards, magazines, books, newspapers, window signs, dolls, and drinking cups. Morrison's novel deals with the most subtle implications of the general society's definition of beauty, and the novel shows us the depth and complexity of those implications. But unlike most novels that take issue with society, the novel argues with itself, clarifying rather than simplifying, uncovering and grappling with the most problematical facets of the subject, and undercutting easily held values in order to reveal complication. The novel's text is inscribed with a countertext, an oppositional discourse so intricately intertwined with text as to render it finally incapable of independent existence, transforming each by turn into the counter of the other. While text and countertext contend for dominance, the one melds into the opposite, and at midpoint between the exchange neither is independently discernible though both are present, like an optical illusion which may alternately assume one form then another, then perhaps varying degrees of both and neither depending upon the disposition of the observer's eye and mind.

The countertextual dynamic of the novel begins with the quotation from the Dick and Jane primer, an introductory gesture, which is in fact and by implication not unlike the prefatory essay to Richard Wright's *Uncle Tom's Children*, "The Ethics of Living Jim Crow" (1938) in that it introduces what is to follow, offers evidence to comment upon and support the thematic implications of the main text, and at the same time informs the main text at each point along its course, its implications engraved within every aspect of plot, character, and description. Morrison's self-consciously epigraphical introduction, the primer text, exists as text and countertext: text in that it has no apparent relation to the major text but lies in the background, the mere genesis of the problem exemplified by Pecola's wanting blue eyes and exemplary, by indirection, of the causes underlying the problematical nature of the lives of the characters in its world; countertext, by turns, in that the epigraphical introduction implies one of the primary and most insidious ways that the dominant culture exercises its hegemony, through the educational system. It reveals the role of education in both oppressing the victim—and more to the point—teaching the victim how to oppress her own black self by internalizing the values that dictate the standards of beauty. "Don't give the girl a fishing pole," the prefatory material tells us, "teach her how to fish," teach her how to enact self-oppression while ostensibly learning to read a simple, unproblematic text. To put this in another way the act of learning to read and write means exposure to the values of the culture from which the reading material emanates. If one wants to read or write, then one must pay for the privilege. The cost of learning to read and write carries with it the necessity to submit to values beyond and other than literacy *per se*, for words do not exist independent of value. One cannot simply learn to read without being subjected to the values engraved in the text.

The introduction to *The Bluest Eye* is also an enabling act, setting up, defining, and effectively writing or reinscribing the nature of what is to be written against. It is the obverse of what in the slave narrative was the act of authentication. Here the author seizes the authority of the authenticator by appropriating and subverting the role of authenticator. That is, the authenticator's role is an authoritative role deriving its authority from socially derived power. The superiority assumed by Charles Sumner and Wendell Philips as authenticators of Frederick Douglass's *Narrative*, for example, is assumed by Morrison herself in her text. Douglass's text is authenticated by Sumner and Philips in the *Narrative* (though he struggles mightily both literarily and historically before wresting away their implied authority). Wright authenticates his own text in "Ethics"; Morrison authenticates her text in the enabling act of her introduction. This is the less complicated aspect of Morrison's discourse in *The Bluest Eye*.

The complications arise when we see that Morrison's sense of the meaning of "bluest eye" is not confined to the meaning we immediately ascribe. The text of the Dick and Jane primer, the epigraphical introduction to Morrison's narrative, is rendered by Morrison in three versions (1–3), each printed in such a way as to appear to grow less comprehensible. The second version omits punctuation, decreasing the space between the lines and running the sentences together; the third omits spaces between the words entirely and arbitrarily breaks words at the end of a line, even words of one syllable. The inference to be drawn is that the final version is incomprehensible. But that is not true. It is, arguably, perfectly comprehensible. The difference between the first and third versions is that the third forces us to participate in the reading in a more active way by demanding that we identify individual words and supply from our own past experience of reading the first version the proper punctuation. The reader is once again, in the very act of reading, taught to read. The meaning is not, as it appears, drained away from first to final draft, but simply concentrated. The implication is that just as Pecola—and all black children—are subjected to the value scheme implied in the primer, so they have imposed upon them whole schemes of value, political, religious, moral, aesthetic, that have little or nothing to do with their actual lives. They are measured using standards they cannot possibly meet—because of genetics and economics—and are found wanting. Yet a paradox arises when we consider that Morrison organizes her text around the primer passage. The sections focusing on Pecola and her family are headed by a line or two from the primer text, the text standing in countertextual relation to the actuality of Pecola's and her family's lives. The final chapter of the novel opens with the primer lines "Look, look. Here comes a friend," and we of course recall that Pecola's friend is hallucinated, the product of her madness. But she does, after all, as the countertext has it, have her blue eyes.

The implication of the novel's structure is that our lives are contained within the framework of the values of the dominant culture and subjected to those values. We have all (there is reason to believe the author does not exclude herself nor anyone else) internalized those values, and to the extent that we have, we are instruments of our own oppression. The text says we are oppressed by the values of the ruling class; the countertext says we participate in our own oppression usually to the extent of being literally the very hand or arm of that oppression.

Such a conclusion is born out by Claudia's (the sometime narrator's) relating her response as a young child to dolls. The reader will recall her literal deconstruction of a white, blue-eyed, yellow-haired doll, an act intended as a means of discovery, and performed on the childish assumption that whatever caused the doll to appear to everyone except herself an object of great value lay within the thing itself, a reasonable assumption since she has concluded that the difference between her and the white doll is an essential, intrinsic difference, not a superficial, extrinsic one. To discover the doll's reality by taking it apart is not to demystify it—it has not yet become mystified for her—but rather to wreak vengeance on it and to discover that the difference between her and the doll lies elsewhere than in the doll's innards.

The countertext has Claudia subsequently join those who approve of little white girls and disapprove of her.

> Adults, older girls, shops, magazines, newspapers, window signs—all the world had agreed that a blue-eyed, yellow-haired, pink-skinned doll was what every child treasured.

These adults are not only white but black as well.

> What made people look at them and say "Awwwww," but not for me? The eye slide of black women as they approached them on the street, and the possessive gentleness of their touch as they handled them.

Her antipathy toward white dolls and little white girls does not, as noted, last forever. Claudia's admission of the fact, however, turns out to be a low-keyed indictment, but devastating in its implications, of the whole scheme of sociopolitical values held by the ruling classes and informing their ideology. She fantasizes about doing the same violence to little white girls that she does to her dolls, the closest she can come to revolt against a vicious value scheme that threatens her very being.

> If I pinched them, their eyes—unlike the crazed glint of the baby doll's eyes—would fold in pain, and their cry would not be the sound of an icebox door, but a fascinating cry of pain. When I learned how repulsive this disinterested violence was, that it was repulsive because it was disinterested, my shame floundered about for refuge. The best hiding place was love. Thus the conversion from pristine sadism to fabricated hatred, to fraudulent love. It was a small step to Shirley Temple. I learned much later to worship her, just as I learned to delight in cleanliness, knowing, even as I learned, that the change was adjustment without improvement.

Claudia expresses here her understanding, a retrospective understanding and not one achieved in childhood, that social values are arbitrary, socially derived, and not existent in nature. It is not natural to have or want blue eyes, but a society may hold such a standard and through its power—its control of images through control of the means of the presentation of imagery, control of "magazines, newspapers, window signs," of current iconography—impress the reality of its values on those not having the wherewithal to resist, not having the facilities to counter the assault.

But herein lies the power of Toni Morrison's argument, for she undercuts the validity of the proposition of the dominant culture that blue eyes and cleanliness are inherently valuable by historicizing social value. Claudia "learned" to worship Shirley Temple just as she "learned" to delight in cleanliness. The text, it is implied, is that blue eyes and cleanliness are valuable because in this society such values are imposed upon its members. The countertext reads that such values are not so much relative as arbitrary. They have no reality in and of themselves. The image of Shirley Temple as representing a standard of beauty came about not because of anything inherent within Shirley Temple but because she exists as icon in movies and on, of all things, a common drinking cup, a trivial commercial item, that for Pecola becomes something entirely other, a chalice, a grail whose milk-white content will allow her to take in the blood of the goddess, a white blood of milk—not a red blood of wine. The milk is the blood of the goddess because it is contained within the cup. Pecola gorges herself on the blood of the goddess; she indulges an insatiable appetite. If she drinks enough white milk from the chalice, she may become like the stuff she imbibes and as well become like the image adorning the container itself. One ingests the blood of the goddess in order to become her. Pecola performs a kind of masturbatory communion, a self-administered version of the ritual in which she is both priestess and communicant.

This initial ritualistic act of communion prefigures a later one, later in the sequence of the book's episodes though in fact earlier in time than the communion of graham crackers and milk, bread and wine. By the time Pecola comes to live briefly with Claudia and Frieda, she has already learned to indulge the rituals, the third of which (her interaction with Soaphead Church) will lead to her transformation into the creature of her desire. She devours the candy, little yellow caramels called Mary Janes, a conflation, given the immediate context of their description in the novel and the more general context of the novel's primer frame, of Christ (Mr. Jacobowski says to Pecola, "Christ. Kantcha talk?"), of the Jane of the primer, and of the Virgin Mary. Pecola is an inverted Virgin Mary, however, a Virgin Mary demystified: not mysteriously and spiritually impregnated by God the father but brutally impregnated by Cholly Breedlove, the father, on the dirty floor of the kitchen of her storefront home. The offspring of this union is the Christ child, the stillborn Christ child, who is incapable of saving the world because incapable of saving himself.

The ritualistic significance of the eating of the Mary Janes and the relation to Shirley Temple, milk, communion, and sexuality are born out in Morrison's description of Pecola's experience with the candy.

> Each pale yellow wrapper has a picture on it. A picture of Mary Jane, for whom the candy is named. Smiling white face. Blond

hair in gentle disarray, blue eyes looking at her out of a world of clean comfort. [Compare the primer Jane.] The eyes are petulant, mischievous. To Pecola they are simply pretty. She eats the candy, and its sweetness is good. To eat the candy is somehow to eat the eyes, eat Mary Jane. Love Mary Jane. Be Mary Jane.

Three pennies had bought her nine lovely orgasms with Mary Jane. Lovely Mary Jane, for whom a candy is named.

The text is what we read of Pecola's experience; the countertext is the central mythology of the dominant culture, a mythology demystified and therefore disempowered by Morrison's analysis of the relation of the experience of specific individuals to the myth. Transubstantiation has occurred; the candy has been transformed into the body and blood of Mary Jane (Shirley Temple). Lest we missed the implications of the ritual signification of Pecola's consumption of her Mary Janes, the reference to communion, to Christian mythology, and to the demystification of Christian ritual, Morrison reiterates the subtextual meaning of the Christian symbology by reference to the trinity: Pecola has three pennies; Mr. Jacobowski "scoots three Mary Janes toward her" (which mysteriously multiply into nine orgasms), "orgasms," not the spiritual transformation and renewal traditionally affected by ingestion of the host, but a suitable equivalent in the world Pecola inhabits.

Morrison comments upon the episode through the first line of the next episode immediately following. One sentence after "Three pennies bought her nine lovely orgasms," we read, "Three whores lived in the apartment above the Breedloves' storefront." Here the text comments upon, analyzes itself. Text and countertext produce a stark indictment of the prevailing values of the dominant society. The "three whores" are named "China," "Poland," and "The Maginot Line," a commentary of its own in that the distance between the trinity (father, son and the Holy Ghost) and the naturalistic fact of Pecola's purchase of penny candy is analogous to the distance between the seemingly insignificant lives of three whores in a small midwestern town and the large-scale geopolitical and geographical dimensions of China, Poland, and The Maginot Line. The root of the analogy is Morrison's awareness in the world of this novel that no human conception, knowledge or understanding has its source outside of individual experience. The most basic myths and the broadest geopolitical conceptions have their origins in the experience of people.

The association in the text of milk and blood and the consequent evocation of the broad range of actual and mythological meanings are clearly demonstrable in the text and are not brought to it by the over-imaginative analyst. In the very midst of Mrs. MacTeer's unremitting tirade against Pecola's consumption of prodigious quantities of milk, Pecola begins to menstruate—as though she is putting back into the world that which she has been accused of unjustly and unreasonably taking away. The association of menstruation and lactation, of bleeding and feeding, is unavoidable and explicit. Mrs. MacTeer speaks.

> "Anybody need three quarts of milk to *live* need to get out of here. They in the wrong place. What is this? Some kind of *dairy* farm?"
>
> Suddenly Pecola bolted straight up, her eyes wide with terror. A whinnying sound came out of her mouth.
>
> "What's the matter with *you*?" Frieda stood up too.
>
> Then we both looked where Pecola was staring. Blood was running down her legs. Some drops were on the steps. I leaped up. "Hey. You cut yourself? Look. It's all over your dress."

Mrs. MacTeer's assault, motherly assault that is, brings about, however unintentionally, the onset of Pecola's menses. It is not, Claudia tells us, the child that the parent attacks but the condition that allows or causes the child to appear to be a problem. It is not Pecola with whom she is angry but the conditions that require her to be concerned about how much milk she drinks. Pecola responds in a way Francis Back has seen as a response reflective of human nature.

> Whosoever hath anything fixed in this person that doth induce contempt hath also a perpetual spur in himself to rescue and deliver himself from scorn.

Pecola rescues and delivers herself from scorn by giving to back the world what she has taken away. She has consumed a natural body fluid, milk; she gives back a natural body fluid, blood. In so doing she appeases Mrs. MacTeer, turning her wrath not into mere tolerance but into a rarely expressed and articulated acceptance, approval, and support.

The reality of the situation is such, however, that initiation and the potential of deliverance (in an entirely secular sense) are available for Pecola. It in any case seems so. The water has as its purpose not to drown but to cleanse; not to inundate but to initiate. Pecola is initiated, baptized into biological female adulthood; Frieda and Claudia are detraumatized, brought into a normalized relation to ordinary biological process.

We could hear the water running into the bathtub.
"You think she's going to drown her?"
"Oh, Claudia. You so dumb. She's just going to wash her clothes and all."

"Should we beat up Rosemary?" [Should we react as our mother reacted when she thought we were "playing nasty"? Does the fact of Pecola's menstruation require the drawing of blood? Does this situation require aggression on our parts?]

"No. [Let us emulate mother.] Leave her alone."

The water gushed, and over its gushing we could hear the music of my mother's laughter.

The meaning of the text at this moment lies in its playing off, one against the other, the total childish ignorance of Claudia and Pecola, the childish half ignorance of Frieda, and the mature, woman's knowledge of Mrs. MacTeer. From the antagonism, anger, misunderstanding, and conflict of the events leading up to this point arises a new understanding and vision, a celebratory confluence of discordant modes. This section of the novel, you will recall, begins with Mrs. MacTeer berating Pecola.

"Three quarts of milk. That's what was in that icebox yesterday. Three whole quarts. Now they ain't none. Not a drop. I don't mind folks coming in and getting what they want, but three quarts of milk! What the devil does *any*body need with *three* quarts of milk?" (Morrison's emphasis)

It ends with "the music of my mother's laughing" as she bestows on Pecola the care and comfort which may be available to the female child entering this new stage from the female parent figure. Embedded within the text, existing at various levels and a form of countertext, are three perspectives. One is the perspective of the child Claudia, the nine-year-old who at first hand witnesses many of the events of the novel. The second is the perspective of the significantly more mature retrospective narrator who understands and interprets those events, events which the younger Claudia could not possibly have understood. We see the disparity between the adult and child perspectives when Claudia asks whether their mother is going to drown Pecola. Because the meaning of the section is obviously shaped, the question could only emanate from a consciousness that knows the question is a childish one. Hence the question betrays a consciousness that has conceived the mind conceiving the question.

The third perspective, whose existence is inferred from the existence of the total text, the novel itself, is the author's perspective—the perspective that knows of the relation between this scene (ending with the "music" of Mrs. MacTeer's laughter) and the final episodes of the novel, sexual intercourse visited upon the virgin Pecola by her father, the issue of that (her stillborn child), and Pecola's ensuing madness. In other words there lies submerged beneath "the music of my mother's laughter" a countertext, a text whose meaning we can know only retrospectively, after having read the novel. Then we know that the apparent blessing, the apparent confluence of positive meaning, value, and feeling, is only "apparent." This positive moment, one of two such moments in the novel, when Pecola relates intensely to another human being, when she is loved and accepted in a way significantly poignant to her, is mirrored on the floor of the Breedlove kitchen when Cholly, as does Mrs. MacTeer here, likewise expresses an adult, parental, sense of relatedness, concern for, and involvement with Pecola. His is *another* initiation involving fluids: not clean, gushing, fresh water, but "cold, greasy dishwater."

Text and countertext are juxtaposed at the moment Pecola responds to the onset of menses, and her response is determined by the fact that she does not know what is happening to her: "her eyes [are] wide with terror." Claudia feels that something negative is occurring; that Pecola has been somehow injured: "You cut yourself?" Frieda normalizes and brings the situation under control by indicating knowledge of what is occurring, naming it: "That's ministratin'." Against Frieda's attempt to wrest the experience from out the chaos of ignorance, to banish fear through knowledge, Pecola pits her own specifically individualized response: "Am I going to die?"

Frieda's response to Pecola's question once again juxtaposes text and countertext, winding up the plot of the novel as though it were the mainspring of a clock whose steady and controlled release of tension will result in the ticking out of the plot. In a very significant sense the center of the novel, insofar as that center is based upon a text-countertext opposition, rests in this moment, this moment of moments, in Frieda's response to Pecola's question, a response less naive than ironic in its implications regarding Pecola's fate: "Noooo. You won't die. It just means you can have a baby!" The implication is that the ability to have a baby is a good thing. The fact is that for Pecola the countertext has it that her ability to have a baby is a curse, a curse not on women in general but on her. The implications of the interaction between Frieda and Pecola at this textual moment are teased out at the chapter's end when the question of the meaning of Pecola's potential to have a baby arises, are further explored by the three girls, however perfunctorily.

That night, in bed, the three of us lay still. We were full of awe and respect for Pecola. Lying next to a real person who was really ministratin' was somehow sacred. She was different from us now—grown-up-like. She, herself, felt the distance, but refused to lord it over us.

After a long while she spoke very softly. "Is it true that I can have a baby now?"

"Sure," said Frieda drowsily. "Sure you can."

"But . . . how?" Her voice was hollow with wonder.

"Oh," said Frieda, "somebody has to love you."

"Oh."

This section of the novel, especially in the two passages quoted above, is the germ from which the remainder of the novel proceeds. Nearly everything that happens in Pecola's life demonstrates to the reader and to herself that nobody loves her and then finally somebody does love her and she does indeed have a baby, though through a process that she neither seeks nor even could imagine. All of that is implicit in the conversation above. All unfolds, from this point on, leading inexorably to the kitchen floor of the Breedlove place and ultimately to the premature birth and death of Pecola's child. Her insanity stands in countertextual relation to the underlying tone of these two passages. The transformation from girl to biologically mature female which seems happy and hopeful, as reflected in Claudia's and Frieda's barely concealed envy, turns horrific, "appalling," in the root sense of that word. The meanings implicit in Claudia's feelings as the three lie abed that "Lying next to a real person who was really ministratin' was somehow *sacred*" (my emphasis) are themselves aborted.

The chief word in the novel's text after this section is "Breedlove," Pecola's family name. "Breed" and "love" clearly exist oppositionally, in countertextual relation: "breed" is the biological phenomenon, a physiological occurrence having no affective source or consequence; "love" is a social, religious, or spiritual phenomenon, implying meaning beyond the simply phenomenal. The two definitions of relatedness are intertwined in the name. The fact of the tension brought about by the disparate meanings of the two words comprising the name, yet their having been yoked together to produce one name, replicates the character of the text itself. It is a text which ultimately does not allow us clearly to distinguish (nor does it invite awareness of the possible distinctions to be made) between the historical meanings of the words "breed" and "love." The novel at once maintains and breaks down the distinctions: the distinction between breeding and loving is a linguistic, moralistic distinction and not a distinction to be sustained by reference to any appeal to what is, to actuality. That is to say, Morrison suggests that the concepts are easily enough distinguished, but experience is not identical with our abstractions about it. Felt experience, Morrison insists, is far too complex and different in character from idea to correspond to our concepts regarding it. Specifically, our lexicon distinguishes "breed" and "love," but "love" in actuality, as experienced, may not be distinguishable from animalistic "breed," and the element of "breed" may lie inextricably buried within the experience of love.

The implications of the meaning of the family name, a name which comes to the family through Cholly ("Charles Breedlove," a good Anglo-Saxon name, is entombed within his full name as well as a host of other meanings), conflate in the narrative's climax, the sexual abuse of Pecola on a Saturday afternoon on the kitchen floor of the storefront the Breedloves occupy. All thematic and plot lines, the text-countertextual movement of the novel as well, converge at that particular juncture in time and space.

Cholly, during this scene, is allowed by Morrison to appropriate narrative authority insofar as he is permitted the privilege of having what occurs told from his vantage point. He does not usurp narrative authority, for his control stems entirely from the author's self-imposed limitation: she restricts herself at this point to the third person limited narration. Whatever authority Cholly possesses accrues not because it comes to him by nature, or because he is male, but because Morrison chooses to give it to him. She grants this black male a voice, and in allowing him voice, she again expresses countertextuality. There is some degree of distance between the perspective of Cholly and that of Morrison. Whereas Morrison is not Cholly, Cholly is likewise not Morrison. Yet, Morrison allows Claudia to be something other than simply evil. We know in the abstract that there are no circumstances under which a father may justifiably, knowingly have sexual intercourse with his daughter. Morrison does not tell us that what Cholly does to Pecola is all right; rather she says that what happens is very complicated, and that though Cholly is not without blame for what happens to Pecola, he is no less a victim than she.

The factors motivating him on that Saturday afternoon in the Breedlove kitchen stem from the whole of his past experience, his experience as a poor, black youth, victimized by white and black oppression. It is not clear where oppression begins or ends: his mother abandons him on a garbage heap, but his grandmother rescues him. Abandonment is text; rescue is countertext. The first act of oppression against him is counteracted by his grandmother. Is his abandonment an act of racial oppression? Yes, it is—however indirectly. But it is also personal oppression. There cannot be any such abstraction as "oppression" if it does not find expression through the actions of specific humans. (The first act of oppression committed directly against him is his mother's abandonment.)

The entirety of his sexual life is colored by his first experience of sexual intercourse, an experience utterly entwined with, entirely inseparable from, race. He is thoroughly humiliated by the two white hunters who threaten him with bodily harm if he does not continue sexual intercourse with Darlene. They look on bemused and contemptuous. The hatred and hostility that would be directed at the hunters under normal circumstances is displaced onto Darlene because Cholly is unable to disobey the two white men. The relation between that early experience with Darlene and the later sexual encounter with Pecola is clear enough. We learn that during the episode involving Darlene and the white hunters that he "hated" her and wished he could hurt her. He hated Pecola too and wished "to break her neck." On both occasions the same "biliousness" arises within him.

As the text reads, Cholly's voice tells the unremitting, unvarnished truth of his knowledge, understanding of, and feeling about what happens in that kitchen on that Saturday afternoon. As we have it, what we see is not clearly a rape because of the circumstances surrounding it. We know exactly why Cholly responds to Pecola as he does and that fact along with others gives rise to a countertext. Had he simply felt anger toward Pecola, then the case would be more easily judged. As it is, however, he feels hostility and love, both at the same time. He does want "to break her neck," but he wants to do it "tenderly." Nothing in the tone of the text suggest that these contrary feelings are not utterly genuine. The worst is yet to come: "He wanted to fuck her—tenderly."

In his drunken stupor he confuses Pecola not only with Darlene, whom he hated, but with Pauline, Pecola's mother, whom he loved. The encounter is in fact a reenactment, a reliving of his first meeting with Pauline but tinged with the experience with Darlene. The text makes that abundantly clear. The text also indicates that Morrison does not allow us as readers to get off as easily as we might if it were as clearly sexual abuse as his second attack on her is. We know what to think of fathers who fuck their daughter; perhaps we do not know so easily what to think when we learn of Cholly's thoughts at the time: "Not the usual lust to part tight legs with his own but a tenderness, a protectiveness. A desire to cover the foot with his teeth. He did it then, and started Pauline into laughter. He did it now."

It would be on the whole easier to judge Cholly if we knew less about him and if we could isolate the kitchen floor episode from the social context in which it occurs and from Cholly's past. But we cannot; we are neither invited nor allowed. It is especially evident that this is the case as the episode moves toward termination. We need especially distinguish between what

Morrison, as a function of the particular technical point of view at this juncture, tells us and does not tell us. Consider such a passage as this:: "Following the disintegration—the falling away—of sexual desire, he was conscious of her wet, soapy hands on his wrists, the fingers clenching, but whether her grip was from a hopeless but stubborn struggle to be free, or from some other emotion, he could not tell." The countertext arises from the possibilities of interpretation provoked by the technical point of view. What, in fact, was Pecola feeling at this point? Morrison allows myriad possibilities, among them that Pecola has now been loved, setting out the text and countertext as in the existing shady grammatical and lexical distinction between "being loved" and "being made love to." Of course the opposite is implied as well, for her father's expression of love is by all received standards anything but that. The problematic is intensified when Pecola's other self, the voice arising within her psyche when she becomes psychotic, an alter ego, questions her response to her father's two assaults, introducing the possibility that she wanted and needed them. The text, whereas it does not imply anything like seduction on Pecola's part, at the same time allows the possibility that she is participant and not simply victim, victim and at the same moment participant.

Text-countertextual and counter-countertextual juxtaposition inform the novel throughout. The portion of the primer book text beginning the scene just discussed reads: "SEEFATHERHEISBIGANDSTRONGFATHER WILLYOUPLAYWITHJANEFATHERISSMIINGSMILEFHERSMILE." Of course the father about to "play with" Jane is not the inane, sterile, stereotypical stick figure of the primer text but a blood and bone human out of a different world than that of Dick and Jane, a world in fact, and in some sense unhappily, more real than theirs.

One final example of countertextuality exists in the complexity of attitude demonstrated in the novel's dialogue. Consider the array of attitudes reflected in the response of the ticket agent at the bus terminal when Cholly at fourteen seeks to buy a ticket at the rate for children twelve or younger. Cholly pretends to be twelve and though the ticket agent hardly believes him, still he sells him the reduced rate ticket.

> "I reckon I knows a lying nigger when I sees one, but just in case
> you ain't, jest in case one of them mammies is really dyin' and
> wants to see her little old smoke before she meets her maker, I
> gone do it."

How are we to react to this? The agent's response to Cholly is to the reader ambiguous, though not to the agent. Rattling around inside the empty shell of racist rhetoric is a decent human impulse. But how can we separate the decency from its container? How can we not respond to the humor of the passage and how do we regard the humor in relation to the other, not humorous elements of the response? I don't think we can react simply, and I think this is Morrison's point, a point brilliantly made in a tiny corner of her edifice.

Every element of Morrison's text has its countertext. The notion of "the bluest eye," for example, suggests that her primary concern is with the culture's standard of beauty. That, as a matter of fact, is the way that this novel has been generally understood. But if this is so, what are we to do with Claudia's observations and conclusions at the novel's end?

> All of us—all who knew her—felt so wholesome after we cleansed ourselves on her. We were so beautiful when we stood astride her ugliness. [What does the word "astride" suggest here? A species of masculine dominance? Cholly's rape?] Her simplicity decorated us, her guilt sanctified us, her pain made us glow with health.

The indictment of the society stands, but it is conceived far more realistically than the conception allows that erroneously contends that the racial issue involves simply black and white. The novel has, as countertext, its class ramifications too. Claudia conceives of the world in terms of race alone when she deconstructs white dolls. Eventually she learns to have the regard for those dolls that her parents have. She understands the limitations of her perspective. That is, she recognizes that she is, because of her economic status, subject to the same social forces molding others. Her experience demonstrates that in a land where the bluest eye holds hegemony none of the dispossessed escapes its gaze.

LINDA DITTMAR

"Will the Circle Be Unbroken?": The Politics of Form in The Bluest Eye

Our metaphors of self cannot then rest in stasis, but will glory in difference
and overflow into everything that belongs to us.

Deborah E. McDowell

Deborah McDowell introduces her recent essay on *Sula* with the
following quotation from Henry James: "What shall we call our 'Self'?
Where does it begin? Where does it end? It overflows into everything that
belongs to us." My own epigraph—her concluding sentence in that same
essay—reworks James's concern with "self" and "overflow" so as to highlight the mingled awe and anxiety which Toni Morrison's writing tends to
elicit. McDowell's emphasis on the mediation of knowledge touches on
what is at once inspirational and unsettling in Morrison's work: the verbal
abundance in which this writing glories is tinged with skepticism. Its "overflow" touches off a feeling that meanings are unstable, at once elusive and
in formation. In part, this effect concerns the "readerly" stance of
Morrison's writing (in Barthes's sense), in that her self-reflective narration
refracts and defers meanings. In part it also concerns political issues—
notably racial and sexual. In this respect, the issues of difference which
McDowell identifies as operating in *Sula* are political, not just literary or

From *Novel: A Forum on Fiction* 23, no. 2 (Winter 1990). © 1990 Novel Corp. Reprinted with
permission.

121

personal. "Difference," it turns out, is a site of struggle which involves the material as well as theoretical consequences of ideology.

This converging of *difference* in its linguistic-philosophical sense (i.e. Derrida's endlessly displaced meanings) and "difference" as a political reading of abusively inegalitarian social institutions underlies the following discussion. On the one hand, Morrison's writing invokes a modernist concern with language, epistemology, and the constructed nature of art. In this respect, the ineffable quality Nelly McKay admires in her prose is not unrelated to the luminous evanescence that haunts the pages of Conrad and Faulkner, E. M. Forster and Virginia Woolf. Morrison, like them, foregrounds narrative indirection, and for her, too, this is traceable to yearnings checked by prohibition and to a will to utter checked by doubt. At the same time, McKay is right to set Morrison apart from the modernist tradition. As she notes, the ineffable quality of Morrison's writing is politically and culturally inflected through a specifically Afro-American tradition. The yearnings Morrison articulates and the prohibitions she faces are inscribed racially, as are the expressive modes she adapts from Afro-American oral, narrative, and musical traditions, notably women's culture. Ultimately, Morrison's writing insists on a double-reading which recognizes, at once, her place within the history of Western narrative in general and her place within a specifically Afro-American tradition.

The following discussion applies this double-reading to Morrison's first novel, *The Bluest Eye* (1970). Though Morrison herself has commented on this book somewhat disavowingly as the novel in which she learned to write, it is a richly-crafted work that deserves study in its own right. Moreover, attention to it is useful as a paradigm for issues which come up in her subsequent novels, notably *Beloved* (1987), which is formally closer to *The Bluest Eye* and *Sula* (1973) than it is to the intervening novels—*The Song of Solomon* (1977) and *Tar Baby* (1981). My aim here is, then, to start laying the groundwork for an overview of Morrison's novels as an evolving body of work and to highlight the particular ways the formal operations of her writing function ideologically. In this respect, her novels require more than a critique of characters and plots as hypothetical instances of social actuality (Bakerman, Bishoff, Christian, Davis, Johnson, Miner, et al.). However problematic, *The Bluest Eye*'s displacing of social pathology and failed human values into the black community (a process Wallace Thurman calls "intra-racism") must be understood in relation to Morrison's craft as it guides the reception of her novel.

Seen this way, *The Bluest Eye* is not as far from *Beloved* as their plotlines might suggest. Especially in the case of a writer whose performative virtuosity so insistently determines sense, we must be careful to register the complex modulations of meaning and judgment built into her writing. As Audre Lorde puts it, the problem is that Morrison's "vigorous and evocative language which sings out like legends beneath our skin," sings of a "love that can be misshapen and frightened into hatred." Lorde is registering the contradictory quality of this writing, and her use of a musical trope to describe Morrison's language and the reception it elicits anticipates Morrison's subsequent comment to McKay (interview) that she is aiming for narrative procedures which, like jazz, will resist closure:

> Jazz always keeps you on the edge. There is no final chord. . . .
> There is something underneath that is incomplete. There is
> always something else that you want from the music. I want my
> books to be like that—because I want that feeling of something
> held in reserve and the sense that there is more—that you can't
> have it all right now.
>
> ....
>
> [Lena Horne and Aretha Franklin] have the ability to make you
> want it, and remember the want. That is a part of what I want
> to put in my books. They will never fully satisfy—never fully.

Such withholding of closure is the essence of narrative desire—a desire knowable mainly through the medium of formal articulation, be it musical or verbal.

It is Morrison's emphasis on the ineffable that beckons readers towards enthusiasm, conflict, and avoidance of conflict. The desiring state she instills in them invites all this precisely because such desire haunts and agitates, just as she intended. Readers may respond differently to the history, culture, and politics inscribed in Morrison's race, gender, and subject-matter, but the process of desiring reception she builds into her narratives forces all of them into yearning which they can either acknowledge or suppress. In part, this embattled reception simply registers her insistence on the opaque and self-referential nature of language. There is nothing humbly "transparent" and self-effacing about her style, point-of-view, and narrative structure. But this desiring reception also has to do with the fact that she sings of aberrations, and beautifully, at that. Each is important, of course, but it is only by understanding how the two interact that we gain full access to her writing.

From *The Bluest Eye* to *Beloved,* Morrison's way with words asserts itself as at once deductive and elusive. While her writing is, indeed, sensorily specific, the actual events it conveys shimmer with a suggestiveness that ultimately withholds at least as much as it gives. Her looping narrative lines, flashbacks, and anticipatory predictions similarly veil and qualify meaning.

The cumulative effect of all this indirection is that it encodes hesitation. Morrison's treatment of Cholly's incestuous rape of Pecola, for example, ends up foregrounding an awareness of the complexity of judgment and feeling, and this is true of *The Bluest Eye* as a whole. The construction of *Beloved* is similarly predicated on a pattern of oblique predictions, backward loopings, and indirection, all of which assert urgency about at once telling, judging, and suppressing that which needs to be told. In short, the difficulty Morrison creates for her readers is not just that Cholly rapes his daughter or that Sethe kills hers, and what these acts say about racism, slavery, poverty, and related abuses. The difficulty is also that Morrison's rich syntax, resonant imagery, dispersed chronology, and shifting viewpoints inscribe an ambivalent mode of reading.

In the case of Morrison, such ambivalence is neither the consequence of empty "post-modern" flourishes nor a reflection of a modernist collapse of historical reasoning in the Lukácsian sense. Rather, the contradictory claims of form and content which Morrison strives to negotiate, especially when seen in relation to her particular ways of resisting closure raise questions of narrative strategy and ideology to her work as a black woman writer and, by extension, to minority and female writing in general. The following discussion explores the point at which questions of form and content, art and politics, converge in *The Bluest Eye*. My hope is that unraveling the tangled political commitments and formal deflections of this novel will help us read all of Morrison's fiction more complexly and alert us to ways in which narrative form, like thematic content, is never politically neutral.

II

That *The Bluest Eye* has been criticized for being mired in the pathology of Afro-American experience is hardly surprising. Violence, madness, and incest are some of the extreme forms this pathology takes here, though the racism which pushes people to such extremes is Morrison's underlying concern. Describing a society where whiteness is the yardstick of personal worth, where Shirley Temple and Jeanne Harlow set standards for beauty and "Dick and Jane" readers prescribe an oppressive notion of normalcy, where Pecola's shame at her mother's race serves as a model for self-improvement, where fathers deny their sons, mothers deny their daughters, and God denies the communal prayer for the privilege of blue eyes—in such a society, Morrison argues, marigolds cannot bloom. The marigolds are metaphoric, of course. The barrenness they signify goes beyond agriculture to include scapegoating and intraracism, "deeply rooted in the primitive history and prehistory of the human struggle with the environment, specifically the struggle for agricultural maintenance symbolized by the seasons and the marigolds."

There are several problems with this metaphor: it leaves the barrenness unaccounted for; it situates social and psychological oppression in the community that receives them (the "soil" in which the seeds were sown); it presents racism as an inescapable atavism; and it provides no means of recovery. In fact, when one surveys the tale of inhumanity *The Bluest Eye* unfolds, it is hard not to question the ideology of its thematics. Readers worry that the microcosm Morrison locates in her Ohio town includes few venues for anger directed beyond the black community and almost no potential for regeneration within it. Read thematically, this novel does indeed seem overwhelmingly pessimistic, given its relentless piling up of abuses and betrayals. Its formal devices partly deflect but never quite extinguish the wish for a plot-based judgment. It is the tension between the two that makes *The Bluest Eye* a problematic novel.

Morrison does not let this tension subside or drop out of view. If anything, this novel's very structure accentuates it precisely because the novel remains inconclusive to the very end. For while *The Bluest Eye* is, indeed, a brilliant orchestration of a complex, multi-formed narrative, the ideological thrust of its structure is ambiguous. Morrison orders her materials into four seasonal parts—autumn, winter, spring, and summer—but within this design nothing is simple or stable. Excerpts from a "Dick and Jane" reader serve as a framing point of reference for Claudia's ostensibly autobiographical narrative; Claudia's account frames Pecola's story; and Pecola's story, in its turn, frames the three long flashbacks which trace the stories of Pauline, Cholly, and Soaphead Church. This elaborate patterning of framing devices attenuates textual accountability. Its mediations deflect attribution, disperse sympathy and identification, and thus question judgment in ways that echo rather than counter the plot's pessimism. They pass on to readers the task of gathering the novel's parts into a signifying whole, even as their ever-shifting modulations of stance assert that the effect is doomed to remain inconclusive.

Inside this Chinese-box arrangement, an obtrusive use of varied typographies further undermines the conventions which normally efface authors' control of their story-telling. Portions of Pauline's narrative are set apart from the rest as oral history; they are italicized first-person accounts which have a distinctly spoken grammar and cadence. Cholly's and Soaphead's narratives are also foreign elements, for they are third-person accounts unattributable to Claudia or any other dramatized narrator. The opening segment in each seasonal division has uneven right hand margins, as does Pauline's narrative in its entirety. While such margins may serve to suggest the text's informal, possibly spoken origins, the mere use of this unusual device is attention-getting, especially given its recurrent suspension and re-introduction. Such intrusion is most noticeable in the "Dick and Jane" passages, where an obtrusive and increasingly unreadable typography emphasizes their role as hostile assaults on Claudia's account. Using "found objects" in apposition to poeticized ones, these passages create an angry dialectic between documentation and fictionality and between the public domain of early childhood acculturation and the private one of personal experience. Numbing the imagination with their simplifications of grammar and life, both the form and the substance of the "Dick and Jane" passages violate the integrity of the life Morrison depicts.

The overall effect of this complexly structured work is to foreground the authorial project of orchestrating a fluid, multi-voiced novel, where the parts sometimes jostle against one another, sometimes complement or blend with each other, and at all times project a dense sense of the multiplicity of narration. Since the function of the story-telling act is, as Claudia puts it, to explain, Morrison's juxtaposition of diverse voices asserts that understanding is collective. In this respect, *The Bluest Eye*'s design supplements its thematic focus on communities as sites of meaning, for it posits that meanings get constructed dialogically. Maureen Peel and Geraldine, the MacTeers as well as the Breedloves, Mr. Henry and Soaphead Church, the Fishers, Hollywood, and the Maginot Line—these and others collaborate in the production of ideology within the plot. At the same time, *The Bluest Eye*'s very structure parallels the construction of meaning undertaken by its characters. Its shifting points-of-view, flashbacks, and digressions inscribe into the novel's very organization the dialogism evident in its plot. The emphasis here is on understanding and judgment as restless, dynamic, and interactive processes of meaning-production, forever open to modification and change.

This foregrounding of the unstable and constructed nature of knowledge, and of the collaborative processes which guide it, affirms the possibility of positive change. Individual characters may not participate in such change; certainly Claudia, for all her adult retrospection, provides no empowerment. But the dialogic interchange among these voices shifts the center of activity away from any one character to the readers who assemble and interpret the novel's diverse segments. Depicting and enacting ways we produce and reproduce ideology, the text reminds us that we can take charge of our future. Thus, Claudia's role as the young narrator coming of age only partly shapes the novel. Interacting with adjacent voices, she contributes to a larger process of formation. At the same time, Morrison's parcelling out of narrative authority suggests qualification. The issue is not that dialogism is inherently open-ended, but that in Morrison's writing—which is committed to a desiring openness on all levels—this open form is particularly prone to dispersal. Given that *The Bluest Eye* focuses its concern with the production of meanings on the valuation of race, gender, and social class, the danger latent in its procedures is one of ambivalence and evasion. The danger is that the pleasurable resistance to closure Morrison uses to elicit desire will also cloud our judgment.

Not surprisingly, both the hopefulness and the anxiety inherent in Morrison's treatment of the construction of meaning coexist in this novel. Thus, while for Claudia the initiating impetus for narration is the need to account for the fact that, "Quiet as it's kept, there were no marigolds in the fall of 1941," neither Claudia nor Morrison project confidence about the possibility of doing so. The narrative may originate in the need to account for this mystery, but it never fulfills its promise. "There is really nothing more to say," Claudia notes at the end of her brief introduction, "except why. But since why is difficult to handle, one must take refuge in *how*." At the very outset of story-telling, Morrison already questions the act of telling—first by moving Claudia from "why" to "how," next by being vague about what she is trying to do (for "to handle" the "why" is more evasive and non-commital than "to answer" it), and finally by shifting from Claudia's first person "I" to the impersonal "one" and by admitting that the "one" is "taking refuge" in description as a substitute for explanation.

Of course, this groping can be attributed to Claudia, who comes across as a still developing young person despite her seemingly powerful position as a retrospective narrator. The trouble is not in Claudia's *persona*, but in Morrison's reluctance to supplement Claudia's incomplete vision forcefully. This reluctance manifests itself through Morrison's ambivalent turning to the community in which the seeds withered. For though the novel's use of a multi-voiced community affirms the rehabilitating gift of sharing and belonging, its orchestration also disperses power, deflects responsibility, and questions the efficacy of the story-telling act. It is the pleasure in voicing and the desire for its products, more than meaning, that takes over.

Morrison's use of an orchestrated narrative design belongs in a long and dazzling tradition of experimentation, where disrupted chronology, splintered plots, decentered accountablility, and disparate modes of narration can lead to a panic about the loss of center. Yet in most multi-layered narratives, and in *The Bluest Eye* alongside them, such a dismantling foregrounds reconstitution. Though putting Humpty Dumpty together again may be impossible, in that the glue joining the shards will always be visible, the process of engaging in reconstitution and, thus, in re-possession is the important recuperative activity in which such texts engage their readers. Morrison's "Dick and Jane" typography belies the text's claim to transparency, as do her leaps in chronology, in location, and in narrating view-points and modalities. All these devices insist on the reader's self-conscious participation in the reconstitution of the text. Of course, there are ways in which Morrison counters the disruption with stabilizing devices: she uses Claudia's narrating persona as a regularizing force, and she uses the inexorability and predictability of the Breedlove story to divert readers from the text's dismantling operations to the more pressing urgency of compassion. But on the whole, *The Bluest Eye*'s disrupted construction works to undermine the text's illusionism. Instead, it elicits a reading which subordinates the claims of realism, including the authenticating use of narrative viewpoints, to the dynamic interaction of the parts within the text as a whole. This dismantling design acknowledges the insufficient of any one voice. It posits, rather, that knowledge is constructed by the many and that reading is a process of active re-shaping by readers.

The four-seasons organization of *The Bluest Eye* adds another complication to this already difficult patterning. For while the march of the seasons is reassuringly predictable, it also checks the fluidity of the narrative. Here is the novel's constant—a natural force that antedates the depicted events by millennia, a reminder that the withering of seeds, babies, and minds in Lorain, Ohio of 1941 fits into a much larger picture. Given the heterogeneity of *The Bluest Eye*'s materials, having such a regularizing force would be a help were it not that using the seasons as a structuring device also posits a suffocatingly cyclical design. Inherent in the notion of seasons is the fact that they are an annually recurring condition from which there is no escape. As a metaphor, they are a closed form, sufficient unto itself and allowing for only minor variations. Even the sequence Morrison sets up for these reasons, starting with autumn's decline and ending with a summer edging once again towards such a decline, accentuates the negative aspects of this metaphor. Indeed, in Morrison's treatment, spring is a time of beatings and the narrative section which contains Soaphead's perversion, while summer is "a season of storms," where the mere thought of eating a strawberry bears an uncanny resemblance to violent deflowering ("I . . . break into the tightness of a strawberry"). Avoiding both the positive use of spring and summer as symbols of renewal and the epic use of the seasons to punctuate a historical process of struggle and change, Morrison's four-part design implies a trap.

The book's ending adds to this sense of futility. A hundred and fifty pages after Morrison equivocates about the why and how of story-telling, she has Claudia dismiss the strengths Claudia and others do possess:

> And fantasy it was, for we were not strong, only aggressive; we
> were not free, merely licensed; were not compassionate, we were

polite; not good, but well behaved. We courted death in order to call ourselves brave, and hid like thieves from life. We substituted good grammar for intellect; we switched habits to simulate maturity; we rearranged lies and called it truth, seeing in the new pattern of an old idea the Revelation and the Word.

A page later Morrison uses the following paragraph to bring the book to a close:

And now when I see her searching for garbage—for what? The thing we assassinated? I talk about how I did not plant the seeds too deeply, how it was the fault of the earth, the land, of our town. I even think now that the land of the entire country was hostile to marigolds that year. This soil is bad for certain kinds of flowers. Certain seeds it will not nurture, certain fruit it will not bear, and when the land kills of its own volition, we acquiesce and say the victim had no right to live. We are wrong, of course, but it doesn't matter. It's too late. At least on the edge of my town, among the garbage and the sunflowers of my town, it's much, much, much too late.

The despair here is overwhelming. Mired in this sense of the wrong, each betrayal *The Bluest Eye* depicts, each brutalization and denial, aches with a yearning for what could have been but never came to pass. Ultimately, Morrison dodges the very questions she raises. She starts the passage accepting responsibility for assassination, even if only of an unspecified "thing," but within two lines she transfers this responsibility to a land which seems to kill "of its own volition." Depicting people as passively acquiescing in brutalizations they, presumably, never initiated, she veers from social criticism to natural disaster. Even her acknowledgment that "we were wrong" ends up linked to "it doesn't matter. It is too late." Considering that *The Bluest Eye* was written during a period of race awareness and political activism, such an ending feels particularly negative.

In fact, an overview of Morrison's work suggests an ongoing malaise in this respect. In her second novel *Sula*, the use of Shadrach, the mad prophet of self-annihilation, to frame the disintegration of Medallion's Black Bottom promises an apocalypse which never happens, and by its ending echoes the resistance to closure evident in *The Bluest Eye*:

"All that time, all that time, I thought I was missing Jude." And the loss pressed down on her chest and came up into her throat.

> "We was girls together," she said as though explaining some-
> thing. "O Lord, Sula," she cried, "girl, girl, girlgirlgirl."
>   It was a fine cry—loud and long—but it had no bottom and
> it had no top, just circles and circles of sorrow.

The Song of Solomon and *Tar Baby* avoid such open-endedness, but only by
focusing on those whose wealth discolors color and whose questionable
myths of levitation claim to transcend economic and political disenfran-
chisement. That these two novels are more simply structured and, thus,
more readable on the level of chronology and narrating viewpoint makes
sense, given their remove from the pressing political concerns of black
communities at the time of their publication. Their relative thematic safe-
ness, it would seem, frees them to be direct. In all these respects *Beloved* is at
once a new departure and a return. Its use of history is pointedly specific and
anchored in protest, but its narrative procedures once again refract
chronology, point-of-view, and stylistic directness so as to highlight the
mediated nature of telling and the elusive process of reception. Here, in
contrast with *The Song of Solomon* and *Tar Baby*, thematic anguish seems to
call forth a more elaborate strategy of deflection.

While my use of "seem" above cautions that the novels at hand may not
constitute the critical mass needed for sound generalization, the correlation
between the thematic risk and formal strategies of deflection in Morrison's
work nonetheless raises important questions about her address to readers.
For though Morrison sees her formal resistance to closure as a uniquely
black aesthetic mode akin to black music, and though she uses it as an opportunity to free readers to tap new capabilities within themselves (e.g. compassion for Cholly, Tate), the question also arises whether some of this
deflection may not have something to do with the fact that Morrison is a
black woman writer whose "implied reader," to borrow Wolfgang Iser's term,
is educated, middle class and not infrequently white. That is, beyond questions of Afro-American art, at issue here are also questions of address as a
personal and political, not just literary, practice. In this respect, Raymond
Hedin's essay, "The Structuring of Emotion in Black American Fiction," is
particularly illuminating, for Hedin argues persuasively that Afro-American
novelists have traditionally turned to strategies of evasion and indirection in
order to suppress or disguise racial anger.

That Hedin's analysis mainly focuses on earlier writers makes historical
sense, and he is right to note that even in their novels a "revolutionary threat
remains, held in check but not eliminated by the structuring context of plot
and character." However, his reading of *The Bluest Eye* is more positive than
mine. He sees its form as clarifying Morrison's anger because it brings the

causes of Pecola's suffering into sharp focus. "The coherence of Morrison's vision," he writes, "and the structure which parses out its logic into repeated patterns offer the reader no solace, no refuge from Morrison's anger." Hedin is right about the anger; Morrison is much more direct and unrelenting than most of her predecessors. But I question his view that she brings the causes of Pecola's suffering into sharp focus and that her narrative offers us no refuge. Morrison locates too much of Pecola's suffering in the black community, while the luminous style and predictive backward loopings with which she mediates the plot work quite deliberately to provide solace.

Beloved, in contrast, works better; it distinguishes pointedly between white brutalization of black Americans and its intra-racist carry-overs. Cincinnati's black residents may hold diverse views of Sethe and the whites who caused such massive suffering to so many blacks, but their views are clear and they are able to join in acts of resistance and recovery in ways the residents of Medallion do not quite match. (Exceptions in *The Bluest Eye* include Aunt Jimmy's friends, the prostitutes, and church women, but only peripherally to the main plot.) Still, while thematically this novel is clearer and more optimistic, formally it nonetheless offers solace by way of narrative strategies whose mediation continues to displace the pain and anger of being defined as "other." Ben Shan's comment that "a society is molded upon its epics, and . . . imagines in terms of its created things" is worth noting in this connection, precisely because it urges awareness of the ideology inscribed in the artifacts we allow to shape and unite us. When reading any work, then, we must be conscious of the ways its form, not just its theme, molds us in its own image. We must note, finally, that *The Bluest Eye* exists within the power structures which control our lives. In this respect, Ben Shan anticipates Althusser: the contradictory forces at work in Morrison's writing reflect the contradictions at work in the society out of which she writes.

III

It is Ben Shan's reminder that society imagines in terms of its created things that brings me back to the revivalist tone of my title. In part, "Will the Circle be Unbroken?" registers my interest in Morrison's use of the seasons as a value-laden construct. But the initial impulse behind this choice was musical. Alluding to the song, "Will the Circle be Unbroken?", it pays tribute to Morrison's voice. For hers is, indeed, a powerfully regenerative voice that brings out the essence beneath the surface and the heritage which defines identity. It is, indeed, a voice that tells of circles of recurrent loss, but it also displaces the pain from the realm of the physical to that of the spiritual and, thus, edges towards redemption. The impulse behind my title, then, was the need to acknowledge the voice as regenerative, even in the face of the despair inscribed in the novel's cyclical structure and wrenching plot.

Only after completing a draft of this essay did I come across Henry Dumas' story "Will the Circle be Unbroken?", which uses the same title to signify a very different meaning. Though there is considerable irony in Dumas' reversal of racist exclusionary practices ("I'm sorry, but for your own safety we cannot allow you [in]," etc.), his story concerns internal power at least as much as the social structure in which that power gets enacted. For Dumas, that power has its source in Africa's timeless heritage. It is a force—a charmed circle—that grows out of shared understanding. The "vibration" which arises from it finds its voice in jazz music in general and in a mythic afro-horn in particular:

> Inside the center of the gyrations is an atom stripped of time, black. The gathering of the hunters, deeper. Coming, laced in the energy of the sun. He is blowing. Magwa's hands. Reverence of skin. Under the single voice is the child of a woman, black. They are building back the wall, crumbling under the disturbance.

For both Dumas and Morrison, the voice is the source of regeneration, and for both it is the interaction of diverse voices—diverse musical instruments—that complements the power of the single voice and makes reconstitution possible. Yet despite this shared emphasis on the empowering origins of Afro-American identity and on the political imperative of collective action, Morrison and Dumas head in different directions. His story uses the circle as a metaphor for an unblemished and inviolable essence, while her novel uses the seasons' cyclicality to signal a trap. His afro-horn functions as a lethal but also as a clearly regenerative symbol, while her "miracle" of blue eyes functions ambivalently. Mediated as it is through a deflecting treatment of point-of-view and narrative reliability, and placed too late in the novel to allow for adequate recuperation of deferred judgment, it edges towards articulating defeat. The extended Soaphead chapter, previously anthologized as a short story in its own right, further separates the plot's ending from what leads up to it; it disrupts Claudia's narrative just at the point where one would expect her to gain new insight. Thus, while Dumas' "Will the Circle be Unbroken?" repossesses the song, my own use of this allusion echoes but also questions the oracular opacity of Morrison's narrative strategies.

The problem with Morrison's circles is, finally, that in *The Bluest Eye* circularity functions as a structuring metaphor which runs counter to other aspects of her text. The story-line and seasonal cyclicality posit an entrapment at odds with the empowering coral organization and eloquence of her writing. Of course, cyclicality is only one organizing metaphor among several here. Alongside it is a multi-voiced orchestration which does make powerful claims for the needs of the many, cumulative reiterations which do express great anger, and a Chinese-box structure which does insist on linking the specific to its context. In all respects design signifies and signifies constructively. At the same time, though, the fatalism inscribed in the cyclical organization of this novel cannot be denied, especially given the way Morrison foregrounds the cleavage between one season and the next. The book's format sets the season apart, and at the opening of each section Claudia's narrative occurs in an indeterminate present tense, as if in a-temporal space. Each opening mythologizes its materials. Each season breaks with the preceding narration, and each promises a new beginning which, the subsequent narrative shows, offers no change. The problem with this design is that it severs events from their causes and holds back the possibility of recovery. The thematic urgency the text establishes about finding ways to escape the tyranny of racist values gets undermined by uncertainty.

It is especially *The Bluest Eye*'s verbal exuberance that counters the skepticism inscribed in this seasonal metaphor. Morrison's syntax belies her fatalism. Her cadences spill into long sentences in which flexible syntactical structures enact the capacity for change. Her short sentences and sentence fragments are close systems, self-sufficient, well-placed, and punchy. Her descriptive passages are rich with images, especially organic ones, which make facts resonate with latent meanings, and her mythic allusions elevate the ordinary and ascribe to the insignificant epic scope. The overall impression such writing creates is of an echoing, shimmering, reverberating experience, where each utterance initiates an ever-expanding sequence of interrelations. Note, for example, the following passage:

> They come from Mobile. Aiken. From Newport News. From Marietta. From Meridian. And the sounds of these places in their mouths makes you think of love. When you ask them where they are from, they tilt their heads and say "Mobile" and you think you've been kissed. They say "Aiken" and you see a white butterfly glance off a fence with a torn wing. They say "Nagadoces" and you want to say "Yes, I will." You don't know what these towns are like, but you love what happens to the air when they open their lips and let the names ease out.

The "they" Morrison describes here are a type; they are certain "brown girls" particularized in Geraldine—a character she condemns with special anger.

Yet the writing in this passage mostly beautifies these women. It is a writing that sways with their sensuous voices and caresses their nuanced gestures. Mostly it is the information which emerges later that challenges this seduction, and even then the cadences and images of Morrison's prose continue to rehabilitate the facts.

Pauline's description of her lovemaking with Cholly is one of this novel's extraordinary passages. The rainbow metaphor she assigns to orgasm is, indeed, a covenant—a broken covenant, as it turns out, given the world she and Cholly inhabit, but also a circle opened and a provisional declaration of faith. Tapping the Bible's recurrent concern with broken covenants and new possibilities for regeneration, the metaphor suggest grace. The very language Morrison uses to describe Pauline's experience inscribes this affirmation. She transmutes Pauline's tactile and visual sensations into an eroticized prose free of grammatical inhibitions and revelling in counterpointed repetitions, delays, and variations evocative of Molly Bloom's soliloquy at the end of *Ulysses*. Linked to Pauline's orgasm, this stylistic articulation of desire is indeed erotic. But seen in relation to the rainbow metaphor, Morrison's style here invokes the notion of jouissance in its full range of associations, at once physical and metaphysical. In this respect, *The Bluest Eye* in general and the rainbow passage in particular anticipate Alice Walker's use of Celie in *The Color Purple* (1982) as well as the work of Toni Cade Bambara, Ntozake Shange, and Gloria Naylor. Pauline, Celie, and others would have been social and linguistically disenfranchised speakers were it not for their author's retrieving Afro-American vernacular as a medium of empowerment that runs counter to the normalcy posited by Dick's and Jane's parents and their dog, Spot.

In short, *The Bluest Eye* counters the muting of Pecola's voice with the empowerment of other voices in her community. Rather than make readers restore diachrony so as to realize a historic dialectic, the novel elicits a relational, "dialogic" reading. To Aunt Jimmy's friends, Morrison ascribes a conversation spanning lifetimes of struggle, where the blending of utterances orchestrates individual experiences into a multi-layered account which parallels her own work as a novelist:

> Their voices blended into a threnody of nostalgia about pain.
> Rising and falling, complex in harmony, uncertain in pitch, but
> constant in the recitative of pain.

This musicalization of experience is Morrison's theme once more when commenting on Cholly's epic journey in search of his father:

> The pieces of Cholly's life could become coherent only in the
> head of a musician. Only those who talk their talk through the

gold of curved metal, or in the touch of black-and-white rectangles and taut skins and strings echoing from wooden corridors, could give true form to his life. Only they would know how to connect the heart of a red watermelon to the asafetida bag to the muscadine to the flashlight on his behind to the fists of money to the lemonade in a Mason jar to a man called Blue and come up with what all of that meant in joy, in pain, in anger, in love, and give it its final and pervading ache of freedom. Only a musician would sense, know, without even knowing that he knew, that Cholly was free.

Morrison's writing registers this view of music as an expressive but also clarifying medium formally as well as thematically. Here and in numerous other passages, including Pauline's rainbow and the full Aunt Jimmy section, the very syntax builds up sequences of repetition and variation which lead readers through a cumulative, patterned reception akin to listening. Morrison's very writing is a performance which celebrates the free play of language and the power of the voice to utter. Finally, it is her own virtuosity that guides readers, line by line, to affirmation. Thus, when she uses the Aunt Jimmy and Cholly episodes to explore the concept of freedom, her conclusions are questionable; the freedom of old age she bestows on rural black women and the "Godlike" freedom she grants Cholly when she leaves him with nothing left to lose entail such extreme bereavement that the benefits are hardly worth having. At the same time, the writing through which Morrison lays out this proposition is so sinuous and seductive that, like the "brown girls" from Mobile, Aiken, and Newport News, she makes us want to say, "Yes, I will."

This writing just about begs to be read aloud. Its diction, rhythms, and incremental patterning almost seem propelled by sound. Repeating key words, and stringing along sentences, clauses, and phrases which share syntactical structure and which do not always group into punctuated units, this writing creates an echo-chamber effect where the very fact of reiteration becomes all powerful. This is the "verbal delirium" Patricia Yaeger sees as women writers' linguistic resistance to the despair inscribed in plots of victimization, but it is also a verbal mode rooted in Afro-American secular and religious oral traditions. Though Morrison's roots in these traditions deserve the kind of close reading which this essay cannot undertake, it is important to notice that this specificity (O'Shaughnessy). Like a griot, preacher, or blues singer, Morrison uses inventories and variations to make her case. The richness of her language, organized as it is into infinitely expandable sequences, suggests a wealth of possibilities and an ungovernable

verbal fecundity which belie the social desolation she depicts. Such regenerative writing is not about retrieving and explaining, as *The Bluest Eye*'s
opening claims, but about saying as cure. Naming her ghosts and, indeed,
ours, she diminishes their power over us. Embroidering on actuality as
much as China, Poland, and Miss Marie do, she makes the speaker repossess the spoken.

The power of the voice to retrieve and re-shape is the moving force of
Beloved, too, where the entire narrative is motivated by a process of reconstitution. Though *The Bluest Eye* lacks this controlling purpose, its overall
effect is similar. Claudia captures this power when she describes her mother
singing the blues:

> If my mother was in a singing mood, it wasn't so bad. She would
> sing about hard times, bad times, and somebody-done-gone-
> and-left-me times. But her voice was so sweet and her singing-
> eyes so melty I found myself longing for those hard times,
> yearning to be grown without "a thin di-i-ime to my name." I
> looked forward to the delicious time when "my man" would leave
> me, when I would "hate to see that evening sun go down . . ."
> 'cause then I would know "my man has left this town." Misery
> colored by the greens and blues in my mother's voice took all of
> the grief out of the words and left me with a conviction that pain
> was not only endurable, it was sweet.

Describing women's pain as not only endurable but even sweet is hardly the
lesson to teach an adolescent girl. It presupposes stasis and advocates resig-
nation, not change. However, as Claudia sees it, it is the singing voice, and
nothing else, that colors misery and cleanses out the grief. Beyond naming
and mourning, singing proves an act of resistance. Turning to a long tradition of women's blues, it is the empowering act, not the acceptance, that is
Morrison's focus. Linking Mrs. MacTeer to Bessie Smith, she celebrates the
courage and the imagination which allow one to re-possess one's experience.

IV

The relation Morrison's poeticized voice has to the dismantling operations
of her text and the relation between this dismantling structure and the
exegetic content of her story-line are at the heart of both the trouble and the
delight her writing creates for her readers. *The Bluest Eye*, like all novels,
consists of an interrelation of narrative elements. Characters, story-line,

structure, images, mythic allusions, syntax, diction, and more are all parts of a patterned whole. The way they interact constitutes a system of knowledge which centers neither on content alone nor on pure form, but on the interpretive transactions each text's patterning lays out for its readers. In the case of *The Bluest Eye*, this dynamic is key to both its strengths and its equivocations. For while this novel's story-line is distressingly naturalistic in its sordid subject-matter and fatalism, and while its seasonal cyclicality underscores this pessimism, the choral structuring of the novel, the a-temporal and often mythologizing quality of the narrative, and the fecundity of Morrison's writing counter the despair with affirmation. Clearly, *The Bluest Eye* does not suffer from a simple form and content contradiction. Rather, a close reading shows that in this text it is the free-play of the constituting parts that leads to tensions Morrison does not resolve.

One might argue that the elusiveness at work in Morrison's writing is inherent in the nature of the language, where the fact that utterances are always other than that to which they refer forever severs the gesture from its subject. In this sense, free-play is inevitable. Signifiers will never quite correlate with the signified. Still, while this position is not inapplicable to Morrison, it does not fully account for the specific effects of her writing. Writing which foregrounds "narrative desire" is always friendly to linguistically-based deconstructive and psychoanalytical readings, and one can certainly make a strong case for readings of *The Bluest Eye* that foreground its fragile place in the symbolic order as key to its "ineffable" quality. But Morrison's writing is too specifically Afro-American in its subject matter and form to be cut off from its cultural and political specificity. Its invocation of a rich heritage which has long been the source of power and hope for Afro-Americans requires that we cherish that in her writing which resists assimilation into a universalizing reading. Seen from this perspective, the difficulties Morrison creates for her readers register a slippage in political ideology, not the shifty nature of the signifying process.

The Bluest Eye is, in fact, a composite of different sets of values which need to be understood historically, in that it embodies both the achievement and the equivocation of the society in which it originated. It is a revolutionary novel in the ways its form assaults conventions and empowers normally disenfranchised speakers. It is a remarkable novel, too, in the ways it "sings out like legends beneath our skin," as Audre Lorde puts it. At the same time, the skepticism it evinces concerning its own revolutionary message testifies to the constraints under which it came into being. Thus, seen in terms of Roland Barthes's definition of narrative sequence as "a logical succession of nuclei bound together by a relation of solidarity," it is the wavering of solidarity here that is ideologically important. On the one hand, the dismantling operations of this text refuse to lull conservative readers into a complacent acceptance of the *status quo* and cohere formally in their complexly counterpointed patterning. On the other hand, narrative cannot be drained of referentiality, and in this novel the referentiality of both content and form is at odds with itself. As a "fugued" composition (Barthes's term), *The Bluest Eye* inspires; as a referential construct—as a guide to the practical choices we make in our daily lives—*The Bluest Eye* equivocates.

Morrison's elusive strategies suggest, finally, one balanced tenuously between faith and despair, action and entrapment. In her later fiction, these extremes move towards resolution. Especially in *Beloved*, it is the word itself—the freedom to utter and the capacity to shape imagined possibilities—that provides a redemptive vision. The fact that these extremes are laid out so distinctly in *The Bluest Eye* is useful precisely because it helps us to read Morrison's subsequent novels with a clearer grasp of the relation between form and ideology. The skepticism and even pessimism of *The Bluest Eye* cannot be denied, but neither can its richness. In one sense, this dialectic is inevitable. After all, this is not a utopian novel. It is no better than the society in which it germinated. Still, the book does offer a critique of our society; it does validate anger as an appropriate response to brutalizing inequalities; and it does normalize and dignify aspects of our humanity which we often deny. Affirming the imagination's ability to repossess chaos and create coherence, Morrison colors the misery she depicts with the blues and greens of her voice. The ideological hesitations in her writing must be acknowledged, but so, too, must the message of resilience and regeneration.

SHELLEY WONG

Transgression as Poesis in The Bluest Eye

In the opening pages of *The Bluest Eye*, Toni Morrison writes that since the "why" of Pecola and Cholly Breedlove's situation is "difficult to handle, one must take refuge in how." This admission, hardly the admission of a lack of technique or craft, is, instead, Morrison's admission that she is interested in, not questions of final causes, but questions of process, questions about how process comes to be shut down. Not surprisingly then, *The Bluest Eye* opens with a tuition in closure. In a passage rendered in the style of the Dick and Jane series of primers, the novel lays bare the syntax of static isolation at the center of our cultural texts:

> Here is the house. It is green and white. It has a red door. It is very pretty. Here is the family. Mother, Father, Dick, and Jane live in the green-and-white house. They are very happy. See Jane. She has a red dress. She wants to play. Who will play with Jane? See the cat. It goes meow-meow. Come and play. Come and play with Jane. The kitten will not play. See Mother. Mother is very nice. Mother, will you play with Jane? Mother laughs. Laugh, Mother, Laugh. See Father. He is big and strong. Father, will you play with Jane? Father is smiling. Smile, Father, smile. See the dog. Bowwow goes the dog. Do you want to play with Jane? See the dog run. Run, dog, run. Look, look. Here comes a

From *Callaloo* 13, no. 3 (Summer 1990) pp. 471–81. © 1990 The Johns Hopkins University Press.

friend. The friend will play with Jane. They will play a good game. Play, Jane, play.

With the exception of Jane, each character—Mother, Father, Dick (who is absent from the narrative after the first mention of his name), the dog and the cat—maintains himself in a self-enclosed unity, "each member of the family in his own cell of consciousness." The short, clipped sentences accentuate their discreteness. Each of their respective actions—again, with the exception of Jane—is marked by an intransitive verb: "laugh, smile, run," and the conventional sound signatures ascribed to cats and dogs—"meow-meow" and "bowwow." While the verbs "laugh," "smile," and "run" can function as transitive verbs, they do not do so in this passage. These verbs—including "see"—are also imperatives, suggesting the presence of, though never naming, the controlling authority that directs both the reader and the characters of the story. Only Jane (and the unnamed "friend"), who "wants to play," expresses a desire, or a capacity, to engage a world beyond the self. The family is purportedly "very happy." However, the laughing and smiling, seen in the context of the characters' atomized condition, seem not to express joyful affirmation but, rather, almost scornful repudiation. They refuse to play.

In an interview, Morrison commented that she had "used the primer, with its picture of a happy family, as a frame acknowledging the outer civilization. The primer with white children was the way life was presented to black people." The lesson of this passage in fact goes well beyond acknowledging or presenting white bourgeois values—it goes as far as enacting the very conditions of alienated self-containment which underlie those values. We might note, for instance, that the "house" precedes the "family" in order of both appearance and discussion. In this scheme of things, human relations are preempted by property and commodity relations. The space of ownership engulfs the time of human development and fellowship. The body of human relationships is drawn into the marketplace of being, an essentially timeless space which fosters a frightening commensurability between people and units of exchange, a commensurability which renders family members falsely individualized moments of a social and material whole. In the school of bourgeois economics, the child's first lesson in cultural literacy teaches the primacy of the singular and the discrete. The lesson works against memory and history, and collapses the structure of desire and *communitas*, while simultaneously promoting the desirability of discrete repetition, the wish to be always equal to some measure of ideality divorced from one's own physical and spiritual needs.

The primer passage itself is subsequently repeated twice (though with quite another lesson in mind): the first time without punctuation or capitalization, and the second time without punctuation, capitalization, or spaces between words or sentences. Again, in an interview, Morrison offers a reason for this particular arrangement: "As the novel proceeded I wanted that primer version broken up and confused, which explains the typographical running together of words." The brevity and the apparent simplicity of this explanation belie the dynamic complexity of a formal practice. "Broken up" means into pieces, ceasing to exist as a unified whole. "Confused" means mixed indiscriminately, blurred, from the Latin root *confundere* meaning "to pour together." Out of this seeming contradiction, it is possible to locate a two-fold process which marks the trajectory of Morrison's narrative prac- tice—i.e., the practice of taking apart and then pouring back together to form the ground of a new order of signification.

Formal considerations notwithstanding, some critics have read these typographical arrangements as symbolic representations of three different kinds of family situations. The first typographically "correct" version formally represents the idea (or close to ideal) American family typified in the novel by the white Fisher family (Pauline Breedlove's employers), or the aspiring black bourgeois household of Geraldine, Louis, and Louis Junior. The second version is then associated with the family of the young narrator, Claudia MacTeer, a family admitting of some "disorder," but which "still has some order, some form of control, some love." The final run-on version is said to depict the "utter breakdown of order among the Breedloves."

What these critics have overlooked, however, in their rush to establish thematic equivalencies, is the actuating potential of Morrison's formal textual strategies. They focus on the facts of the story but do not attend to the tech- nique through which the story is told. The omission is problematic because while the story itself may fall within the thematic bounds of bleakness, the way in which it is told can constitute a means of resistance to both personal despair and cultural oppression. By omitting punctuation and capitalization, Morrison begins to break up—and down—conventional syntactic hierar- chies, conventional ways of ordering private and public narratives.

The practical effect of this omission is to force one to reevaluate the cultural signposts which give measure to one's life. By also omitting conven- tional spacing between words and sentences and breaking lines without respect for the integrity of the word, Morrison collapses those measures alto- gether, forcing one to pick one's way through a welter of potential significa- tion. The progressive elimination of markers and the running together of words at once defamiliarizes and refamiliarizes the signifying terrain. In refusing the terms of the dominant culture's patterning of experience, one is in a position to restate the familiar, that is, to retrace the particular contours of one's own experience, to regain the practice of one's own narrative. This refusal of ready-made terms, and the responsibility it entails, plays itself out through other art forms, such as music—in particular, jazz. Some time ago, in answer to an interview question, the jazz pianist Thelonious Monk offered the following:

> Jazz and freedom go hand in hand. That explains it. There isn't anything to add to it. If I do add something to it, it gets complicated. That's something for you to think about. You think about it. *You* dig it.

The refusal of the dominant culture's ready-made terms also challenged that culture's monopoly of meaning. The singular authority of the self-contained word threatens always to hypostatize and monopolize the very process of signification itself. As Morrison notes in conversation:

> It's terrible to think that a child with five different present tenses comes to school to be faced with those books that are less than his own language. And then to be told things about his language, which is him, that are sometimes permanently damaging. He may never know the etymology of Africanisms in his language, not even know that "hip" is a real word or that "the dozens" meant something. This is a really cruel fallout of racism. I know the standard English. I want to use it to help restore the other language, the lingua franca.

It is indeed a fallout of racism, but it is also a fallout of a way of organizing social and economic relations. It is a fallout of what one Chinese American writer has called—and called into question—a "Christian esthetic of one god, one good, one voice, one thing happening, one talk at a time," in short, an ideology and an aesthetic of authoritarian closure.

The single image of the ideal, the single meaning of the word, command either silence or mute repetition, and produce people "who know not what they do / but know that what they do / is not illegal." Against a contemporary mood wherein, as Morrison notes, "everybody is trying to be 'right,'" *The Bluest Eye* launches a critique of received norms of beauty and morality. The novel accomplishes this, in part, through its structural affinity with jazz, in particular, with a jazz practice which insists on overstepping conventional boundaries. Working out of an aesthetic of transgression, such music is frequently misunderstood, and mistaken for the stammered expression of past and/or present oppressions. When Theodor Adorno condemns jazz for its perpetuation of slave rhythms, its integration of "stumbling and coming-too-soon into the collective march-step," he mishears the music because he conflates "slave"—black American in bondage—with "slavish"—being imitative, submissive, or spineless. Adorno considers jazz's incorporation of slave rhythms to be black America's self-mocking responses to, and affirmation of, past and present oppressions. For Adorno, syncopation involves the "coming-too-soon" into an enforced march-step, the self-lacerating eagerness which rushes headlong into servitude. But syncopation is not always a matter of being ahead of the beat; syncopation can also involve dragging the beat, resisting the perceived measure by deliberately working behind the beat. While acknowledging other critics' ideas concerning the transformative power of "stumbling," the sometimes rapid and unexpected rhythmic shifts, are not ways of reflecting or accommodation victimage but are, instead, ways of negotiating a cultural minefield. To stumble the way Monk stumbles is to recognize the constant necessity of picking one's way through that minefield, refusing to be pinned down by the enemy, to be where the enemy expects you to be, or to be caught within the range of their oppressive cultural instrumentation. It can be a terrifying freedom—the freedom to be blown apart by a careless step, by an extravagant hubris. But at the same time, "stumbling" remains one of the few honest motions left in a world that demands a collective march-step. Decrying the tendency amongst young people today to give themselves up to a totally administered existence, Morrison peoples her novels with characters such as Cholly Breedlove in *The Bluest Eye* and Sula and Ajax in *Sula* who try to resist such pervasive administration:

> They are the misunderstood people in the world. There's a wildness that they have, a nice wildness. It has bad effects in a society such as the one in which we live. It's pre-Christ in the best sense. It's Eve. When I see this wildness gone in a person, it's sad. This special lack of restraint, which is a part of human life and is best typified in certain black males, is of particular interest to me. . . . Everybody knows who "that man" is, and they may give him bad names and call him a "street nigger"; but when you take away the vocabulary of denigration, what you have is somebody who is fearless and who is comfortable with that fearlessness. It's not about meanness. It's a kind of self-flagellant resistance to certain kinds of control, which is fascinating. Opposed to accepted notions of progress, the lockstep life, they live in the world unreconstructed and that's it.

The word "unreconstructed" is crucial here, for it points up and elaborates on that two-fold process characterizing both Morrison's use of the primer passage and an analogous jazz practice. An "unreconstructed" world suggests a world that has, first of all, been taken apart and then not—or not yet—put back together in any definitive sense of a final unity. The world unreconstructed refuses the matter-of-factness with which the administered world fixes a permanent name to an object, choosing instead to remain plural and fissiparous, requiring constant naming and constant articulation. Whether that articulation evolves into the blues, jazz, or other modes of formal expression, the impulse behind it is to express the mutable extravagance of materiality and to eschew the restraining paucity of all forms of ideality. In blues and jazz, improvising becomes a way of keeping the world open to its own potentiality. Jazz articulates meaning through attention to the particulars of the moment, to the work under hand, rather than through any strict adherence to received, and preconceived, notions of the bar or the line. Musicians such as the pianist Cecil Taylor or the alto saxophonist Ornette Coleman have, in their early work, even called into question the very notion of tonal centers:

> [The resulting music is] in many cases atonal (meaning that its tonal "centers" are constantly redefined according to the needs, or shape and direction, of the particular music being played, and not formally fixed as is generally the case . . .).

> [Through jazz improvization] music and musician have been brought, in a manner of speaking, face to face, without the strict and often grim hindrances of overused Western musical concepts; it is the overall musical intelligence of the musician which is responsible for shaping the music.

The improvised piece, if it is to be articulate, requires not only attention to the immediate complex of sound and feeling begin worked out but, also, attention to the total field of composition, to the "*total area* of its existence as a means to evolve, to move, as an intelligently shaped musical concept, from its beginning to end."

"Intelligence," I might note, takes its etymological cue from an agricultural vocabulary, from the Latin for "gleaning," the gather ing together of meanings. Much of Morrison's writing comes back repeatedly to this concern with her characters' abilities to gather meaning from the ragtag details of a life. Pauline Breedlove "like, most of all, to arrange things," but that impulse was never able to find an appropriate outlet: "she missed—without knowing what she missed—paints and crayons." In Morrison's second novel, *Sula*, we find Sula Peace without a way to perform herself in the world:

[Sula's] strangeness, her naiveté, her craving for the other half of her equation was the consequence of an idle imagination. Had she paints, or clay, or knew the discipline of the dance, or strings; had she anything to engage her tremendous curiosity and her gift for metaphor, she might have exchanged the restlessness and preoccupation with all she yearned for. And like any artist with no art form, she became dangerous.

Similarly, for Cholly Breedlove in *The Bluest Eye*, the inability to articulate the disparate moments of a life results in a hysteria of freedom:

The pieces of Cholly's life could become coherent only in the head of a musician. Only those who talk their talk through the gold of curved metal, or in the touch of black-and-white rectangles and taut skins and strings echoing from wooden corridors, could give true form to his life. Only they would know how to connect the heart of a red watermelon to the asafetida bag to the muscadine to the flashlight on his behind to the fists of money to the lemonade in a Mason jar to a man called Blue and come up with what all that meant in joy, in pain, in anger, in love, and give it its final and pervading ache of freedom. Only a musician would sense, know, without even knowing that he knew, that Cholly was free. Dangerously free.

Cholly was free in the sense that he was not bound by responsibility (or response-ability) to anyone but himself. Having been "abandoned in a junk heap by his mother, rejected for a crap game by his father, there was nothing more to lose." For Cholly, in this "godlike state," the world remained unconstructed. Having lost all measures of relatedness to others, he was free to remake, or free to not make at all, his own ties to the world. In this sense, the unreconstructed narrative of his life resembles the third primer passage where all hierarchies, all conventional ordering has been collapsed. Using the analogy of a tape recording played back at high speed, or a film shown in fast motion, the seeming absence of cultural markers requires one either to create new orders of signification or to risk losing one's way altogether. In a nation which has historically insisted upon some people "shar[ing] all the horrors but none of the privileges of our civilization," what passes for cultural measures can, when taken up by the disinherited, quickly be revealed as a hysteria of mismeasure.

For Cholly, the inability to ground himself in new measures results in despair. Initially unfitted, by way of race and class, for the dominant culture's patterning of experience, and then fitted too tightly into the "constantness, varietylessness, [and] sheer weight of sameness" of his marriage, Cholly was soon smothered by his own "inarticulate fury and aborted desires." "Only in drink was there some break" from the relentless routinization of body and soul. The eight of sameness, the tyranny of repetition—at home and at the mill—destroys for him the sense of time as a generative, forwarding process. The destruction, however, actually begins much earlier than his marriage. Cholly's abandonment by his parents radically disconnects him from the time of family. Later the interruption and the frustration of his first sexual encounter by two white hunters further highlights his separation from the world of generative and reproductive time. This intrusion of the white world maintains a historical precedent in slavery. The slave trade had disrupted generative, and genealogical, time by breaking up families and by rendering family members commodities, that is, by reducing the ever-changing, ever-proliferating body to the status of exchangeable homogeneous units. Nowhere in this novel is the legacy of slavery—the disfigurement of human relationships by the marketplace—more ironically stated than in Morrison's decision to locate a family by the name of "Breedlove" in a converted (and poorly converted at that) storefront.

In the Breedloves' lives, repetition as the time of "flesh on unsurprised flesh," as the copying of a static ideal, or as the submission to slave or factory time, results only in a stopped narrative, an arrested history. As Cholly moves to rape her, Pecola's "shocked body" startles Cholly out of the miasma of routinized desire that was his marriage, setting in motion a "confused mixture" of his memories of his first encounter with Pauline and his hatred for Darlene, the young girl who had witnessed his humiliation in front of the white hunters. Pecola's "shocked body" excites him, perhaps because it recalls for him a time before the freezing of his bodily imagination. Thus, while trying to break out of the stultifying confines of his quotidian existence by doing "a wild and forbidden thing," Cholly succeeds only in copying those two earlier moments. In turning back process through raping his own daughter, Cholly breaks with and thwarts genealogical time. Within this context, their baby cannot possibly live, for nothing can issue from a stopped narrative.

The pathos of the Breedloves' lives lies in their complete alienation from each other and from the world; locked in their individual cells of consciousness, they are unable to give birth to each other, unable to bring each other into the world of generative time. In *The Bluest Eye*, Morrison allows the reader to see how the Breedloves arrive at their atomized conditions. The subsequent revelation points up how a metaphysics, a socioeconomic system, a society and a community, can interact in a mutual frenzy of blind ideality to mutilate people, particularly girls and women. The destructiveness of culturally sanctioned closures is implicit in the very title of the novel, where the "eye" is decidedly singular. There can, after all, only be one bluest eye, not a pair of eyes that are the bluest in the world, but a single eye. The impossibility of Pecola's wish is rooted in the singularity of the superlative. In order to achieve the bluest eye, she has to sacrifice the other—the result, self-mutilation. Pecola's subsequent derangement, the splitting up of her psyche and the splitting off of herself from the world, provides the only route to the superlative.

The Bluest Eye emerges as the indictment and the uncrowning of a social and economic order which upholds and implements a metaphysics of isolate unity. The world of discrete facts spawned by such a metaphysics refuses the ambivalence of the material world; it refuses to acknowledge the mutuality of material being that reveals itself in a newborn baby whose eyes "all soft and wet," are a "cross between a puppy and a dying man"; in a dog who coughs the "cough of a phlegmy old man"; in men who are dogs; in cats who take the place of men; in an old woman who "yelps" like a dog; in a pregnant woman who "foals"; in a young girl who "whinnies" when she begins to menstruate; in all the ways that the material body asserts its transformative possibilities in an unfinished world of metamorphosis:

> The unfinished and open body (dying, bringing forth and being born) is not separated from the world by clearly defined boundaries; it is blended with the world, with animals, with objects . . . it represents the entire material bodily world in all its elements.

In con-fusing, in running together, the usually discrete states of birth and death and the discrete orders of humans and animals, Morrison breaks down the false and isolating solidity of self-contained identities and, at the same time, answers with an emphatic "No" Soaphead Church's question to God: "Is the name the real thing then? And the person only what his name says?" In refusing the fixed identity of word and object, Morrison reveals the inanity at the center of the authoritarian word:

> Is that why to the simplest and friendliest of questions "What is your name?" put to you by Moses, You would not say, and said "I Am Who I Am." Like Popeye? I Yam What I Yam? Afraid you were, weren't you, to give out your name? Afraid they would know the name and then know you? Then they wouldn't fear you?

One way Morrison breaks open the secretive, evasive nature of the solitary word is by acknowledging the physicality of the words themselves. Words are not dead letters on the page but live sounds in the mouth and in the ear. She pays careful attention to not only the connotations of words, but also to the cadences of the language itself. Through the repetition of words, images, and grammatical structures, she affirms and enacts the resonance of materiality. To repeat in this way is not to yearn after the exactness of a copy but, rather, to follow up the traces of a family resemblance. In *The Bluest Eye*, Morrison uses the repeated phrase in much the same way a musician uses a riff—i.e., as a way of grounding, without prescribing, the entire composition; it is as much a point of departure as it is a point of return. On one level, the riff bears structural affinities with the rhetorical device of anaphora, a device which Morrison uses throughout the novel. Anaphora literally means "a bringing again" and refers to the practice of beginning successive sentences or clauses with the same word or sound. Each "bringing again" of the concrete word or sound offers another look, another hearing, another context, and another shifting around and gathering of meanings. "Truth" is to be found, not in semantics alone, but also in "timbre" and cadence.

For Morrison, language is material; language "is the thing that black people love so much—the saying of words, holding them on the tongue, experimenting with them, playing with them." The same could be said of a jazz musician's relationship to the musical phrase, particularly in the practice of the riff-solo sequence, the riff, here, being the occasion of collective playing which launches the individual musician on his own solo improvisation. The musician will take up the phrase and play with it, extending it and turning it over and over again until he extracts from it all the meaning that his own desires and questionings can call up. In Morrison's writing, the riffing frequently takes the form of a kind of rhyming, not of sounds necessarily (though this is often the case), but of occasions. This rhyming manifests itself temporally and spatially. In temporal terms, the novel is composed in such a way that it continually folds back on itself, replaying certain themes, images, or words. When we encounter Maureen Peal in the "Winter" section of the novel, we realize that her appearance had in fact been prepared for in the "Autumn" section, when Pecola, savoring the thought of eating Mary Jane candies, feels a "peal of anticipation unsett[ling] her stomach." The sonic rhyme in "peal" signals the occasional rhyme—both the eating of the Mary Jane candies and the appearance of Maureen Peal in mid-winter promise false springs. Maureen is the "disrupter of seasons," and for Pecola, the Mary Janes will ultimately be the disrupters of generative time, the seasonal time of the body. The repetition also throws us forward into Pecola's later encounter with Soaphead. There, on the verge of achieving the much desired transubstantiation, of achieving the beauty and the popularity of a Maureen Peal, Pecola's stomach is unsettled by the odor of the poisoned meat and by Bob's subsequent death throes.

In spatial terms, Morrison rhymes by distributing human and animal characteristics amongst her characters in such a way that the human and animal worlds are unmistakably linked through a shared materiality. When humans "nest" and dogs cough like old men, and when a "high-yellow dream child" has a "dog-tooth" and another girl "whinnies" in fear, the hierarchical boundaries between the human and the animal are no longer absolute and human pretensions to the contrary are exposed as self-delusions.

In her writing, Morrison dethrones isolate unity and, instead, artic-ulates the connectedness of people, animals, objects, and words—in short, all the manifestations of material being. The very act of articulating—of "making [one's] own patchwork quilt of reality—collecting fragments of experience here, pieces of information there"—becomes a means of survival. For some of Morrison's characters—such as Mrs. MacTeer and Poland, one of the three whores who live in the apartment above the Breedloves—the blues provide a means to gather and to transmute the pain of daily existence. Mrs. MacTeer, Claudia tells us, "having told every-body and everything off . . . would burst into song and sing the rest of the day," singing about "hard times, bad times, and somebody-done-gone-and-left-me times." In his essay, "Richard Wright's Blues," Ralph Ellison writes this:

> blues is an impulse to keep the painful details of and episodes of a brutal experience alive in one's aching consciousness, to finger its jagged grain, and to transcend it, not by the consola-tion of philosophy but by squeezing from it a near-tragic, near-comic lyricism.

Ellison's choice of the word "transcend" seems to jar against the rest of his observations, and in its place, I would insert the word "transform," for the blues do not rise above the pain but bear witness to it and make it livable. Morrison's own writing stems from a similar impulse. After Soaphead has performed Pecola's miracle, he writes a letter to God. As he prepares to do so, he reaches for a "bottle of ink [that] was on the same shelf that held the poison." The juxtaposition of the ink and the poison is far from gratuitous. The literal poison on the shelf here merely underscores the novel's repeated concern with a metaphorical poisoning which works through the American culture industry's projection—from the movie screen, from

Mary Jane candy wrappers, and from Shirley Temple mugs—of a single image of ideal beauty, one that is decidedly white and devoid of any "dreadful funkiness." The writing-out of pain remains inseparable from the cause itself.

There are those, however, without the means to transform their experience. The criminal failure to be equal to the dominant culture's image of beauty, to be equal to any imposed measure of ideality, leaves Morrison's characters scrambling for refuge in what are often destructive alibis. When it becomes known that Cholly has raped his own daughter, and that she is pregnant as a result of it, the black community's response ranges over disgust, amusement, shock, titillation, and outrage. Their moral outrage, while purportedly based on the violation of the incest taboo, is also clearly based on the violation of culturally sanctioned standards of beauty: "Ought to be a law: two ugly people doubling up like that to make more ugly. Be better off in the ground." Any child of Cholly and Pecola's was "bound to be the ugliest thing walking," and it would be better, for all concerned, if the baby didn't live to remind them of their own tenuous relationship to white America's standards of beauty. The baby doesn't live. And the community's alibi, created to deflect their own complicity in its death and in Pecola's psychological death, remains intact:

> All of us—all who knew her—felt so wholesome after we cleaned ourselves on her. We were so beautiful when we stood astride her ugliness. Her simplicity decorated us, her guilt sanctified us, her pain made us glow with health, her awkwardness made us think we had a sense of humor. Her inarticulateness made us believe we were eloquent. Her poverty kept us generous. Even her waking dreams we used—to silence our own nightmares. And she let us, and thereby deserved our contempt. We honed our egos on her, padded our character with her frailty, and yawned in the fantasy of our strength.
>
> And fantasy it was, for we were not strong, only aggressive; we were not free, merely licensed; we were not compassionate, we were polite; not good, but well behaved. We courted death in order to call ourselves brave, and hid like thieves from life. We substituted good grammar for intellect; we switched hats to simulate maturity; we rearranged lies and called it truth, seeking in the new pattern of an old idea the Revelation and the Word.

"Quiet as it's kept," the narrator tells us at the beginning of the novel, leaving us to anticipate the "big lie [that] was about to be told." From that moment on, the novel bears witness to the lie that is closure itself. In bearing witness, Morrison will tell the tale of "who survived under what circumstances and why." Through the telling, the dominant culture's monologue on itself will be challenged and ruptured by the lingua franca of an ambivalent materiality itself. In this sense, the telling becomes a liberating pedagogy. In commenting on her function as a writer, Morrison says:

> I write what I have recently begun to call village literature, fiction that is really for the village, for the tribe . . . [my novels] ought to identify those things in the past that are useful and those things that are not; and they ought to give nourishment.

According to the tenets of an older Platonic tradition of rhetorical theory, the function of the rhetorician was to move the soul of another in order that the soul begin to move itself. In more recent terms, the American poet Charles Olson has formulated another conception of that function for the contemporary writer: "he who can tell the story right has actually not only, like, given you something, but has moved you on your own narrative." In bearing accurate witness to the "big lie," Morrison has reopened the tale of the tribe, reopened for the members of her tribe and for her readers the points of entry to a private and public narrative. Telling and freedom go hand in hand, we can hear Morrison saying—"*You* dig it."

DOREATHA DRUMMOND MBALIA

The Bluest Eye: *The Need for Racial Approbation*

In *The Bluest Eye*, Toni Morrison's emphasis is on racism. Specifically, she investigates the effects of the beauty standards of the dominant culture on the self-image of the African female adolescent. The role of class, the primary form of exploitation experienced by African people that will become the focus of later works, is only relevant insofar as it exacerbates self-image. Of the three main characters—all African female adolescents—it is Pecola Breedlove who is the primary focus. It is she who is most affected by the dominant culture's beauty standards because it is she who is the poorest and, consequently, the most vulnerable. Thus, even with this early work, Morrison is conscious of the role economics plays in the African's having a wholesome self-image. For it is the Breedloves' fight for survival that weakens the family structure and makes the family members more vulnerable to the propaganda of the dominant culture. Still, it is clear that in *The Bluest Eye* Morrison regards racism as the African's primary obstacle. Describing the Breedloves, she writes "Although their poverty was traditional and stultifying, it was not unique. But their ugliness was unique." This comment demonstrates that in the late 1960s, when this novel was written, Morrison's level of consciousness about the primary cause of the nature of the African's oppression in the United States as well as in the rest of the world was considerably weak, for she not only subordinates the role of economics to

From *Toni Morrison's Developing Class Consciousness*. © 1991 by Associated University Presses, Inc.

racism, but also neglects to show a causal relationship between them, that an exploitive economic system gives rise to racist ideology.

The thesis of the novel is that racism devastates the self-image of the African female in general and the African female child in particular. Toni Morrison's emphasis is on the society, not the family unit. According to her, the African's self-image is destroyed at an early age as a result of the ruling class's (i.e., the European capitalist class's) promotion of its own standard of beauty: long, stringy hair, preferably blond; keen nose, thin lips; and light eyes, preferably blue. By analogy, if the physical features of the European are accepted as the standard of beauty, then the African must be ugly. This is the type of logic that the Breedloves use to convince themselves of their ugliness:

> They had looked about themselves and saw nothing to contradict the statement: saw, in fact, support for it leaning at them from every billboard, every movie, every glance. "Yes," they had said. "You are right." And they took the ugliness in their hands, threw it as a mantle over them, and went about the world with it.

Although Morrison clearly and correctly understands that the concept of beauty is a learned one— Claudia MacTeer learns to love the big, blue-eyed baby doll she is given for Christmas; Maureen Peal learns she is beautiful from the propaganda of the dominant society as well as from the African adult world; and Pauline Breedlove learns from the silver screen that every face must be assigned some category on the scale of absolute beauty— Morrison does not yet understand that this concept will change depending on the racial makeup of the dominant class. That is, her immature class consciousness at this point in her writing career precludes her understanding of three important facts: first, that the ruling class, whether of European, African, or Asian descent, possesses the major instruments of economic production and distribution as well as the means of establishing its socio-economic dominance (i.e., all forms of media including books, billboards, and movies); second, that possessing such means, the ruling class uses and promotes its own image as a measurement of beauty for the entire society; and third, that the success of this promotion ensures the continual domi-nance of this ruling class.

Although her class analysis is immature at this point, Morrison is at least conscious of a limited role that economics plays in the exploitation of African people. For example, Morrison begins *The Bluest Eye* with a page and a half of one passage repeated in three different ways. Each of the passages reflects the three primary families in the novel: the Dick-Jane primary reader family, the MacTeer family, and the Breedlove family. The first family is symbolic of the ruling class; it is an economically stable family. Both the MacTeers and the Breedloves symbolize the exploited class although the Breedloves are less economically stable than the MacTeers. In fact, the spacing of the passages reflects the varying economic levels of these families. Although the MacTeers are poor, the father works and provides some shelter, food, and clothing for the economic survival of the family. On the other hand, the Breedloves are dirt poor, and it is the extent of their poverty that strips them of their sense of human worth and leaves them more vulnerable to the cultural propaganda of the ruling class. Their house, significantly a run-down, abandoned store, reflects no stability. The family members come and go like store patrons, having no sense of family love and unity. That Morrison takes the time to describe and explain the poor economic conditions of the Breedlove family, and the effects of these conditions on it, reflects her awareness of the class question. At least she informs the reader that the MacTeers and Breedloves do not suffer simply because of racism, but because of poverty as well.

Additionally, Morrison reveals her class consciousness by exploring the intraracial prejudices caused by petty bourgeois Africans, those who aspire for the same goals and aspirations of the ruling class. In *The Bluest Eye*, she creates three "minor" African families who, because they benefit economically, politically, and/or socially from the exploitation of their own people, disassociate themselves from poor Africans and associate themselves with the ruling class.

One such family is the Peals. Although the reader is introduced to only one member of this family, Maureen, her appearance, behavioral patterns, and remarks about the nature of her family's "business" offer sufficient glimpses of the Peals to reflect their class interests. Physically, Maureen looks and dresses like a little European-American girl, the storybook Jane or the child actress Shirley Temple. Her hairstyle, "long brown hair braided into two lynch ropes that hung down her back" resembles that of little European girls. In fact, the description of her hair as lynch ropes clearly associates her with the African's oppressors. Her "high-yellow" complexion and her clothes make this association even more pronounced. She wears "Kelly-green knee socks," "lemon-drop sweaters," "brown velvet coat trimmed in white rabbit fur, and a matching muff."

Socially, Maureen's behavior patterns reflect the way in which some within the dominant class relate to poor African people. She pities Pecola when she is humiliated by Bay Boy and Junie Bug, and she humors Claudia by speaking to her on one occasion after neglecting her on many others. Economically, the Peal family appears to make money by exploiting the race issue. They initiate suits against European-American establishments (e.g.,

Isaley's ice cream store in Akron) that refuse to serve Africans. Although, according to Maureen, her "family does it all the time," apparently these suits are benefitting financially no other African family but the Peals.

Still, Morrison is more interested in developing the skin-color conflict (race) than the class conflict (capitalism). For the emphasis in the Peal section is on "unearned haughtiness," Maureen's physical appearance. She looks like the doll that Claudia has had to learn to love; she is the person whom the teachers smile at encouragingly, the parents talk to in honey-coated voices, the boys leave alone; she is Shirley Temple; she is Jane. Moreover, Maureen's last appearance in the novel is clearly associated with the question of intraracial prejudice based on skin color. When Maureen is verbally attacked by Claudia, she responds by using the same dehumanizing name calling that Bay Boy used against Pecola: "I *am* cute! And you ugly! Back and ugly black e mos. I *am* cute!" Clearly, Maureen sees herself as superior because she looks more like her oppressors.

By disassociating itself from the African community, the second family—Geraldine, Louis, and Louis Junior—also reflects ruling class aspirations. The family members consider themselves to be *colored*, a term that for them signifies some nebulous group of Africans who are neither European nor African: "Colored people were neat and quiet; niggers were dirty and loud." So Louis Jr. plays with European-American children; his hair is cut short to deemphasize its wooliness; his skin is continually lotioned to keep him from revealing his ashy Africanness. When Geraldine sees Pecola, she is reminded of everything she has sought to escape—everything associated with the poor, struggling African masses: their physical appearance, their behavioral patterns, their lifestyle, and their speech patterns. Her calling Pecola, a little girl of ten, a "nasty little black bitch" and commanding her to "get out of my house" illustrate the extent of Geraldine's isolation from her people and her association with her oppressors. Perhaps even more significant is the fact that she showers love on her black cat, but not on her "black" son. Clearly, for her, the blue eyes of the cat make it easier to love the animal than her own son. All in all, her thoughts, words, and actions parrot those of the ruling class.

The third family, the Elihue Micah Whitcombs, are so obsessed with the physical appearance of Europeans that they jeopardize their mental stability by intermarrying to maintain some semblance of whiteness. They are grateful that their ancestor, a decaying British nobleman, chose to whiten them, and they enthusiastically separate themselves "in body, mind, and spirit from all that suggested Africa" while developing "Anglophilia." They are, in fact, convinced of De Gobineau's hypothesis that "all civilizations derive from the white race, that none can exist without its help, and that a great society is great and brilliant only so far as it preserves the blood of the noble group that created it." Not only do the Whitcombs strive for the "whiteness" of the ruling class, but they imitate the exploitive nature of this class as well; they exploit their own people, the Africans who live in the West Indies: "That they were corrupt in public and private practice, both lecherous and lascivious, was considered their noble right."

Clearly, Morrison's class consciousness, however weak, is reflected in her condemnation of these families who share the class aspirations of these oppressors. All suffer from what Kwame Nkrumah called the crisis of the African personality—Africans so bereft of their own national identity that they exhibit distorted, even psychopathic, behavioral patterns. Morrison is certainly aware of this crisis, for in this work as in later ones, she harshly criticizes those characters who divorce themselves from the African community. In fact, she considers this petty bourgeois sector of the African population the living dead, a buffer group between the ruling and the oppressed classes who are always portrayed as abnormal in some sense. In *The Bluest Eye*, Geraldine lavishes love on her black cat, but withholds it from her son; the Whitcombs become a family of morons and perverts. Quite appropriately, Elihue is donned Soaphead Wilson by the community for he is a pervert who is incapable of healthy love. Instead, he loves worn things and little girls; Pecola is both worn (loss of virginity) and a little girl.

Morrison's characterization of these three "minor" families—the Peals, the "Geraldines," and the Whitcombs—certainly substantiates the premise that she does possess some class consciousness even in this first novel. However, that these are not major families in the novel indicates that her class consciousness is decidedly weak. Moreover, even though Morrison is conscious of the role class aspirations play in these minor families, she often discusses these aspirations as if they were intraracial prejudices based on skin color rather than class conflicts. That is, discussions of class conflicts are couched within, and thus overshadowed by, her discussions on racial prejudices. Indeed, it is interesting to note that just as Africans in the United States in the 1960s and early 1970s viewed the primary enemy of African people as "the white man," so does Morrison, writing *The Bluest Eye* in the late 1960s, see the issue as one of European versus African. However, as she continues to think about, write about, and experience the ongoing oppression of African people despite the gains of the Civil Rights Movement, she will become more conscious of the fact that capitalism, not racism, is the African's greatest enemy.

It is interesting to surmise that the limited focus on the issue of class as the primary problem confronting African people in *The Bluest Eye* and the primary focus on racism as the major concern may be dialectically related to the novel's inorganic structure. The structural limitations of the novel can be gleaned through the many artificial props that Morrison relies on to help her develop her theme. First, she includes two prefaces, one to inform the reader of the conflict in the novel, the other to present the outcome. The first preface, extracted from the Dick-Jane primary reader, presents the three dominant families that will be contrasted in the novel: The Dick-Jane family, the MacTeers, and the Breedloves. Each is represented by one of the three storybook passages that Morrison places at the beginning of the novel to give the reader his first clue as to the economic and social well-being—or lack thereof—of the families. The structure of the first passage, representing the Dick-Jane household, is correct according to the double spacing and punctuation requirements of a standard typewritten page. The next passage lacks the traditional structure of the first. It is single spaced. Representing the MacTeer household, it signifies neither the ideal nor complete chaos. Rather, it reflects a struggling household, one that manages to survive despite its economic hardships. The third passage is completely devoid of spacing and punctuation. Its words are run together, reflecting the chaos found in the Breedlove household. Therefore, just as the second two passages are presented to enable the reader to compare and contrast them with the first, so the MacTeer and Breedlove families are presented to enable the reader to compare and contrast their condition in society with that of the standard or ideal European-American family, the Dick-Jane family. The structural layout of the passages enhances the theme that as Africans born in a racist society, neither the MacTeers nor the Breedloves enjoy the benefits of America that their European counterparts do.

The second preface, the marigold page, presents the outcome of the novel—the unfortunate and irreparable demise of Pecola Breedlove in particular and of the Breedlove family in general. It also reveals the reason for this demise; the infertile soil of Lorain, Ohio, symbolic of the United States, precludes the healthy, normal growth of the marigolds, symbolic of African-American people.

Another prop used by Morrison to help tell her story is the use of three different levels of time. First, the reader is introduced to a present that exists outside of the novel proper, the present of the adult Claudia. Second, the reader is given a glimpse of the future within the context of the novel, the marigold preface. Third, the story proper actually begins in the present on page twelve. However, by page seventeen, with the introduction of Pecola, and certainly by page thirty, with the description of the Breedlove's store house, the reader does not know what time period exists. Does Pecola come to live with the MacTeers after the Breedlove's abandoned store is burned, or does Cholly burn some other, prior dwelling place, and then the Breedloves move into the abandoned store? Such questions arise because of Morrison's clumsy handling of time throughout the novel. She is not yet skilled in structuring plots.

The use of names of season to indicate the major parts of the novel also aids Morrison in telling her story. By beginning the novel with autumn, she informs us that the world of the novel is topsy turvey. Spring usually symbolizes the beginning of things, the time of birth and rebirth. Autumn, in contrast, is the time of death and decay. Summer, commonly associated with life in full bloom, ripeness, is a time of death, life in its final moments. These seasonal divisions aid the reader in understanding the fundamental decadence of life for the African living in the United States. They help tell Morrison's story of the warped psyche of an adolescent African female living in a racist society.

A fourth structural crutch is Morrison's reliance on a series of passage chapter headings primarily to let the reader know that the Breedlove family will be the focus of the chapters and, secondarily, to let the reader know what specific aspect of the family will be the focus. For example, chapter 2, the first section that concerns the Breedloves, has as its heading a run-together passage describing the house of Dick and Jane. By using this particular passage as the heading, Morrison informs the reader that the contents of the chapter will be devoted to a description of the Breedlove house. When a heading includes all the members of the Dick-Jane family, as in chapter 3, the reader knows that all the Breedloves will be discussed. Admittedly, Morrison has created an interesting and unique structural device. Still, these headings do in fact simplify her task as a writer, for she can rely on them to help organize her material, i.e., to help develop the plot of *The Bluest Eye*. In later works, such devices are omitted because they are unnecessary. Moreover, they distract the reader from concentrating on the narrative itself. In later works, Morrison demonstrates her developed consciousness, her developed writing ability, and her developed confidence by relying only on the narrative to tell her story. In other words, the act of writing itself helps her class consciousness develop, and her developed class consciousness enhances her writing skills. The two are dialectically related.

Morrison's reliance on three narrators—Claudia the child, Claudia the adult, and an omniscient narrator—is problematic as well. For instance, as narrator, Claudia the adult at times ascribes her adult feelings and adult analytical ability to Claudia the child. The reader is amazed, for instance, that a nine-year-old can understand that U.S. capitalist society is to blame for creating the standard of beauty: "And all the time we knew that Maureen Peal was not the Enemy and not worthy of such intense hatred. The *Thing* to fear was the *Thing* that made *her* beautiful, and not us." For most, this realization does not come until adulthood. Phyllis Klotman attempts to offer a logical explanation for this shift in point of view from the child to the adult Claudia when she writes: "The narrative voice shifts . . . when the author wants us to have a more mature and objective view of the characters and their situations. . . . There is not only a progression in Claudia's point of view from youth to age, but also from ignorance to perception." Contrarily, Morrison's narrative structure is more illogical than logical since Claudia the child thinks like an adult at times and child at others. There is not what Klotman refers to as "a progression in Claudia's point of view." Throughout the novel, the reader constantly asks the following question: "Is Claudia, the adult narrator, looking back on her childhood and telling us the story, or is she telling the story as a nine-year-old participant and an adult observer?

The use of the omniscient narrator adds to this narrative confusion and awkwardness. It is the omniscient narrator who tells the Breedlove's story; Claudia, the child and/or adult, relates the events within the remaining chapters. What prevents the reader from being totally confused by this arrangement is the inclusion or omission of chapter headings. Chapters without headings are told by Claudia; those with headings are told by the omniscient narrator. However, this understanding of Morrison's narrative structure does not rid it of its awkwardness. On the contrary, the division of the story in such a way contributes to the reader's impression that Morrison, at this early stage in her writing career, must rely on artificial or external textural devices to organize her material.

Just as there are weaknesses between chapters, so are there weaknesses within chapters. In interviews with both Jane Bakerman and Robert Stepto, Morrison admits that she had difficulty with the Pauline Breedlove section of the novel. Unable to have either of her three narrators—the omniscient narrator, the adult Claudia, or the child Claudia—tell Pauline's story, Morrison is forced to use italics to symbolize Mrs. Breedlove's own thoughts. Morrison admits this writing weakness to Bakerman:

> When I wrote the section in *The Bluest Eye* about Pecola's mother, I thought I would have no trouble. First I wrote it out as an "I" story, . . . then I wrote it out as a "she" story. . . . I was never able to resolve that, so I used both. The author said a little bit and then she said a little bit. But I wish I had been able to do the "I" thing with her. I really wanted to.

To Robert Stepto, she says: "I sort of copped out . . . because I used two voices."

Having to oscillate between Pauline's thoughts within italics and the omniscient narrator's comments within a single chapter is only one instance of Morrison's inability to make the text cohere. The introduction of Pecola is another. At the end of one paragraph, Morrison completes a discussion of Mr. Henry Washington, the MacTeer's new boarder. At the beginning of the next, Pecola is introduced by the following ambiguous statement: "She slept in the bed with us." There is no transition from the discussion on Mr. Henry to that on Pecola. Neither is there a legitimate stylistic reason for this textual gap since for the reader it creates confusion, not clarity.

Too, there is at least one chapter—the Geraldine-Junior chapter—that seems superfluous to the rest of the text because it is not clearly integrated with the other chapters. Unlike the Maureen Peal section, which clearly helps to explain the effects of racism within the African race, and unlike the Soaphead Wilson section, which is relevant in providing the conditions under which Pecola imagines she has blue eyes, the Geraldine-Junior section does not advance the plot of *The Bluest Eye*. At first glance, it appears merely as a repetition of an already established fact: Pecola has an all-consuming desire to have blue eyes. However, it actually moves beyond repetition by relating the circumstances under which Pecola becomes convinced that she can be "black" and have blue eyes and, by convincing her of this fact, helps to seal her fate. But for Morrison to use an entire chapter to make this point (and then to make it so unclearly) is a mark of her undeveloped writing skills.

Later works evidence a symbiosis between text and structure, for as Morrison better understands capitalism/imperialism—the exploitation of one class of people by another class—she will structure her text to represent the type of economic system that condemns exploitation and promotes collectivism: socialism. Thus, by the time she writes *Tar Baby*, her story will be told equally by all of the main characters in the novel as well as by the omniscient narrator. Each will have the opportunity and the responsibility to contribute to the organic whole. And by the time she writes *Beloved*, she will so expertly manipulate past, present, and future as to demonstrate to African people that there is no significant difference between the quality of their life now and that experienced in slavery. This devotion to creating a dialectical relationship between text and structure will, in turn, point the way to the solution: collectivism.

TONI MORRISON

Afterword

We had just started elementary school. She said she wanted blue eyes. I looked around to picture her with them and was violently repelled by what I imagined she would look like if she had her wish. The sorrow in her voice seemed to call for sympathy, and I faked it for her, but, astonished by the desecration she proposed, I "got mad" at her instead.

Until that moment I had seen the pretty, the lovely, the nice, the ugly, and although I had certainly used the word "beautiful," I had never experienced its shock—the force of which was equaled by the knowledge that no one else recognized it, not even, or especially, the one who possessed it.

It must have been more than the face I was examining: the silence of the street in the early afternoon, the light, the atmosphere of confession. In any case it was the first time I knew beautiful. Had imagined it for myself. Beauty was not simply something to behold; it was something one could *do*.

The Bluest Eye was my effort to say something about that; to say something about why she had not, or possibly ever would have, the experience of what she possessed and why she prayed for so radical an alteration. Implicit in her desire was racial self-loathing. And twenty years later I was still wondering about how one learns that. Who told her? Who made her feel that it was better to be a freak than what she was? Who had looked at her and found her so wanting, so small a weight on the beauty scale? The novel pecks away at the gaze that condemned her.

From the 1994 Edition of *The Bluest Eye*. © 1993 by Toni Morrison. Reprinted by permission of International Creative Management, Inc.

The reclamation of racial beauty in the sixties stirred these thoughts, made me think about the necessity for the claim. Why, although reviled by others, could this beauty not be taken for granted within the community? Why did it need wide public articulation to exist? These are not clever questions. But in 1962 when I began this story, and in 1965 when it began to be a book, the answers were not as obvious to me as they quickly became and are now. The assertion of racial beauty was not a reaction to the self-mocking, humorous critique of cultural/racial foibles common in all groups, but against the damaging internalization of assumptions of immutable inferiority originating in an outside gaze. I focused, therefore, on how something as grotesque as the demonization of an entire race could take root inside the most delicate member of society: a child; the most vulnerable member: a female. In trying to dramatize the devastation that even casual racial contempt can cause, I chose a unique situation, not a representative one. The extremity of Pecola's case stemmed largely from a crippled and crippling family—unlike the average black family and unlike the narrator's. But singular as Pecola's life was, I believed some aspects of her woundability were lodged in all young girls. In exploring the social and domestic aggression that could cause a child to literally fall apart, I mounted a series of rejections, some routine, some exceptional, some monstrous, all the while trying hard to avoid complicity in the demonization process Pecola was subjected to. That is, I did not want to dehumanize the characters who trashed Pecola and contributed to her collapse.

One problem was centering: the weight of the novel's inquiry on so delicate and vulnerable a character could smash her and lead readers into the comfort of pitying her rather than into an interrogation of themselves for the smashing. My solution—break the narrative into parts that had to be reassembled by the reader—seemed to me a good idea, the execution of which does not satisfy me now. Besides, it didn't work: many readers remain touched but not moved.

The other problem, of course, was language. Holding the despising glance while sabotaging it was difficult. The novel tries to hit the raw nerve of racial self-contempt, expose it, and then soothe it not with narcotics but with language that replicated the agency I discovered in my first experience of beauty. Because that moment was so racially infused (my revulsion at what my school friend wanted: very blue eyes in a very black skin; the harm she was doing to *my* concept of the beautiful), the struggle was for writing that was indisputably black. I don't yet know quite what that is, but neither that nor the attempts to disqualify an effort to find out keeps me from trying to pursue it.

Some time ago I did the best job I could of describing strategies for grounding my work in race-specific yet race-free prose. Prose free of hierarchy and triumphalism. Parts of that description are as follows.

The opening phrase of the first sentence, "Quiet as it's kept," had several attractions for me. First, it was a familiar phrase, familiar to me as a child listening to adults; to black women conversing with one another, telling a story, an anecdote, gossip about some one or event within the circle, the family, the neighborhood. The words are conspiratorial. "Shh, don't tell anyone else," and "No one is allowed to know this." It is a secret between us and a secret that is being kept from us. The conspiracy is both held and withheld, exposed and sustained. In some sense it was precisely what the act of writing the book was: the public exposure of a private confidence. In order to comprehend fully the duality of that position, one needs to be reminded of the political climate in which the writing took place, 1965–69, a time of great social upheaval in the lives of black people. The publication (as opposed to the writing) involved the exposure; the writing was the disclosure of secrets, secrets "we" shared and those withheld from us by ourselves and by the world outside the community.

"Quiet as it's kept" is also a figure of speech that is written, in this instance, but clearly chosen for how speakerly it is, how it speaks and bespeaks a particular world and its ambiance. Further, in addition to its "back fence" connotation, its suggestion of illicit gossip, of thrilling revelation, there is also, in the "whisper," the assumption (on the part of the reader) that the teller is on the inside, knows something others do not, and is going to be generous with this privileged information. The intimacy I was aiming for, the intimacy between the reader and the page, could start up immediately because the secret is being shared, at best, and eavesdropped upon, at the least. Sudden familiarity or instant intimacy seemed crucial to me. I did not want the reader to have time to wonder, "What do I have to do, to give up, in order to read this? What defense do I need, what distance maintain?" Because I know (and the reader does not—he or she had to wait for the second sentence) that this is a terrible story about things one would rather not know anything about.

What, then, is the Big Secret about to be shared? The thing we (reader and I) are "in" on? A botanical aberration. Pollution, perhaps. A skip, perhaps, in the natural order of things: a September, an autumn, a fall without marigolds. Bright, common, strong and sturdy marigolds. When? In 1941, and since that is a momentous year (the beginning of World War II for the United States), the "fall" of 1941, just before the declaration of war, has a "closet" innuendo. In the temperate zone where there is a season known as "fall" during which one expects marigolds to be at their peak, in the months

before the beginning of U.S. participation in World War II, something grim
is about to be divulged. The next sentence will make it clear that the sayer,
the one who knows, is a child speaking, mimicking the adult black women on
the porch or in the backyard. The opening phrase is an effort to be grown-
up about this shocking information. The point of view of a child alters the
priority an adult would assign the information. "We thought . . . it was
because Pecola was having her father's baby that the marigolds did not grow"
foregrounds the flowers, backgrounds illicit, traumatic, incomprehensible
sex coming to its dreaded fruition. This foregrounding of "trivial" information and backgrounding of shocking knowledge secures the point of view but
gives the reader pause about whether the voice of children can be trusted at
all or is more trustworthy than an adult's. The reader is thereby protected
from a confrontation too soon with the painful details, while simultaneously
provoked into a desire to know them. The novelty, I thought, would be in
having this story of a female violation revealed from the vantage point of the
victims or could-be victims or rape—the persons no one inquired of
(certainly not in 1965): the girls themselves. And since the victim does not
have the vocabulary to understand the violence or its context, gullible,
vulnerable girlfriends, looking back as the knowing adults they pretended to
be in the beginning, would have to do that for her, and would have to fill
those silences with their own reflective lives. Thus, the opening provides the
stroke that announces something more than a secret shared, but a silence
broken, a void filled, an unspeakable thing spoken at last. And it draws the
connection between a minor destabilization in seasonal flora and the
insignificant destruction of a black girl. Of course "minor" and "insignificant" represent the outside world's view—for the girls, both phenomena are
earthshaking depositories of information they spend that whole year of
childhood (and afterward) trying to fathom, and cannot. If they have any
success, it will be in transferring the problem of fathoming to the presumably adult reader, to the inner circle of listeners. At least they have distrib-
uted the weight of these problematical questions to a larger constituency,
and justified the public exposure of a privacy. If the conspiracy that the
opening words announce is entered into by the reader, then the book can be
seen to open with its close: a speculation on the disruption of "nature" as
being a social disruption with tragic individual consequences in which the
reader, as part of the population of the text, is implicated.

However, a problem lies in the central chamber of the novel. The shat-
tered world I built (to complement what is happening to Pecola), its pieces
held together by seasons in childtime and commenting at every turn on the
incompatible and barren white-family primer, does not in its present form
handle effectively the silence at its center: the void that is Pecola's "unbeing."

It should have had a shape—like the emptiness left by a boom or a cry. It required a sophistication unavailable to me, and some deft manipulation of the voices around her. She is not seen by herself until she hallucinates a self. And the fact of her hallucination becomes a kind of outside-the-book conversation.

Also, although I was pressing for a female expressiveness, it eluded me for the most part, and I had to content myself with female personae because I was not able to secure throughout the work the feminine subtext that is present in the opening sentence (the women gossiping, eager and aghast in "Quiet as it's kept"). The shambles this struggle became is most evident in the section on Pauline Breedlove, where I resorted to two voices, hers and the urging narrator's, both of which are extremely unsatisfactory to me. It is interesting to me now that where I thought I would have the most difficulty subverting the language to a feminine mode, I had the least: connecting Cholly's "rape" by the whitemen to his own of his daughter. This most masculine act of aggression becomes feminized in my language, "passive," and, I think, more accurately repellent when deprived of the male "glamour of shame" rape is (or once was) routinely given.

My choices of language (speakerly, aural, colloquial), my reliance for full comprehension on codes embedded in black culture, my effort to effect immediate co-conspiracy and intimacy (without any distancing, explanatory fabric), as well as my attempt to shape a silence while breaking it are attempts to transfigure the complexity and the wealth of Black-American culture into a language worthy of the culture.

Thinking back now on the problems expressive language presented to me, I am amazed by their currency, their tenacity. Hearing "civilized" languages debase humans, watching cultural exorcisms debase literature, seeing oneself preserved on the amber of disqualifying metaphors—I can say that my narrative project is as difficult today as it was thirty years ago.

With very few exceptions, the initial publication of *The Bluest Eye* was like Pecola's life: dismissed, trivialized, misread. And it has taken twenty-five years to gain for her the respectful publication this edition is.

Princeton, New Jersey
November, 1993

LINDEN PEACH

The Bluest Eye *(1970)*

The innovatory nature of Morrison's first two novels is derived from the ways in which their radical content is allowed to determine their experiment with form. Ostensibly *The Bluest Eye* is about a lonely, victimised, black girl, Pecola Breedlove, who is driven insane by her desire to have white skin, blonde hair, and blue eyes, and the interplay between her disintegration and a number of black characters who are more fully integrated into white society. But even a casual reader cannot help but notice that there is more to the book than this. At the outset of the novel Morrison adapts the eighteenth and nineteenth-century convention whereby work by a black American often carried a preface from a white writer confirming the authenticity of the black authorship. In its preface, which provides an introduction to some of the chapters, extracts from a Dick-Jane American primer present a standardised, white American family embracing Euro-American views of beauty and happiness. This introduces the major theme of *The Bluest Eye*, that the white voice is inappropriate to dictate the contours of African-American life. At the end of the novel Claudia and Frieda overhear snippets of gossip about the Breedloves that summarize the social consequence of this imposition: none of them seem 'right'; they don't have relatives; they are ugly. Beauty is as much a political as an aesthetic concept whilst ugliness is not merely a matter of appearance; it is

From *Modern Novelists: Toni Morrison*. © 1995 by Linden Peach. Reprinted with permission of St. Martin's Press, Inc.

169

a manifestation in Western thinking of an inner ugliness, a spiritual and moral failure, if not an innate evil:

> That which was 'white' (or Anglo, male, Christian, wealthy) was extolled and infused with connotations of benevolence and superiority, while that which was not white (or not Anglo, female, non-Christian, poor) was debased and associated with malevolence and inferiority.

Claudia herself, as the mature narrator, condemns the American concept of blonde beauty as one of 'the most destructive ideas in the history of human thought.' As de Weever (1991) points out, the insistence upon one standard of beauty contradicts the pluralistic nature of contemporary America where African standards of beauty are frequently adopted by African-Americans, for example, the dashiki, ancient Egyptian long braids and cornrow hairstyles. She also surmises that there may have been secret societies in some African countries in the seventeenth and eighteenth centuries concerned to inculcate a confident centre of being in young girls and young women which was then destroyed by slavery and racism.

This chapter examines how the novel's structure is driven by its exploration of the impact of white ideologies on the black community. In particular it focuses on the ironic juxtaposition of the white mythology of the Dick-Jane primer and the lives of African-American as part of a larger interplay of differences within the novel and on how the exploration of the nature of whiteness provides its arguments about the embourgeoisement of black culture with a special slant. The order and the apparent moral certainty of the white world is contrasted with the inner dislocation and search for coherence in the lives of Pecola and her parents. The novel itself is organised into four sequences, each associated with a season and beginning with Claudia's memories of that season. There are seven subsections, introduced by lines taken from the primer extract in the preface, related from the perspective of an omniscient narrator. The lines, reprinted with punctuation and spaces removed, are ostensibly unintelligible so as to emphasise the dislocation between the white Dick-Jane mythology and the norms of black experience. The retrospective nature of Claudia's narrative is an important device in deconstructing the embourgeoisement of black people in the novel. At the end of the book we realise that the voice of Claudia, which becomes fused with that of the omniscient narrator, is that of an older Claudia who, now living in the North, is looking back and tracing the stages which have led to her maturity of outlook. Thus, on one level, the narrative takes us backwards from the present in the North into the past and the South, whilst, on another level, taking us forward in the events of Pecola's tragedy.

II

The text pursues ironies created by the interplay between two levels of artic-ulation in the narrative. One level of articulation arises from the role of Claudia as survivor and her retrospective account of episodes introduced within the context of a season; the other derives from the black kinswoman who narrates the episodes introduced by extracts from the primer. She is an omniscient narrator who is able to provide access to information which Claudia could not have and is able to involve characters outside of Claudia's immediate range of experience. The ironies arising from these two levels of narration are developed within a wider framework provided by the mismatch between what the primer suggests is the norm and the lived experience of the black families.

In discussing the levels of irony within *The Bluest Eye* it is important to remember that Toni Morrison's works are not easily approached through reading habits developed in relation to the realist novel where language often gives the impression of transparency, that is where the representation and the represented are seen as the same thing. In Morrison's novels, language, as the French critic Roland Barthes recognised, is enmeshed with the power struc-tures and forces underlying what we might call 'social reality': 'And the reason why power is invincible is that the object in which it is carried for all human eternity is language: the language that we speak and write.' In Morrison's novels, ideology is not, as envisaged by Marx, an illusion or false consciousness but, as conceived by the French Marxist theorist, Louis Althusser, it is the staple of daily living, embodied in language and in social institutions such as the school, the family and the media.

As we said in the introduction, the dialectic between inherited codes of representation and imagined codes is one of the features which Morrison's work shares with novels from Latin America classified as 'magic realist.' This dialectic emerges in *The Bluest Eye*, as in subsequent novels, from the reali-sation of the black culture out of which Morrison is writing and of the distor-tion of the self created by the imposition of white norms on black people. The effect of this imposition is to create a profound sense of fracture. The concept of black in the novel is a construct partly of the characters' own making but mostly social, based on white definitions of blackness which asso-ciate it with violence, poverty, dirt and lack of education, whilst Africa is perceived as uncivilised and (negatively) tribal. Black people developed as a social category of low status when Arab trade in African slaves increased, but it was with the European subordination of world peoples as labouring classes that blacks came to form, as McLaughlin says, part of an oppositional and hierarchical system of cultural constructs that justified a coloniser/colonised power system.

In Morrison's novels the struggle to define and create a notion of selfhood in ways which are different from the stereotypical expectations of behaviour carried by the larger symbolic order as whole inevitably involves a process of inner dislocation. As in, for example, *Song of Solomon*, this sense of inner disruption is sometimes resolved positively by the intervention of a female or androgynous figure in the central character's life. But this is not true of Morrison's first two novels where Pecola, suffering from a sense of self-loathing and false identity, retreats into schizophrenia after being raped by her father and where Sula withdraws into her grandmother's room to die alone and unfulfilled.

Although *The Bluest Eye* demonstrates Morrison's abiding interest, like that of many novelists, in dislocation, alienation, gaps and ellipses, these features arise out of the distortion of self created by the imposition of Euro-American cultural ideals on black people, including white concepts of beauty. Wilkerson (1988) has conveniently summarised three of the key characteristics of Morrison's narratives: they are rooted in arresting events (for example, a child having her father's baby, an insurance salesman attempting to fly off a roof, a First World War veteran announcing National Suicide Day, a slave mother killing her own child who later returns to haunt her); they involve personal histories which have been made tangled and complex; and they feature personal lives which skirt the edge of madness. However, whereas Wilkerson argues that the familiar in black folk lore is made strange in the telling, I would argue that in Morrison's work the eccentric (perhaps the ex-centric?) is often made explicable (or centred?). Both the first two novels are retrospective narratives: in *The Bluest Eye*, Claudia tries to understand her own involvement in Pecola's tragedy as the narrative also seeks to explain why a father in the ironically-named Breedlove family should impregnate his own daughter; in *Sula*, the people of a black neighborhood, Medallion, retain and try to understand the implications for themselves and their community of the bizarre history and behaviour of the equally ironically named Peace family.

The explanation for many of the behaviours in the novel lies in the impact of prevailing white ideologies and dominant social structures on the black community, the negative consequence of which are inevitable as Claudia, partly in an attempt to abrogate her own responsibility, observes:

'This soil is bad for certain kinds of flowers. Certain seeds it will not nurture, certain fruit it will not bear . . .' As we shall see, the authentic black self is buried so deep in some of the characters that their perceptions of themselves amount to self-hatred. This self-loathing is strongest in those characters who are farthest from their communities; for what they hate the most is being different since difference brings about abuse and cruelty. The self-hatred is often focused on the body as the most obvious indicator of race; hair and colour, for example, are recurrent concerns.

The black community is envisaged as existing like a cell within the larger white body of America, sustained by traditional strengths and values but being weakened by divisions within it. These divisions are the result of the gradual embourgeoisement of black people, as a consequence of a complicated process of adjustment and accommodation to white norms. In LeClair (1981), Morrison explains: "The music kept us alive, but it's not enough any more. My people are being devoured'. The structure of *The Bluest Eye* is one of the means by which the novel explores how and why black people are being devoured and is best approached from this perspective. In speaking of African-Americans as being consumed, Morrison is inverting how whites, since earliest colonialist times, represented blacks as bestial. She is ironically adapting how African mythologies about slavery posited the whites as cannibals because blacks taken by them never returned; here perceiving the exploitation of blacks by whites as economic cannibalism. It is a view, however, which ignores how African-Americans have influenced language, dress, manners, and culture in America, even in the South.

Not all critics have recognised the success of the novel in deconstructing the impact of white values on African-American people. Valerie Smith (1987) complains that *The Bluest Eye* does not 'address hard questions directly'; by this she means that it does not undertake to explain, for example, why black Americans aspire to unattainable standards of beauty. Her claims would seem to be borne out by Pecola's conclusion: 'There's really nothing more to say—except why. But since why is difficult to handle, one must take refuge in how.' However, this is not the conclusion of the ostensibly omniscient narrator, but the view of Claudia as an adult trying to come to terms with her own role in Pecola's tragedy. What Claudia says does not suggest, as Smith argues, that the novel will take refuge in 'how;' it is a warning that what the narrative will uncover by means of explanation may be unpalatable.

The difference between the white and African-American cultures and between the sociopolitical contexts of the lives shaped within those cultures are pursued throughout *The Bluest Eye*, in the persistent contrasting of the Dick-Jane mythology of the primer with the Breedloves, the African-American family. The chapters which are introduced by lines from the primer extract, sometimes with a very subtle but significant variation, provide particularly bitter glosses on the bourgeois myth of the ideal family life. Each chapter enlarges on the Breedlove family while the themes are developed further with reference to a range of minor characters.

Black people are visible to whites in *The Bluest Eye* only in so far as they fit the white frame of society. The novel deconstructs this frame literally through dismembering the American Dick-Jane mythology: essential features of their world—house, family, cat, mother, father, dog and friend—are separated from each other and their ideological plot elements in the Breedlove narrative. This process of dismemberment is analogous to Claudia's increasing dismemberment of a white doll in an attempt to discover the superiority of white culture:

> I fingered the face, wondering at the single-stroke eyebrows; picked at the pearly teeth stuck like two piano keys between red bowline lips. Traced the turned-up nose, poked the glassy blue eyeballs, twisted the yellow hair. I could not love it. But I could examine it to see what it was that all the world said was lovable.

Claudia's destruction of the doll is a complex response which requires us to understand how Western culture, as McLaughlin explains, 'inspires hatred toward and among people of African descent, inducing destructive behaviours and an equally adverse disconnections from anything not western.' In removing the various parts of the toy, Claudia dismantles the structure which constitutes and sustains it as an emblem of white beauty. Again, this is anticipated in the way in which the mythology of the primer is increasingly dismantled in the preface—the extract is reprinted, first without the punctuation and then with the spacing removed as well until all the letters run into each other. Claudia's obsession with discovering the source of the superiority of white culture leads her initially to torture the white girls whom the dolls represent but later to recoil in horror from this disinterested violence.

Within the ironic interplay of difference, the text dramatises and explores the consequences of enforced or voluntary abatement to white society, though in a sense no abatement can be entirely voluntary where black people exist in a world defined by the surrounding white society in terms of its blackness. Following Claudia's recollections of autumn 1940, in which she dismembers the white doll, the first chapter introduced by a primer extract develops the ironic differences between the pretty house of the primer and the abandoned store in which the Breedlove family lives. The store consists of rooms which have partitions that do not reach the ceiling; there is no bathroom but there is a toilet bowl which is out of sight though within earshot of the inhabitants. The irony is underscored by the repetition of the world 'pretty' which occurs only once in the preface and the way in which the extract breaks off, rather manically, with the first letter of that word.

The stress placed on the word 'pretty' also anticipates the misery endured by the Breedloves, and especially Pecola, in the following chapter because they believed they were ugly. That chapter is introduced with a primer extract that talks of family happiness and which breaks off equally significantly with the first letter of 'happy'. Unlike the ideal, sanitized family of Dick and Jane, the Breedlove's marriage is quarrelsome and violent, though both Pauline and Cholly need this kind of relationship. Mrs. Breedlove finds zest and passion in her formalised battles with her husband, whilst he projects on to her a sense of an innate inferiority arising from the way he has been treated by whites.

Whilst Claudia at this time dismembers the white doll in order to discover the nature of white superiority, Pecola regularly stares into her mirror 'trying to discover the secret of ugliness, the ugliness that made her ignored or despised at school, by teachers and classmates alike'. The irony here is that the secret is not going to be found within herself, but within the culture that defines her as ugly. The focus of the novel is on the nature of whiteness: what Pecola sees in the eyes of the shopkeeper, Mr. Yacobowski— 'the total absence of human recognition—the glazed separateness'—who as a Jew should understand prejudice sufficiently to transcend it.

The world of the primer is very ordered and controlled as the short, tight sentences suggest, a world in which the middle-class, suburban home stands compartmentalized. Even the verbs are held in check—there are no adverbs and the sentences do not expand to embrace of convey the excitement of laughing or smiling or running; not even the dog's bark appears to interrupt this carefully constructed and ordered world. Claudia remembers the segregated Lake Shore Park for being well laid out and ordered, a quality embodied in the 'clean, white, well-behaved children and parents'. It has an illusory air to it which anticipates the interior of the 'proud' white house where Pauline becomes a servant. There its unreality for black people is conveyed in the details; the pink nighties, the embroidered pillow slips, the blue cornflowers in the top hems of the sheets, the 'fluffy' white towels and the 'cuddly' night clothes.

III

As we intimated at the outset, exploring the nature of whiteness in order to expose the negative consequences of the embourgeoisement of black culture gives *The Bluest Eye* a special slant. On one level, Geraldine, who has taken advantage of what little opportunity exists for black women from her background, is an example of a middle-class black woman who has become divorced from her African-American roots:

> They go to land-grant colleges, normal schools, and learn how to do the white man's work with refinement: home economics to prepare his food; teacher education to instruct black children in obedience; music to soothe the weary master and entertain his blunted soul.

On another level, her history suggests that African-American women in her position surrender a deep-rooted passion which whites both envy and fear: 'The dreadful funkiness of passion, the funkiness of nature, the funkiness of the wide range of human emotions'. The word 'dreadful' here does not convey the views of the black kinswoman narrator but of the land-grant colleges which inculcate black students in white values.

In placing 'funk' at the centre of the African-American sensibility Morrison's text risks confirming a white stereotype of black women. But Geraldine's loss of passion is an indicator of the erosion of her black identity. Her physical being within the cultural frame she has adopted is described in terms of absences. The closest she comes to experiencing an orgasm is when her napkin slips free of her sanitary belt. In Geraldine's life the family kitten of the Dick-Jane mythology also becomes the object of displaced emotions. The cat, which she cradles in 'the deeply private areas of her lap', is the only thing to which she can show any kind of warmth. Geraldine's marriage is described as building a nest; it seems to consist only of ironed shirts and the phrase 'birthed Louis Junior' suggests that parenthood, too, for her is a cold affair. Even the black cat which with blue eyes seems to signify the ideology to which Geraldine aspires, is as cold as an iceberg. The colours of Geraldine's home, of which we become aware when Junior invites Pecola in to torment her, are those of the primer; there is a red-and-gold Bible and lamps with green-and-gold bases. The word 'pretty' is strategically repeated throughout and the boy himself wears a white shirt and blue trousers.

Pecola disturbs Geraldine because she represents disorder: 'Hair uncombed, dresses falling apart, shoes untied and caked with dirt', while the impact of white standardised concepts of beauty upon young women like

Pecola is epitomised in the way in which the blue-eyed black cat when thrown at Pecola claws at her face. Geraldine's final words to Pecola pointedly recall Maureen's to Frieda and Claudia: 'Get out . . . You nasty little black bitch. Get out of my house'.

Instead of passing on ancestral wisdom, the traditional function of the African mother, a role assumed by Pilate in the later novel *Song of Solomon*, Geraldine passes on divisiveness. Ironically, her son, Junior, would like to be accepted by the black boys; he would like to roll in the dirt with them and share their wildness, in effect overthrowing the control and order of the primer. Unable to do so, he takes his frustration out on brown-skinned girls as black men displace the humiliation which they suffer at the hands of whites on their wives and children. Significantly he is also afraid of black girls who are said to hunt in packs. The animal metaphor, suggesting how *he* sees them not how the narrator perceives them, is an index of the extent to which Junior has assumed the derogatory white view of blacks as animals rather than people. The metaphor also suggests that there is defence in solidarity and highlights the vulnerability of those who try to go it alone. The image of the dead cat with its blue eyes closed, 'leaving only an empty, black, and helpless face', suggest the cultural vacuum in which blacks who aspire to white norms may eventually find themselves.

The counterpoints to Geraldine in the novel are the three prostitutes: China, Poland, and Miss Marie. Not only do they have a sexual autonomy which Geraldine has surrendered but they have economic independence. As such, they are also a counterpoint to other petty bourgeois African-Americans who benefit from the exploitations of their own people: the Peal family makes money out of racial law suits while the Whitcombs exploit Africans who live in the West Indies.

The novel focuses not only on the interracial prejudices caused by the black petty bourgeoisie but also on the obsessive nature of their fixation with white values and the lengths to which they sometimes go to deny their blackness. The Whitcombs are so obsessed with not being black, grateful to the decaying British nobleman who gave them their whiteness, that they continue to intermarry to maintain it. Louis Junior's hair is deliberately cut short to hide its wooliness whilst his skin is lotioned to disguise its ashy Africanness. The most ironic example of all, however, is Maureen, the counterpoint to Pecola's humiliation and victimisation. Maureen looks and dresses like Jane, the archetypal Euro-American girl. Whilst Pecola is ignored by her teachers, Maureen is encouraged. Ironically, the lynch rope into which Maureen's hair is said to have been braided reminds us of slavery and oppression, the past on which black solidarity ought to be transformed into an adornment and robbed of its power. This kind of inversion is demonstrated also by the law suits which her parents issue for racism in order to make money, a perverse parody of the real struggles for civil rights.

The inner dislocation which the influence of white values creates in African-Americans, anticipating Pecola's eventual breakdown at the end of the novel, is embodied most obviously in the case of Pauline. In the movies which provide her with an escape from loneliness and alienation, Pauline encounters and assimilates a value system that classifies her and her family as ugly. The films present her with the white Dick-Jane mythology: 'White men taking such good care of they women, and they all dressed up in big clean houses with the bathtubs right in the same room with the toilet'. The line from the primer which introduces this chapter concerns how 'nice' the white mother is and how much she laughs. It is anticipated and contradicted by Claudia's own recollections of spring in the preceding chapter. Although she doesn't hate her mother for it, her memories of the season are shot through with the recollections of the sting left by beatings from thin, green and supple twigs. Green was one of the cheerful colours of the house in the primer extract, but for Claudia, the colour, like the season, brings no cheer; it caused her to miss the 'steady stroke of a strap or the firm but honest slap of a hairbrush'. Ironically, it is the way in which the white myths create an inner dislocation within Pauline Williams that causes her to be less than 'nice' with her own daughter. In the white house in which she becomes a servant she finds an order and beauty that causes her to deny her own family and especially her daughter. When Pecola, her daughter, inadvertently enters the white home and frightens the 'little pink-and-yellow girl', Pauline punishes her and comforts the white girl. Pauline has moved with her husband to a community that is more obviously white than that from which she came. Her schizophrenia is a product of the enforced isolation, exaggerated by the way in which the other black women she meets are amused by her for not straightening her hair, as they have done in imitation of white women, and for retaining the dialect of the South. The novel contrasts not only the isolation of the white, nuclear family with the community of the South—evidenced in the attention Aunt Jimmy receives from her neighbours during her illness and in the community gathering at her funeral—but the isolation of the African-American in the North.

Even though Pauline's marriage collapses into a cycle of violence and unsatisfying sex, she refuses to leave Cholly for the white woman and a romanticised concept of 'sisterhood'. For Pauline race becomes more important than gender: 'But later on it didn't seem none too bright for a black woman to leave a black man for a white woman'. As becomes clear from the monologues which betray the complexity of her situation, her experience of how white doctors treat white women differently from black women is crucial to her rejection of the concept of 'sisterhood'. Once again, the point is made that cultural dislocation, as for Geraldine, brings about an emotional and sexual dislocation. The implication that her white employee has married a man with 'a slash in his face instead of a mouth', is that she has never experienced the passion which Pauline used to find with Cholly, encapsulated in the description of orgasm from a woman's point of view:

> I begin to feel those little bits of color floating up into me—deep into me. That streak of green from the june-bug light, the purple from the berries trickling alone my thighs, Mama's lemonade yellow runs sweet in me. Then I feel like I'm laughing between my legs, and the laughing gets all mixed up with the colors, and I'm afraid I'll come and I'm afraid I won't. But I know I will. And I do. And it be all rainbow all inside. And it lasts and lasts and lasts . . .

IV

The order of the white world, its coherence and moral certainty, is juxtaposed throughout with the disunity and search for coherence in the lives of African-Americans. The chapter which contrasts the white, mythical mother of the primer with Pauline is followed by a chapter that takes up the description of the father as big, strong and protective in the primer extract. This is itself ironic in the light of the text's subsequent celebration of the inner strength and fortitude not of black fathers but of black women:

> Everybody in the world was in a position to give them orders. White women said, 'Do this.' White children said, 'Give me that.' White men said, 'Come here.' Black men said, 'Lay down.' The only people they need not take orders from were black children and each other. But they took all of that and re-created it in their own image. . . . They patted biscuits into flaky ovals of innocence—and shrouded the dead. They plowed all day and came home to nestle like plums under the limbs of their men.

The chapter, in contrasting Cholly with the strong, protective father of the primer, begins by fleshing out his past and concludes with his rape of his own daughter, an incident which can only be understood, if not excused, in light of this background. Compounding the irony, the primer extract begins by asking the white father if he will 'play' with his daughter, Jane, a verb which in the Breedlove episode acquires a much less innocent connotation. There is a further irony in the way in which Claudia's recollections are of Frieda relating how her father beat up Mr. Henry because he touched her breasts and of being dragged to the doctor by her mother in case she had been 'ruined'. Within this account, Cholly is remembered not for being a strong, protective father but for being always drunk. As Hernton observes, it is concomitant with the black literary heritage that black women write about the violence and abuse which they have suffered at the hands of black men. This has created problems, however, for black women writers. When they document the violence and rape they have suffered, even as young girls, they are sometimes accused of sowing the seeds of division in what should be perceived of as a homogeneous community in the face of white oppression. As Hernton says, 'one of the most galvanizing examples of this is the hostility black men have toward Toni Morrison'. This makes it all the more important to understand the complexity of what Morrison is trying to do.

In *The Bluest Eye*, the white father of the primer is invoked as a contrast not only to Cholly but also to Cholly's own father who abandoned him to his mother. The way in which the text returns to Cholly's past to contextualise what has happened is a device used in several of Morrison's novels to illustrate and explore how what appears to be immoral behaviour is actually the result of unnatural experiences imposed on black people by whites. The opening sentence of this chapter sharply contrasts Cholly's childhood with the way in which Pauline's white charges have been brought up; he was left on a junk heap wrapped in two blankets and an old newspaper. This rejection is compounded by some of his later experiences. His grandmother takes him to her bed for warmth in winter, an act which the reference to the way in which he could see her wrinkled, sagging breasts suggests is unnatural, and it is with her that he witnesses violence for the first time when she takes a razor strap to his mother. Here the novel is not only concerned with the way in which Cholly's relationship with his father has been obliterated, but with the way in which white racism and colonialism fractured relationships between mother and child, an increasing and recurring theme in Morrison's work as we shall see in discussions of her subsequent novels. At the beginning of her final narrated section, the adult Claudia recalls her mother as she was in 1929, so that her newfound appreciation of her black identity and of how Pecola's tragedy involved them all is concomitant with a renewal of her bond with her female ancestral line. After she has been raped by her father, Pecola lies on the kitchen floor trying to connect the pain between her legs with the face of her mother looming over her. The connection is complex, but it is one that the reader as much as Pecola has to make through the way in which Pauline denied her daughter the mother/daughter bonding which in Morrison's novels, as we shall see in the discussion of *Beloved*, is crucial to black women's self-definition.

Cholly's rape of his daughter is as much rooted in the past as in the present. His young daughter's helpless presence arouses a range of emotions within him, culminating before the rape in a hatred reminiscent of that which years earlier he had transferred to Darlene when the white hunters forced him to 'perform' sexually with her in front of them. Pecola's innocent gesture of scratching the back of her leg with her foot reminds him of the first occasion he was aroused by Pauline. The whole episode is shot through with confusion: between memories of Pauline and the excitement of what is forbidden; between the past with Darlene and the present with Pecola; between desire for Pecola and tenderness for her. When Cholly approaches his daughter he does so crawling on all fours like a child of the animal which whites have made him feel. Nibbling the back of her leg he regresses into the most primal of experiences, while his closed eyes suggest how he is unable to see the full moral implications of what he is doing. Right up until the act of penetration, though, he retains some semblance of moral being, albeit confused, wanting to 'fuck her—tenderly'. When he enters and impregnates her, the text makes clear that all moral responsibility and familial dignity have been abandoned: 'His soul seemed to slip down to his guts . . .' After he has finished, he stands at the end of the chapter as a pathetic figure made limp as the sight of Pecola's 'grayish panties' emphasises, as much by the realisation of what he has done as by his ejaculation. Yet he is also a tragic figure broken, as the final references to his hatred make clear, by what white society has done to him and this is reinforced by the way the account of his rape of Pecola brings the incident with Darlene in the woods to mind. When he and Darlene began to make love together, she tickled his ribs and grabbed his ribcage while he dug his fingers into the neck of her dress; his assault on Pecola begins in earnest when he digs his fingers into her waist. The description of how his soul had fallen down to his guts recalls how the flashlight of the white hunters, forcing him to penetrate Darlene, 'wormed its way into his guts' while 'the gigantic thrust' he makes into his daughter reminds us of how with Darlene 'he almost wished he could do it—hard, long, and painfully . . .'

The women who gossip about the rape perpetrate the contempt which led to it. The novel comes full circle from its initial questioning of the mode of perception that labels some plants flowers and others weeds. Claudia conjures up an image of Pecola's child that is not ugly, as the gossips suggest, but a counterpoint to the white doll of the beginning and to Pauline's pink-white charges: 'It was in a dark, wet place, its head covered with great O's of wool, the black face holding like nickels, two clean black eyes, the flared nose, kissing-thick lips, and the living, breathing silk of black skin'. Claudia's memory of Pecola's victimization by so many people anticipates the ironic juxtaposition of the primer excerpt which introduces Pecola's schizophrenia and which focuses on the friend who will play with Jane. Of course the effect of this is to underscore Pecola's loneliness and lack of friends.

The Bluest Eye is an innovative novel in which its experiments with form are determined by the perspectives and approaches which it brings to the condition of the African-American at the tense interface between two cultures. One of these perspectives is the way in which language is enmeshed with power structures, pursued throughout the novel by the persistent contrasting of the Dick-Jane mythology of the primer with the Breedlove family. Within this ironic interplay of difference, the text brings a particular perspective not only to the impact of white ideologies on the black community, but also to the nature of whiteness and its inappropriateness to determine the contours of African-American culture and lived experience.

JAN FURMAN

Black Girlhood and Black Womanhood:
The Bluest Eye *and* Sula

From the beginning of her writing career Morrison has exercised a keen scrutiny of women's lives. *The Bluest Eye* and *Sula*, Morrison's first and second novels, are to varying extents about black girlhood and black womanhood, about women's connections to their families, their communities, to the larger social networks outside the community, to men, and to each other. Lending themselves to a reading as companion works, the novels complement one another thematically and may, in several ways, be viewed sequentially. (Morrison calls her first four novels "evolutionary. One comes out of the other." In *The Bluest Eye* she was "interested in talking about black girlhood," and in *Sula* she "wanted to move to the other part of their life." She wanted to ask, "what . . . do those feisty little girls grow up to be?") *The Bluest Eye* directs a critical gaze at the process and symbols of imprinting the self during childhood and at what happens to the self when the process is askew and the symbols are defective. In *Sula*, Morrison builds on the knowledge gained in the first novel, revisits childhood, and then moves her characters and readers a step forward into women's struggles to change delimiting symbols and take control of their lives. But excavating an identity that has been long buried beneath stereotype and convention is a wrenching endeavor, and Morrison demonstrates in *Sula* that although recasting one's role in the community is possible, there is a price to be paid for change.

From *Toni Morrison's Fiction*. © 1996 by the University of South Carolina Press.

The Bluest Eye (1970)

The opening lines of *The Bluest Eye* incorporate two signifying aspects of Morrison's fiction. The first sentence, "Quiet as it's kept, there were no marigolds in the fall of 1941," emanates from the African-American community, capturing the milieu of "black women conversing with one another; telling a story, an anecdote, gossip[ing] about some one or event within the circle, the family, the neighborhood." The line also demonstrates Morrison's urge to connect with her reader by choosing "speakerly" phrasing that has a "back fence connotation." Morrison explains:

> The intimacy I was aiming for, the intimacy between the reader and the page, could start up immediately because the secret is being shared, at best, and eavesdropped upon, at the least. Sudden familiarity or instant intimacy seemed crucial to me. I did not want the reader to have time to wonder, "What do I have to do, to give up, in order to read this? What defense do I need, what distance maintain?" Because I know (and the reader does not—he or she had to wait for the second sentence) that this is a terrible story about things one would rather not know anything about.

The line's foreboding aura charitably prepares the reader for powerful truths soon to be revealed. The pervading absence of flowers in 1941 sets that year off from all others and produces a prophetic and ominous quality which unfolds in the second line: "We thought, at the time, that it was because Pecola was having her father's baby that the marigolds did not grow." Exploiting the child speaker's naive but poignant logic, Morrison requires the reader, during this first encounter, to be accountable, to acknowledge a dreadful deed and respond to its dreadful consequences. "If the conspiracy that the opening words announce is entered into by the reader," Morrison explains, "then the book can be seen to open with its close: a speculation on the disruption of 'nature' as being a social disruption with tragic individual consequences in which the reader, as part of the population of the text, is implicated." This three-way collaboration between author, speaker, and reader is the effect for which Morrison strives in all her novels.

From this profoundly stirring beginning Morrison advances to an equally moving examination of Pecola's life—her unloving childhood, her repudiation by nearly everyone she encounters, and finally the complete disintegration of self. Through it all Morrison exposes and indicts those who promulgate standards of beauty and behavior that devalue Pecola's sensitivities and contribute to her marginalized existence.

The search for culprits is not arduous. The storekeeper who sells Mary Jane candies to Pecola avoids touching her hand when she pays and barely disguises his contempt for her: "She looks up at him and sees the vacuum where curiosity ought to lodge. . . . The total absence of human recognition—the glazed separateness. . . . It has an edge; somewhere in the bottom lid is the distaste. . . . The distaste must be for her, her blackness . . . and it is the blackness that accounts for, that creates, the vacuum edged with distance in the white eyes." The white Yacobowski is condemned for his cultural blindness, but he is not the only one responsible for Pecola's pain. Responsibility must be shared by blacks who assuage their own insults from society by oppressing those like Pecola who are vulnerable. Little black boys jeer and taunt her with "Black e mo, Black e mo, Yadaddsleepsnekked," defensively ignoring the color of their own skins. But "it was their contempt for their own blackness that gave the first insult its teeth. They seem to have taken all of their smoothly cultivated ignorance, their exquisitely learned self-hatred, their elaborately designed hopelessness and sucked it all up into a fiery cone of scorn that had burned for ages in the hollows of their minds . . ."

Teachers ignore Pecola in the classroom, giving their attention instead to a "high-yellow dream child with long brown hair" and "sloe green eyes." And when this same high-yellow Maureen Peal declares to Pecola and the MacTeer sisters "I *am* cute! And you ugly! Black and ugly black e mos," she is dangerously affirming intraracial acceptance of the world's denigration of blackness. "Respectable," "milk-brown" women like Geraldine see Pecola's torn dress and uncombed hair and are confronted with the blackness they have spent lifetimes rejecting. For Morrison these women are antithetical to the village culture she respects. They attend to the "careful development of thrift, patience, high morals and good manners" as these are defined by white society. And they fear "the dreadful funkiness of passion, the funkiness of nature, the funkiness of the wide range of human emotions" because these qualities are defined by black society. They are shamed by the "laugh that is a little too loud, the enunciation a little too round; the gesture a little too generous. They hold their behind in for fear of a sway too free; when they wear lipstick, they never cover the entire mouth for fear of lips too thick, and they worry, worry, worry about the edges of their hair." As one of these women, Geraldine executes the tyranny of standardized beauty that enthralls some in the black community and terrorizes too many others.

When Pecola stands in Geraldine's house—tricked there by Geraldine's hateful son—she transgresses a line demarking "colored people" from "niggers," light-skinned from dark, hand-me-down whiteness from genuine culture. In her innocence Pecola does not perceive the transgression or its consequences. To her, Geraldine's world and house are beautiful. The house's ordered prettiness sharply contrasts the shabby makedo appearance of the Breedlove's storefront. Geraldine, however, does perceive Pecola's outrageous breech, and the hurting child that Pecola is becomes a "nasty little black bitch" in Geraldine's mouth. Geraldine sets her teeth against any recognition of some part of who she is in Pecola. To Pecola, Geraldine is "the pretty milk-brown lady in the pretty gold and green house." To Morrison, she is a shadow image of the Dick-and-Jane life, a sadistic approximation of the storybook people. Through her Morrison demonstrates that such a life as Geraldine's is only validated by exclusion of others.

Michael Awkward discusses this "purgative abuse" of Pecola in terms of the black community's guilt about its own inability to measure up to some external ideal of beauty and behavior. Pecola objectifies this failure (which results in self-hatred) and must be purged. She becomes the black community's shadow of evil (even as the black community is the white community's evil). "In combating the shadow . . . the group is able to rid itself ceremonially of the veil that exists within both the individual member and the community at large. To be fully successful, such exorcism requires a visibly imperfect, shadow-consumed scapegoat" like Pecola.

Even her parents, Cholly and Pauline Breedlove, relate to Pecola in this way. Ironically named since they breed not love but violence and misery, Cholly and Pauline eventually destroy their daughter, whose victimization is a bold symbol of their own despair and frustrations. In the pathos of their defeated lives, Morrison demonstrates the process by which self-hatred becomes scapegoating.

Pauline's lame foot makes her pitiable and invisible until she marries Cholly. But pleasure in marriage lasts only until she moves from Kentucky to Ohio and confronts northern standards of physical beauty and style. She is despised by snooty black women who snicker at her lameness, her unstraightened hair, and her provincial speech. In the movie theaters she seeks relief from these shortcomings through daydreams of Clark Gable and Jean Harlow. But even in high heels, makeup, and a Harlow hairstyle Pauline is a failure. "In equating physical beauty with virtue, she stripped her mind, bound it, and collected self-contempt by the heap," which she deposits on her husband and children who fail by "the scale of absolute beauty . . . she absorbed in full from the silver screen." Eventually, Pauline gives up on her own family and takes refuge in the soft beauty surrounding her in the Fisher home, where she works—the crisp linens, white towels, the little Fisher girl's yellow hair. She cannot afford such beauty and style. In the Fisher house, however, she has dominion over creditors and service people "who humiliated her when she went to them on her own behalf [but] respected her, were even intimidated by her, when she spoke for the Fishers." With the Fishers she had what she could not have at home— "power, praise, and luxury." By the time Pecola finds herself awkwardly standing in the Fisher's kitchen, responsible for the spilled remains of a freshly baked pie at her feet, Pauline is incapable of a mother's love and forgiveness. Her best response is knocking Pecola to the floor and running to console the crying Fisher child.

In substituting fierce intolerance of her family for love, Pauline refuses what she cannot transform. Her husband is an irresponsible drunk; the son and daughter are sloven. Only she has order and beauty and only in the Fisher house. Under these conditions Pauline is reborn as self-righteous martyr with no time for movies, unfulfilled dreams, and foolish notions of romantic love. "All the meaningfulness of her life was in her work. . . . She was an active church woman . . . defended herself mightily against Cholly . . . and felt she was fulfilling a mother's role conscientiously when she pointed out their father's faults to keep them from having them, or punished them when they showed any slovenliness, no matter how slight, when she worked twelve to sixteen hours a day to support them."

Like Pauline, Cholly too is driven by personal demons which he attempts to purge in violence against his family. Pauline does not see or understand Cholly's hurts, but Morrison represents them as remarkably egregious. Callously abandoned on a garbage dump by his mother, years later Cholly searches for the father who also discards him. His response to his father's angry denunciations—crying and soiling his pants—eclipses any opportunity for emotional maturity and returns him, in a sense, to the help-lessness of his abandonment in infancy. After the rejection, in a nearby river he seeks relief, even rebirth, curled for hours in the fetal position with fists in eyes. For a while he finds consolation in "the dark, the warmth, the quiet . . . [engulfing him] like the skin and flesh of an elderberry protecting its own seed." Protection is short-lived, however. There is no prelapsarian innocence available to Cholly.

In marrying Pauline, Cholly seems fully recovered from these earlier traumas. Initially, he is kind, compassionate, protective, but these feelings too are fleeting. He retreats from her emotional dependence, he is humil-iated by economic powerlessness, and he mitigates his frustrations in drink and abuse. In turning on Pauline, Cholly fights whom he can and not whom he should. This is the lesson of childhood learned when he is forced by armed white men who discover him with Darlene in the woods to continue his first act of sexual intimacy while they watch and ridicule. When the men leave in search of other prey, Cholly realizes that hating them is futile, and he decides instead to hate Darlene for witnessing his degradation. He could not protect her so he settles for despising her. Later Pauline comes to stand for Darlene in Cholly's mind: "He poured out on her the sum of all his inarticulate fury and aborted desires." Cholly, then, needs Pauline to objectify his failure.

His treatment of Pecola may also be seen in terms of scapegoating but not entirely. While Pecola's ugliness is an affront to Pauline's surreptitious creation of beauty in the Fisher house, it is a sad reminder to Cholly of not only his unhappiness but Pecola's as well. Such concern makes him a somewhat sympathetic character. He is one of Morrison's traveling men, one whose freedom to do as he pleases is jeopardized by dependent, possessive women. He has roamed around dangerously, carelessly, irresponsibly, lovingly. The appealing contradiction of his life could find expression only in black music. "Only a musician would sense, know, without even knowing that he knew, that Cholly was free. Dangerously free." After his mother's abandonment and his father's rejection, Cholly has little to lose, and his behavior is disdainful of consequences. "It was in this godlike state that he met Pauline Williams," and marriage to her threatens to conquer him.

In romanticizing Cholly, Morrison defies the unflattering orthodoxy of black maleness and makes peace with the conflict between responsibility to family and freedom to leave. Morrison respects the freedom even as she embraces the responsibility. In the freedom she sees "tremendous possibility for masculinity among black men." Sometimes such men are unemployed or in prison, but they have a spirit of adventure and a deep complexity that interests Morrison. No doubt she views their freedom as a residue of the "incredible . . . magic and feistiness in black men that nobody has been able to wipe out." Cholly exercises his freedom, but not before he commits a heinous crime against Pecola. Even his crime, however, is tempered by the author's compassion for Cholly. Coming home drunk and full of self-pity, Cholly sees Pecola and is overcome with love and regret that he has nothing to relieve her hopelessness. "Guilt and impotence rose in a bilious duct. What could he do for her—ever? What give her? What say to her ? What could a burned-out black man say to the hunched back of his eleven-year-old daughter?" His answer is rape—in spite of himself. In rendering this incomprehensible instance, Morrison captures the curious mixture of hate and tenderness that consumes Cholly. "The hatred would not let him pick her up" when the violation is over; "the tenderness forced him to cover her." The awful irony of his position is overwhelming. In the end Cholly's complexity dominates the moment. Having never been parented, "he could not even comprehend what such a relationship should be." And being dangerously free, he has no restraints.

Morrison does have sympathy for Cholly (she admits that she connects "Cholly's 'rape' by the white men to his own of his daughter"), but he is not absolved; he dies soon after in a workhouse. And Morrison does not minimize his crime against his daughter. Pecola's childlike "stunned silence," "the tightness of her vagina," the painfully "gigantic thrust," her "fingers clenching," her "shocked body," and finally her unconsciousness bear witness to Morrison's aim in the novel to represent Pecola's perspective, to translate her heartbreak. "This most masculine act of aggression becomes feminized in my language," Morrison says. It is "passive," she continues, "and I think, more accurately repellent when deprived of the male 'glamor of shame' rape is (or once was) routinely given."

Feminizing language does not lead Morrison to comfortable binary oppositions of good and evil, feminine and masculine. Rather, it leads to a sensitive treatment of the complex emotions that determine character, male and female. In Morrison's writing there are no easy villains to hate; there are no predictable behaviors.

Just as Cholly is not as reprehensible as he might be, Pauline is not as sympathetic as she might be if she were stereotypically portrayed as an abused wife and as a mother. In fact, Pauline in some sense is as culpable as Cholly for Pecola's suffering. Cholly's love is corrupt and tainted, but Pauline is unloving. After the rape Morrison subtly alludes to the difference: "So when the child regained consciousness, she was lying on the kitchen floor under a heavy quilt, trying to connect the pain between her legs with the face of her mother looming over her." Is Pauline associated with the pain? She did not physically rape Pecola, but she has ravaged the child's self-worth and left her vulnerable to assaults of various proportions.

With single-minded determination Pauline survives, but Pecola withdraws into the refuge of insanity. Like the dandelions whose familiar yellow heads she thinks are pretty, Pecola is poisoned by rejection. But unlike the dandelions, she does not have the strength to persist, and in madness she simply substitutes her inchoate reality with a better one: she has blue eyes which everyone admires and envies. In pathetic conversations with an imaginary friend, Pecola repeatedly elicits confirmation that hers are "the bluest eyes in the whole world," that they are "much prettier than the sky. Prettier than Alice-and-Jerry Storybook eyes."

Pecola's sad fantasy expresses Morrison's strongest criticism of a white standard of beauty that excludes most black women and that destroys those who strive to measure up but cannot. Everywhere there are reminders of this failure: the coveted blond-haired, blue-eyed dolls that arrive at Christmas, Shirley Temple movies, high-yellow dream children like Maureen Peal. And for Pecola the smiling white face of little Mary Jane on the candy wrapper, "blond hair in gentle disarray, blue eyes looking at her out of a world of clean comfort." In desperation Pecola believes that nothing bad could be viewed by such eyes. Cholly and Mrs. Breedlove (Pecola's name for her mother) would not fight; her teachers and classmates would not despise her; she would be safe. And, ironically, perhaps Pecola is right. With the blue eyes of her distorted reality comes the awful safety of oblivion.

Pecola's tragedy exposes the fallacy of happily-ever-after storybook life. Morrison repeatedly calls attention to this falseness. In the prologue and chapter headings are recounted the elementary story of Dick and Jane, mother and father:

Here is the house. It is green and white. It has a red door. It is very pretty. Here is the family. Mother, Father, Dick, and Jane live in the green-and-white house. They are very happy. See Jane. She has a red dress. She wants to play. Who will play with Jane? See the cat. It goes meow-meow. Come and play. Come and play with Jane. The kitten will not play. See Mother. Mother is very nice. Mother, will you play with Jane? Mother laughs. Laugh, Mother, laugh. See Father. He is big and strong. Father, will you play with Jane? Father is smiling. Smile, Father, smile. See the dog. Bowwow goes the dog. Do you want to play with Jane? See the dog run. Run, dog, run. Look, look. Here comes a friend. The friend will play with Jane. Play, Jane, play.

In two subsequent versions Morrison distorts the Dick-and-Jane text. In bold print with no spacing between words, these latter passages take on a frenetic tone that signals perversion of communal perfection for Morrison's characters, who do not blithely run and play and live happily ever after. In removing the standard grammatical codes, symbols of Western culture, Morrison expurgates the white text as she constructs the black. Timothy Bell aptly point out that "Morrison is literally deconstructing the essential white text, removing capitalizations, punctuation, and finally the spacing until the white text is nothing more than a fragmentation of its former self at the beginning of the chapter." Home for Pecola is not the green and white picture-perfect house of the white myth. Home is a storefront where mother and father curse and fight, brother runs away from home, and sister wishes with all her soul for blue eyes. Pecola appropriates the storybook version of life because her own is too gruesome. In her life she is subject to other people's cruel whims to which she can offer no voice of protest.

Indeed, she has no voice in this text at all, a condition which loudly echoes her entire existence. She has no control over the events in her life and no authority over the narrative of those events. That authority goes to twelve-year-old Claudia, who narrates major portions of Pecola's story with compassion and understanding. Claudia and her older sister Frieda are the "we" of the opening paragraph. They witness Pecola's despair and try to save her. "Her pain agonized me," Claudia says, "I wanted to open her up, crisp her edges, ram a stick down that hunched and curving spine, force her to stand erect and spit the misery out on the streets." But the sisters fail. They do not save Pecola from her breakup. As the girls mourn their failure, Morrison chronicles the loss of their innocence. But unlike Pecola's short-circuited innocence, their loss is part of a natural ritual of growing up.

Morrison proffers Claudia and Frieda as foils to Pecola. They are strong and sturdy; Pecola is not. Claudia's independence and confidence especially throw Pecola's helplessness into stark relief. For Claudia, blue-eyed dolls at Christmas and Shirley Temple dancing with Bojangles Robinson are unappealing and even insulting. With youthful but penetrating insight, she declares her exemption from "The universal love of white dolls, Shirley Temples, and Maureen Peals."

Claudia and her sister traverse Morrison's landscape of black girlhood. Bound by a social environment that is hostile to their kind, they have "become headstrong, devious and arrogant" enough to dismiss limitations and believe that they can "change the course of events and alter a human life." With ingenious faith in themselves, Claudia and Frieda attempt to rescue Pecola and her baby. They would make beauty where only ugliness resided by planting marigolds deep in the earth and receiving the magic of their beauty as a sign of Pecola's salvation. When neither marigolds nor Pecola survive, the girls blame a community that is seduced by a white standard of beauty and that makes Pecola its scapegoat: "All of us—all who knew her—felt so wholesome after we cleaned ourselves on her. We were beautiful when we stood astride her ugliness. . . . We honed our egos on her, padded our characters with her frailty, and yawned in the fantasy of our strength."

For the most part their parents, Mr. and Mrs. MacTeer, save Claudia and Frieda from this sort of persecution. Mr. MacTeer (unlike Cholly) acts as a father should in protecting his daughter from a lecherous boarder. Mrs. MacTeer's place is not in a white family's kitchen, but in her own, where familiar smells hold sway and where her singing about "hard times, bad times and somebody-done-gone-and-left-me times" proclaims that pain is endurable, even sweet. To her daughters she bequeaths a legacy of compassion for others and defiance in the face of opposition. Her love for them was "thick and dark as Alaga syrup." The MacTeers embody the communal resiliency at the heart of black culture.

Mrs. MacTeer is not one of Morrison's ancestors—a person wise in the ways of life who transmits that wisdom and knowledge of self to the uninitiated. She is, however, one of Morrison's nurturers. Claudia remembers the feel of her mother's hands on her forehead and chest when she is sick: "I think," she says, "of somebody with hands who does not want me to die." Mrs. MacTeer takes Pecola in when Cholly burns his family out. She presides over Pecola's first menses, hugging her reassuringly (the only hug the adolescent Pecola ever receives; Mrs. Breedlove's hugs and assurances are reserved for the little Fisher girl). But Mrs. MacTeer's influence in Pecola's life is short in duration. With no one else available Pecola turns to the whores who live upstairs over the storefront for instruction given lovingly. China, Marie, and Poland stand in opposition to the Geraldines in the community. They are not pretentious heirs to false puritanical values, and Morrison respects their unvarnished natures. "Three merry gargoyles. Three merry harridans," They are quick to laugh or sing. Defying all stereotypes of pitiable women gone wrong, they make no apologies for themselves and seek no sympathy. "They were not young girls in whores' clothing, or whores regretting their loss of innocence. They were whores in whores' clothes, whores who had never been young and had no word for innocence." Pecola loves these women, and they are more than willing to share the lessons they've learned, but their lessons are wrong for Pecola. They can tell her stories that are breezy and rough about lawless men and audacious women. But they cannot teach her what she wants most to know: how to be loved by a mother and a father, by a community, and by a society.

For that she turns to Soaphead Church, the itinerant spiritualist and flawed human being. A pedophile and a con man, Soaphead has not transcended the pain of life's humiliations and is deeply scarred. Morrison describes him as "that kind of black" for whom blackness is a burden to be borne with self-righteous indignation. Of West Indian and colonial English ancestry that has long been in social decline, Soaphead, existing at the bottom of the descent, is "wholly convinced that if black people were more like white people they would be better off." He, therefore, appreciates Pecola's yearning for blue eyes. But Soaphead's powers are fraudulent as are his claims to have helped Pecola by "giving" her blue eyes; he does little more than use her in his own schemes of revenge against God and man. With no one to help her counteract the love of white dolls with blue eyes, Pecola cannot help herself, and she is obliged to be the victim—always.

Indeed the effects of Pecola's devastation are unrelenting as measured in the passing of time in the novel—season after season: Morrison names each of the novel's sections after a season of the year, beginning with autumn and ending with summer. The headings are ironically prophetic preludes to the story segments. They stand out as perverse contradictions of Pecola's experiences: thematic progression is not from dormancy to renewal for Pecola. In spring she is violated; by summer she is annihilated. Morrison uses this disruption of nature to signal the cosmic proportion of Pecola's injury.

Sula (1973)

The Bluest Eye was not commercially successful at the time of its publication (its popularity has risen in tandem with Morrison's reputation). Yet, it did inaugurate its author's public literary life. After writing it, Morrison became a frequent reviewer in the *New York Times* and an authoritative commentator on black culture and women's concerns. Three years later *Sula* was both a commercial and critical triumph. It was excerpted in *Redbook* and widely reviewed. The Book-of-the-Month Club selected it as an alternate, and in 1975 it was nominated for the National Book Award.

If *The Bluest Eye* chronicles to some extent an annihilation of self, *Sula*, on the contrary, validates resiliency in the human spirit and celebrates the self. In *Sula* Morrison returns to the concerns of girlhood explored in her first novel, but this time she approaches her subject in celebration, as if to see what miracles love and friendship may accomplish for Sula and Nel that they could not for Pecola, Claudia, and Frieda.

Sula Peace and Nel Wright are each the only daughter of mothers whose distance leaves the young girls alone with dreams of someone to ease the solitude. When they first met, "they felt the ease and comfort of old friends." Indeed "their meeting was fortunate, for it let them use each other to grown on." Sula's spontaneous intensity is relieved by Nel's passive reserve. Sula loves the ordered neatness of Nel's home and her life, and Nel likes Sula's "household of throbbing disorder constantly awry with things, people, voices and the slamming of doors . . ." Over the years "they found relief in each other's personality."

In examining their friendship, Morrison tests its endurance. As she says, not much had been done with women as friends; men's relationships are often the subject of fiction, but what about women's strongest bonds? As perfect complements, one incomplete without the other, Sula and Nel together face life, death, and marriage, and eventually they also must face separation. Throughout, Morrison affirms the necessity of their collaboration.

Adolescence for Nel and Sula is marked not by individuation, but by merger, as a single, provocative play scene illustrates. In the summer of their twelfth year, with thoughts of boys and with "their small breasts just now beginning to create some pleasant discomfort when they were lying on their stomachs," the girls escape to the park. In silence and without looking at each other, they begin to play in the grass, stroking the blades. "Nel found a thick twig and, with her thumbnail, pulled away its bark until it was stripped to a smooth, creamy innocence." Sula does the same. Soon they begin poking "rhythmically and intensely into the earth," making small neat holes. "Nel began a more strenuous digging and, rising to her knee, was careful to scoop out the dirt as she made her hole deeper. Together they worked until the two holes were one and the same." In their symbolic sexual play, Nel and Sula, unlike Pecola, have absolute control in this necessary right of passage (without the intrusion of a masculine presence) which conjoins them until, like the holes, they are one and the same.

Two other significant moments define their intimacy as well. The first is Sula's cutting off the tip of her finger in response to a threat by a group of white boys whose menacing bodies block the girl's route home. If she could do that to herself, what would she do to them, Sula asks the shocked boys. The second is the death of Chicken Little, the little boy whose body Sula swings around and around in play until her hands slip, and he flies out over the river and drowns. Nel watches, and no one discovers their culpability. At the graveside they hold hands. "At first, as they stood there, their hands were clenched together. They relaxed slowly until during the walk back home their fingers were laced in as gentle a clasp as that of any two young girl-friends trotting up the road on a summer day wondering what happened to butterflies in winter."

Not even Nel's marriage dissolves their "friendship [that] was so close, they themselves had difficulty distinguishing one's thoughts from the other's." They are both happy; Nel becomes a wife, and Sula goes to college. Ten years later Sula's return imparts a magic to Nel's days that marriage had not. "Her old friend had come home. . . . Sula, whose past she had lived through and with whom the present was a constant sharing of perceptions. Talking to Sula had always been a conversation with herself." Their lives resume an easy rhythm until Nel walks into her bedroom and finds her husband and Sula naked. Not surprisingly, this episode supersedes the women's friendship. Jude leaves town, Nel, and their children, and Nel blames Sula. Three years later, when Nel visits a dying Sula, she asks, "Why you didn't love me enough to leave him alone. To let him love me. You had to take him away." Sula replies, "What you mean take him away? . . . If we were such good friends, how come you couldn't get over it?"

With Sula's question Morrison calls into doubt the primacy of Nel's marriage over women's friendship, intimating that their friendship may even supplant the marriage. Years after Sula's death, Nel comes to this realization at her friend's grave. "All that time, all that time, I thought I was missing Jude. . . . We was girls together. . . .O Lord, Sula . . . girl, girl, girlgirlgirl."

Nel and Sula's estrangement offers Morrison an opportunity to examine women's lives in and out of marriage. As girls Nel and Sula had cunningly authored the dimensions of their own existence without the permission or approval of their families or the community. "Because each had discovered years before that they were neither white nor male and that all freedom and triumph was forbidden to them, they had set about creating something else to be." Morrison does not elaborate further on the specific nature of their creation, but clearly each positions herself just outside the village perspective, thinking and behaving with a certain independence. "In the safe harbor of each other's company they could afford to abandon the ways of other people and concentrate on their own perceptions of things."

The experience that determines Nel's perspective is a train ride with her mother. The two travel for days from Ohio to New Orleans for Nel's great-grandmother's funeral. Her mother's shuffling acquiescence in the face of the white conductor's hostility during the trip, the sullen black male passengers whose refusal to help her mother reflects their own helpless humiliation, the indignity of squatting to relieve themselves in the brush in full view of the train, her mother's stiff shame of her own creole mother's life as a prostitute—all these experiences teach Nel lessons about other people's vulnerabilities. Back home in the safety of her bedroom she resolves to develop her strengths. Looking in the mirror, she whispers to herself "I'm me. . . . I'm me. I'm not their daughter. I'm not Nel. I'm me. Me . . ." Adopting me-ness as her mantra, Nel gathers power and joy, and the "strength to cultivate a friend [Sula] in spite of her mother." Nel's daring is eclipsed, however, by marriage to Jude. For Helene Wright, Nel's mother, marriage is one of the neat conditions of living that defines a woman's place, and Nel accepts a similar arrangement for herself. Nel does not choose Jude; she accepts his choosing her as a way of completing himself. Without Nel, Jude is an enraged "waiter hanging around a kitchen like a woman" because bigotry keeps him from doing better. "With her he was head of a household pinned to an unsatisfactory job out of necessity. The two of them together would make one Jude." In marrying Jude, Nel gives up her youthful dreams (before she met Sula) of being "wonderful" and of "trips she would take, alone . . . to faraway places." In marrying Jude, she gives up her me-ness.

Predictably, when Jude leaves, after his betrayal with Sula, Nel suffers psychic disintegration, and later, after a necessary recovery, she endures shrinkage of the self. She considers the release that may come with death, but that will have to wait because she has three children to raise. In this condition Nel wraps herself in the conventional mantle of sacrifice and martyrdom and takes her place with the rest of the women in the community. Although Nel does not discover it until after Sula's death and she is old, the real loss in her life is that of Sula and not Jude. And the real tragedy is that she has allowed herself to become less than she was.

Sula is different from Nel. It is Sula's rebellious spirit that fuels the intermittent moments of originality that Nel manages to have. In Sula's presence Nel has "sparkle or sputter." Sula resists any authority or controls, and

Morrison offers her as one of the lawless individuals whose life she is so fond of examining. From Sula's days in childhood when she retreated to the attic, she rebels against conventionality. She is surprised and saddened by Nel's rejection of her over Jude. She had not expected Nel to behave "the way the others would have." But nothing, not even her closest and only friend's censures will force Sula to abridge herself.

Even near death, Sula will have none of Nel's limitations. To the end she proclaims, "I sure did live in this world. . . . I got my mind. And what goes on in it. Which is to say, I got me." Sula's me-ness remains intact; she has not betrayed herself as Nel has, and any loneliness she feels is a price she is willing to pay for freedom.

By and large, Sula's assessment of her past is credible. Only once has she come close to subsuming herself to some other, named Ajax. Shortly after Ajax shows up at her door with a quart of milk tucked under each arm, Sula begins to think of settling down with him. All of the men in her past had, over the years, "merged into one large personality" of sameness. "She had been looking . . . for a friend, and it took her a while to discover that a lover was not a comrade and could never be—for a woman." But those thoughts exist before she meets Ajax; he is different in some ways. He brings her beautiful and impractical gifts: "clusters of black berries still on their branches, four meal-fried porgies wrapped in a salmon-covered sheet of the Pittsburgh *Courier*, a handful of jacks, two boxes of lime Jell-Well, a hunk of ice-wagon ice . . ." Sula is most interested in him, however, because he talks to her and is never condescending in conversation. "His refusal to baby or protect her, his assumption that she was both tough and wise—all that coupled with a wide generosity of spirit . . . sustained Sula's interest and enthusiasm."

Their interlude ends when Ajax discovers Sula's possessiveness. For the first time Sula wants to be responsible for a man and to protect him from the dangers of life. Giving in to a nesting instinct that is new for her, she is on the verge of making his life her own. But before that happens Ajax leaves, and Sula has only his driver's license as proof of his ever having been there. Sula's sorrow is intense, but short-lived, unlike Nel's enduring suffering for Jude. In the end, when Nel accuses her of never being able to keep a man, Sula counters that she would never waste life trying to keep a man: "They ain't worth more than me. And besides, I never loved no man because he was worth it. Worth didn't have nothing to do with it. . . . My mind did. That's all." Sula had needed Nel, but she had never needed a man to extend herself. Even in lovemaking she had manufactured her own satisfaction, "in the postcoital privateness in which she met herself, welcomed herself, and joined herself in matchless harmony." With Ajax those private moments had not been necessary, but without him Sula abides. The self, Morrison instructs, should not be liable in its own betrayal.

Sula is, without a doubt, a manifesto of freedom, and that fact in large part accounts for its popularity with readers and critics who champion its triumphant chronicle of a black woman's heroism. That does not mean, however, that the novel approximates the ideal or that Sula's character is not flawed. Morrison describes her as an artist without a medium. "Her strangeness . . . was the consequence of an idle imagination. Had she paints, or clay, or knew the discipline of the dance, or strings; had she anything to engage her tremendous curiosity and her gift for metaphor, she might have exchanged the restlessness and preoccupation with whim for an activity that provided him with all she yearned for." An art form augments life by giving it purpose; perhaps it teaches the individual compassion, but without it someone like Sula is, as Morrison describes her, strange, naive, and dangerous.

In this view Sula is without an essential quality of humanity. She has taken little from others, but more important she has *given* little. She does not mean others harm: "She had no thought at all of causing Nel pain when she bedded down with Jude," but without the moderating and mediating influence of her own humanity, Sula is unthinking and childlike. It is as if some crucial element of consciousness had been arrested in childhood when she heard her mother say to a friend that she loved Sula but did not like her or when "her major feeling of responsibility [for Chicken Little's death] had been exorcised." After that, "she had no center, no speck around which to grow." The most bizarre episodes of her conduct may be understood in this context: feeling no emotion but curiosity while watching her mother burn to death, putting her grandmother in a nursing home for no good reason, and, of course, having sex with her best friend's husband.

Imperfect as she is, however, Sula does escape the falseness and emptiness of Nel's life. As Nel takes her place beside the other women in the community, she and they are identified with spiders, whose limitations keep them dangling "in the dark dry places . . . terrified of the free fall." And if they do fall, they envision themselves as victims of someone else's evil. Sula, on the other hand, is one of Morrison's characters who is associated with flight, the metaphor for freedom. Sula is not afraid to use her wings fully to "surrender to the downward flight." She is unafraid of the free fall.

Flight in Morrison is usually associated with men and not with women, who are more often than not Morrison's nurturers. Of course, Morrison offers neither quality by itself as the archetypal model; in the best scenarios the individual is capable of both nurturance and flight. Indeed, Nel and Sula are incomplete without each other. As Morrison says, "Nel knows and believes in all the laws of that community. She is the community. She believes in its values. Sula does not. She does not believe in any of those laws and breaks them all. Or ignores them." But both positions are problematic, Morrison continues: "Nel does not make that 'leap'—she doesn't know about herself [she does not discover until too late, for example that she had watched Chicken Little's drowning with excitement]. . . . Sula, on the other hand, knows all there is to know about herself. . . . But she has trouble making a connection with other people and just feeling that lovely sense of accomplishment of being very close in a very strong way." Nurturance without invention and imagination is analogous to flight without responsibility. Ajax is the only other character in the novel who is identified with flying. He loves airplanes, and he thinks often of airplanes, pilots, "and the deep sky that held them both." When he takes long trips to big cities, other people imagine him pursuing some exotic fun that is unavailable to them; in truth, he is indulging his obsession with flying by standing around airports watching planes take off.

Metaphorically, Ajax is always in flight—from conventionality. Without work, but willing to be responsible for himself, Ajax does not take cover in domesticity. Unlike Jude, who is only half a man without Nel as his refuge from life's injustices, Ajax does not need Sula to kiss his hurts and make them better. Unlike Jude, Ajax has self-esteem that is not diminished by white men's refusal of work, and unlike Jude, he does not run away and leave behind a wife and children. Ajax does leave Sula, but his action is not a betrayal. Ajax and Sula had come together, not as fractional individuals in need of the other to be complete, but as whole people, and when that equation is threatened by Sula's possessiveness, Ajax leaves Dayton and airplanes. Of men like Ajax Morrison writes:

> They are the misunderstood people in the world. There's a wildness that they have, a nice wildness. It has bad effects in a society such as the one in which we live. It's pre-Christ in the best sense. It's Eve. When I see this wildness gone in a person, it's sad. This special lack of restraint, which is a part of human life and is best typified in certain black males, is of particular interest to me. . . . Everybody knows who "that man" is, and they may give him bad names and call him a "street nigger" but when you take away the vocabulary of denigration, what you have is somebody who is fearless and who is comfortable with that fearlessness. It's not about meanness. It's a kind of self-flagellant resistance to certain kinds of control, which is fascinating. Opposed to accepted notions of progress, the lock step life, they live in the world unreconstructed and that's it."

As characters in flight both Ajax and Sula stand in opposition to the community that is firmly rooted in ritual and tradition. As the devoted son of "an evil conjure woman," whom most regarded as a neglectful mother, Ajax is accustomed to rebuffing public opinion, and as a man he is given a license to do so. As a woman Sula must *take* that license, and in the fray she alienates the community. Sula returns to town after ten years and refuses to honor the town's ceremonies: "She came to their church suppers without underwear, bought their steaming platters of food and merely picked at it— relishing nothing, exclaiming over no one's ribs or cobbler. They believed that she was laughing at their God." Soon the town names her a devil and prepares to live with its discovery. In fact, Morrison says, the town's toleration of Sula is in some way a measure of their generosity: "She would have been destroyed by any other place; she was permitted to 'be' only in that context, and no one stoned her or threw her out."

Clearly, however, the town needs Sula as much as or perhaps more than she needs it. In giving the novel an extraordinary sense of place, Morrison builds the community's character around its defense against this internal threat. Sula is not the only danger, but for a time she is the most compelling. Her defiance unifies the community by objectifying its danger. Women protected their husbands; husbands embraced their wives and children. "In general [everyone] band[ed] together against the devil in their midst." No one considered destroying Sula or running her out of town. They had lived with evil and misfortune all of their lives; it "was something to be first recognized, then dealt with, survived, outwitted, triumphed over."

The predominant evil in their lives, more pervasive and enduring than Sula, is the external force of oppression. Morrison's characteristic treatment of bigotry is not to delineate the defining episodes of white hatred but instead to direct attention to the black community's ingenious methods of coping: using humor, garnering strength from folk traditions, and perversely refusing to be surprised or defeated by experience. Residents of the Bottom waste little time complaining and get on with the business of their lives. Morrison captures here, as she does elsewhere, the rhythms of the black community: men on the street corner, in pool halls; women shelling peas, cooking dinner, at the beauty parlor, in church, interpreting dreams, and playing the numbers, working roots.

Yet, Morrison says, the music and dance belie the pain of men without work and of families living on the frayed edges of the prosperous white town below. Each contact with life beyond the borders of the Bottom recalls the isolating constraints of race prejudice: Helene's brutal reminder by the train conductor that her place is in the car with the other blacks; Sula and Nel's encounter with the four white teenagers who determine the physical boundaries of the girl's world by forcing them to walk in round-about circuitous routes home from school; Shadrack's arrest by police who find him "wandering" in the white part of town. Even dead Chicken Little's space is designated by the bargeman who drays the child's body from the river, dumps it into a burlap sack, and tosses it in a corner. The sheriff's reports that "they didn't have no niggers in their country," but that some lived in those hills "cross the river, up above medallion," underscores the expectation that black life will not spill out of the hills. Morrison acknowl-edges the destructiveness of this enforced separation, but she also treats the isolation ironically by converting its negative meaning into a positive one. Cordoned off as they are, the people are self-sufficient; they create a neigh-borhood within those hills "which they could not break" because it gives continuity to their past and present.

In assigning character to the Bottom, Morrison establishes worth in terms of human relationships. As she says:

> there was this life-giving very, very strong sustenance that people got from the neighborhood. . . . All the responsibilities of the neighborhood. So that people were taken care of, or locked up or whatever. If they were sick, other people took care of them; if they were old, other people took care of them; if they needed something to eat, other people took care of them; if they were mad, other people provided a small space for them, or related to their madness or tried to find out the limits of their madness.

Shadrack's presence in the Bottom is evidence of the community's will-ingness to absorb the most bizarre of its own. When Shadrack returns from World War I and does not know "who or what he was . . . with no past, no language, no tribe," he struggles "to order and focus experience" and to conquer his fear of death. The result is National Suicide Day, which Shadrack establishes as the third of January, believing "that if one day a year were devoted to it [death] everybody could get it out of the way and the rest of the year would be safe and free." At first frightened of him, in time people embrace him and his day. Once they "understood the boundaries and nature of his madness, they could fit him, so to speak into the scheme of things." That is, according to Morrison, the black community's way.

Sula's mother, Hannah, and grandmother Eva had borne their share of these community responsibilities in the big house where youth, old age, disease, and insanity kept company. (Eva takes the life of her son, Plum, but Morrison treats it as an act of compassion, not of selfishness.) Sula is different, however. In refusing to become a part of the community, she refuses a part of her cultural and personal history. Her determination to define herself and to redefine a woman's role places her at odds with the community. And yet, the community makes room for her in a way perhaps that no other place would. There are both variety and cohesiveness in the Bottom, where characters as unlike as Sula, Nel, Ajax, and Shadrack coexist. "There are hundreds of small towns" like Medallion, Morrison explains, "and that's where most black people live. . . . And that's where the juices came from and that's where we *made it*, not made it in terms of success but made who we are."

Morrison suggests that this quality of neighborhood life is endangered. As the buildings and trees are leveled in the Bottom to make room for a new golf course and as blacks leave the hills to occupy spaces vacated by whites in the valley below, Morrison wonders if economic and social gains are worth the sacrifice of community, because without community the cultural traditions that inform character are lost to future generations.

LAURIE VICKROY

The Politics of Abuse: The Traumatized Child in Toni Morrison's The Bluest Eye and Marguerite Duras

With the political liberation of various colonies in the 1950s there also came the recognition of the need for a more profound investigation of the dynamics of oppression and subjugation. In particular, cultural theorists began to focus on the psychological effects of colonization and the emotional strategies employed in response to such pressures. Thus, Ashis Nandy drew attention to the way that the relationship between the colonizer and the colonized was constructed as one of "civilizing" parent/"primitive" child; Frantz Fanon demonstrated the way that racist attitudes could be internalized and could transcend any obvious issue of skin color; and Albert Memmi examined the self-loathing emerging from conditions of oppression, i.e., "injustice, insults, humiliation and insecurity." Similarly, literary critics began to show how psychological theory can help to elucidate not merely the artistic depiction of colonized subjects but also the narrative techniques used in politically-conscious fiction. Patrick Colm Hogan, for example, has used Lacan's notions of the socially imposed ego to explore the relations between cultural domination and madness in Bessie Head's *A Question of Power*, and Shoshana Felman and Dori Laub have explored the way that traumatic responses are significant factors in the recovery and narration of Holocaust memories.

From *Mosaic* 29, no. 2 (June 1996). © 1996 *Mosaic*.

My purpose in the following essay is to further this line of research by providing a more detailed analysis of the relationship to trauma to social oppression and by showing how this connection is dramatized in the critiques of colonialism evident in Toni Morrison's and Marguerite Duras's fiction. Although Morrison addresses white American racial dominance in the 1930s and Duras addresses British/French governmental dominance in East Asia during these years, both writers are concerned with the relation between social power and individual psychology and both try to give voice to those who are traumatized by oppressive social and familial forces. In particular I want to focus on Morrison's *The Bluest Eye* (1970) and Duras's *The Vice-Consul* (1966), because both novels introduce a new element into colonialist discourse: they feature as protagonists young subaltern girls not previously presented in the Western literary tradition. For both writers, traumatized children provide not merely poignant metaphors but also concrete examples of the neglect, exploitation, disempowerment and disavowal of certain communities and even entire cultures (e.g., African American or Third World citizens). In this way, these novels encourage us to see "colonialism" as an ongoing problem and in doing so they serve to challenge the abstractness which frequently tends to characterize "postcolonial" theorizing. I will demonstrate particularly how these writers challenge the subordination of women and children by testifying to their experience and by engaging their readers in that experience.

Trauma is an event in an individual's life which is "defined by its intensity, by the subject's incapacity to respond adequately to it, and by the upheaval and long-lasting effects that it brings about in the psychical organization." Kai Erikson emphasizes that trauma can result "from a constellation of life's experiences as well as from a discrete event—from a prolonged exposure to danger as well as from a sudden flash of terror, from a continuing pattern of abuse as well as from a single assault, from a period of attenuation and wearing away as well as from a moment of shock." Prolonged exposure to threats of violence and ongoing abuse are particularly characteristic of oppressed groups and constitute a pernicious from of trauma, because the constant stress and humiliation are associated with being a person of low socioeconomic status.

In *The Bluest Eye* several of Morrison's characters experience the gradual psychic erosion of which Kai Erikson speaks, representing the weakening of whole communities living under an oppressive white cultural dominance. Whether the process of internalizing dominant values occurs psychologically through reinforcement and punishment, or whether it is a reflection of what Lacan saw as a universal process of inscription of individual identity by the social order, Morrison depicts an imposing white culture whose values are enforced through a variety of means (violent, economic, psychological, etc). As she presents it, what has been seen as individualized psychopathological symptoms must be viewed differently when abuse is endured on a larger, systematic level as in 1930s America. *The Bluest Eye* explores how the traumatic experience of social powerlessness and devalued racial identity prevents the African American community from joining together and truthfully evaluating the similarity of their circumstances, much less finding ways to oppose dominant forces.

The epitome of this devalued community, the Breedlove family suffers from trauma caused by single, startling events, but also in the form of daily, grinding oppression, whereby the parents pass their suffering on to their children. The Breedloves' daughter, Pecola, is especially sensitive to the fearful, repetitively ritualized violence that her parents direct toward each other and their children. Her further devaluation by the world, with little relief except from her playmates and the whores who befriend her, includes constant ridicule from other school children because of her dark skin, poverty and ugliness. The black boys who torment her fail to recognize a fellow member of their community. As Michael Awkward observes, their insults ironically reflect "their ability to disregard their similarity to their victim; the verse they compose reflects their own skin color and, quite possibly, familial situations." White attitudes toward blacks are exemplified in Pecola's encounter with the storeowner, Mr. Yacobowski: "She looks up at him and sees the vacuum where curiosity ought to lodge. And something more. The absence of human recognition—the glazed separateness." In this context Pecola becomes especially vulnerable to the sudden, violent traumas of being beaten and rejected by her mother Pauline, and by the more horrific traumas of being raped by her father Cholly and then losing the baby.

Pecola's parents, furthermore, are often powerless themselves, subject to the whites who employ them, victims of their poverty and the culture which invalidates them. In addition, they themselves have been physically or emotionally abandoned by their families—Cholly was rejected by both of his parents, Pauline was made an outsider because of a limp. Traumatized children themselves, they continue the trauma by denying their own weakness in their abuse of parental power, by instilling their own fears of impotence, and by calling upon their children to fulfill their own unmet needs.

Never valued as an individual when she was a child, Pauline continues throughout her life to seek approval in others' eyes, particularly in her position as a servant for whites. In the one place that she feels powerful—the kitchen of the white family for whom she works—she attacks her daughter (who has spilled a cobbler), and in turn denies her own place in the world when she not only fails to acknowledge Pecola but also comforts the white family's child. Pecola's desire for blue eyes is in fact an inheritance from Pauline herself; based on idealized white images—images of acceptance and beauty completely disconnected from herself and her blackness—Pauline's desire is to look like Jean Harlow. Pauline and Pecola, like the rest of the black community, have internalized the pervasive standard of whiteness: in the white dolls they buy their children, in the movies they watch and emulate, and in their privileging of the light-skinned black child, Maureen Peal, over the darker children. Donald Gibson points out that even through narrative, in the use of the school primer as a structuring device, Morrison has foregrounded the way that their lives are "contained within the framework of the values of the dominant culture and subjected to those values." More subtly, she uses the motif of trauma to suggest the overwhelming power that the larger white culture wields in its slow, relentless obliteration of the value of blackness, which forces them to affirm the dominant perspective because cultivating awareness of their own collusion would bring incredible pain, no readily available form of action, and increased hopelessness.

Cholly's traumatized past ultimately leads to consequences that are even more devastating for his daughter. After being abandoned by his parents, the most formatively brutalizing incident in Cholly's youth was the interruption of his first sexual encounter by armed whites. The experience of being forced by the white hunters to continue relations with his partner constitutes a trauma not only in its humiliating intensity, but also in the impossibility of his being able to react to the situation. The displacement of his anger onto his fellow victim Darlene, as Gibson notes, reveals the extent and depth of his psychic wound: "Never did he once consider directing his hatred toward the hunters. Such an emotion would have destroyed him. They were big, white, armed men. He was small, black, helpless." Cholly, in short, cannot assimilate the truth of his subjugation without being annihilated by a sense of his own powerlessness.

When the environment sustains him, i.e., when his marriage and work are stable, Cholly copes well, but when these sources of support and stability are taken away his past returns to plague his present actions. Psychological research indicates that stress causes "state dependent returns to earlier behavior patterns." A stressful situation will cause thoughts to travel along the same pathways as those connected to a previous traumatic event, and if immediate stimuli recall this event, the individual will be transported back to that somatic (bodily) state and react accordingly; responding as if faced with past threat, and losing "the mental synthesis that constitutes reflective will and belief," the individual will simply "transform into automatic wills and beliefs the impulses which are momentarily the strongest." Such is the process which accounts in part for Cholly's rape of Pecola.

When Pecola makes a gesture which reminds him of the tender feelings he once had for Pauline, Pecola's sadness and helplessness and his own inability to make her happy provoke a repetition of the violent impotence and the helpless fear that he and Darlene felt with the white men. His angry response toward Darlene returns and becomes confounded with feelings of love for Pauline and Pecola, and also with self hatred, because Pecola is like Cholly once was, small and impotent. His pessimistic attitudes toward life, himself and his capacity to love return to this traumatic context, and he loses the ability to approach life or his daughter positively. One way for him to rid himself of his fears is to project them onto Pecola, and in part he tries to destroy those fears by raping her.

This type of projection as a manifestation of the trauma victim's dissociation from the truth of his or her situation is not unique to Cholly. The community in which the Breedlove family lives also projects its own sense of devaluation onto the Breedloves, dismissing them for being "low," ugly outsiders, when actually they are merely extreme examples of the larger group's own abasement by white culture. An important example of this projection may be seen in the way that another member of their community, Geraldine, separates herself from "trashy" blacks like Pecola, who she believes threaten her position vis a vis whites.

> She looked back at Pecola, Saw the dirty torn dress, the plaits sticking out on her head, hair matted where the plaits had come undone, the muddy shoes with the wad of gum peeping out from between the cheap soles. . . . She had seen this little girl all of her life. . . .[children like Pecola] crowded into pews at church, taking space from the nice, neat colored children. . . . Like flies they hovered; like flies they settled. And this one had settled in her house.

In her poverty and blackness, Pecola represents everything that Geraldine is "fighting to suppress," and in telling Pecola to leave her house she is "attempting to rid herself of her fears of her own unworthiness, of her own shadow of blackness." Geraldine's disregard of Pecola represents what Donald Gibson sees as Morrison's acknowledgment of the black community's participation in its own oppression. Geraldine and others fail to recognize that they are outsiders in a white world. Not recognizing that they themselves are what Morrison calls a "pariah community," they reject and revile their own members, like the Breedloves, whereas they should examine the condition of such despised members as "useful for the conscience of that community," so that they can realistically evaluate their own subjugation.

Though not specifically addressing trauma, many critics of Morrison's work, in particular Cynthia A. Davis, analyze how oppression is represented in the from of "psychic violence," i.e., the destructiveness of a white racist society which is not always physically brutal, but destroys by engaging in "the systematic denial of the reality of black lives." Roberta Rubenstein also sees Morrison's work as illustrating that the "constriction of the growth of the self is implicitly linked to restrictive or oppressive cultural circumstances." Like Davis and Rubenstein, I believe that the role of scapegoat which is assigned to the abused child Pecola in *The Bluest Eye* reveals the connection between her devastated life and those of the other individuals in her community. Not psychically able to acknowledge their own lack of power, their seeming lack of sympathy with Pecola is really a displacement "onto the Other all that is feared in the self." To avoid a sense of their own victimization, the community projects its sense of inferiority onto Pecola, who "is the epitome of the victim in a world that reduces persons to objects and then makes them feel inferior as objects"; in order to escape from a similar fate their response is to act within "the interlocking hierarchies that allow most to feel superior to someone."

The traumatic context of Duras's *The Vice-Consul* is Third World destitution endured personally by one native character and observed by European colonists living in India. The novel opens with a colonial narrator and character imagining the thoughts and actions of a beggar woman he has seen. He gives an extended account of the beggar, who as a girl had become pregnant through her own ignorance and was subsequently driven away from home by her mother. The narrative follows the beggar's wandering on the roads from Cambodia to Calcutta, surviving despite the experience of being outcast and pregnant and of giving birth to numerous subsequent children who she abandons out of madness and destitution. Throughout the narrative she longs to be a child again, imagining a return to her mother and clinging to all that she has left of the safety of childhood and home, i.e., scraps of memories and word, the name of her town.

Interspersed with the beggar's story is that of a group of European colonists who are appalled at the apparent breakdown of one of their own—specifically the eponymous Vice-Consul, Jean-Marc de H., a colonial official, who has shot at a group of East Indian lepers in the Shalimar Gardens. This incident is not only harmful to his career but disrupts the veneer of control that the colonials have amidst the extreme poverty, disease and misery that lie just outside the walls of their enclaves. The other male colonials, Peter Morgan, Charles Rossett, Michael Richardson, and the French ambassador, Stretter, avoid and abhor the Vice-Consul's instability and betrayal of their social and psychological order. He gets marginal sympathy from the ambassador's wife, Anne Marie Stretter, who, like Jean-Marc, is affected deeply by the misery around her, but who also helps distract and protect her many lovers in the colony from the realities of the Third World: with her, they believe that "all the sorrows of the world wash over them in waves." Although Jean-Marc and Anne Marie never meet the beggar, both are textually linked to her in several ways: by geographic proximity, in being abandoned by parents early in life, and by their manifestations of madness and sorrow. The other men try to keep Anne Marie away from Jean-Marc because his influence would bring on despair and compromise her role as an emotional buffer for them. On at least a subconscious level all these Europeans mirror in a milder way the traumatic responses of the beggar in their denials of and dissociations from reality.

Both Morrison and Duras portray adults as preying on children and destroying their innocence: Pecola is raped by her father, and the fate of Duras' beggar began when she was a young Cambodian girl who became impregnated by a neighbor. "I went into the forest with him," the girls says simply; "I am too young to understand." Like Pecola, the girl is still a child, but menstruating, and so she is treated as an adult for adult needs. When the Cambodian girl's mother rejects her for becoming pregnant and forces her out into the world to beg because of her "adult" behavior, she is refusing to see the girl as still a child and is choosing on behalf of the survival of her younger children. The mother's ruthless detachment from her daughter, like those in Pecola's community, could also be a strategy of survival, an avoidance of the pain of feeling that one is powerless to change one's situation because this truth is too overwhelming. Although the mother inflicts a traumatizing emotional and physical isolation upon her daughter, the text leaves open the possibility that though the mother's anger, like Cholly's toward Pecola, is directed at the daughter, it may stem from the impossibility of any other kind of action, given her own destitute situation and belief in sexual taboos.

The child victims created by Morrison and Duras are the embodiment of traumatic knowledge that, once understood and articulated, would reveal fearful truths about the other characters' lives. This knowledge, denied by victims and observers alike, sets individuals apart from one another, and underlies separations by skin color, cultural affiliation, class, etc., that help to maintain hierarchies of power. The "communities" depicted in *The Bluest Eye* and in *The Vice-Consul* all lack an ability to recognize themselves and their own experience in the outcasts they shun. They illustrate what Judith Herman so aptly describes as the communal expedience of forgetting such truths: "Repression, dissociation, and denial are phenomena of social as well as individual consciousness."

Neither her family nor community offer Pecola support—the latter are embarrassed or revolted by her incestuous pregnancy and madness. They blame the "dog" Cholly, but cannot offer her comfort because her situation is an extreme [example] of their own unacknowledged powerlessness. The narrator Claudia admits: "All of us felt so wholesome after we cleaned ourselves on her. . . . Even her waking dreams we used—to silence our own nightmares. . . . We honed our egos on her. . . . and yawned in the fantasy of our strength." It is this lack of understanding and response that Morrison attacks, the toleration of isolated suffering, which in fact not only reflects but also perpetrates collective suffering. For all the Breedloves, trauma stems from their devastated, love-deprived lives, from a barren cultural landscape, a "soil [which] is bad for certain flowers. Certain seeds it will not nurture, certain fruit it will not bear, and when the land kills of its own volition, we acquiesce and say that the victim had no right to live. We are wrong of course. . ." According to Claudia, in 1930s America the oppressed and traumatized cannot help one another because the only power they have available to them is that of feeling superior to the weakest. This is especially evident in the treatment of children. Alice Miller stresses that the kind of contempt and violence shown to children is really the weapon of the weak to mask their own feelings of helplessness and loneliness. Morrison's work often recognizes the mistreatment of children (e.g., *Sula* and *Beloved*) and, though attributing it to adults who have also been brutalized, she nevertheless does not condone their abuse of power.

The madness brought on by the victimization of the two child protagonists frightens others. The people of her town avoid Pecola and exacerbate her separateness by removing her from school because of her uncanny, staring eyes. The beggar in Duras's novel similarly terrifies other characters, such as the British colonist Charles Rossett. When she approaches him covered with mud, her "unwavering smile is terrifying" as she bites the head off a live fish in his presence. Unable to endure the reality of her madness and her filth, he runs toward the safety of the fence which encloses his hotel, and which separates the whites from the people of color, the rich from the poor, the colonists from the colonized. Rossett is afraid of the beggar because he cannot tolerate that which he cannot act upon, that which would make him despair, i.e., madness, hopelessness, poverty, the forces of nature, all of which the beggar represents. He and other colonists do not want to acknowledge that they might also be vulnerable to these forces. Hence, the beggar— but also the Vice-Consul, one of the few colonials who can empathize and give up the illusion of emotional control—become the objects of others' fear or scorn in order that these others can avoid their own role in the oppression and destitution they witness. In *The Bluest Eye*, avoidance of these individuals enables those in the larger group to mask their fears and their collusion in systems that degraded themselves; in *The Vice-Consul*, the colonizers mask their fear, their privileged status, and their weakness in the face of abjection through denial and avoidance.

In their discussion of trauma, Van der Kolk and Van der Hart explain that "a feeling of helplessness, of physical or emotional paralysis, is fundamental to making an experience traumatic: the person was in a position of being unable to take any action that could effect the outcome of events," and because appropriate categorization of experience was impaired, traumatic experience cannot be integrated into a memory as with normal events. A failure to make sense of these past experiences resulted in fixed ideas which create repetitive and impotent activities around attempted recreations of the event, and leads to dissociation, where the individual becomes "emotionally constricted and cannot experience a full range of affects." At its worst, personality development is arrested and "cannot expand any more by the addition or assimilation of new elements." In a traumatic experience the past remains unresolved and lingering, because it is not processed in the way that normal information is: either cognitively or emotionally. Non-traumatic memories lose their force, for when new ideas and information become stored, they "are constantly with old knowledge to form flexible mental schemas," and once an event is within a larger scheme, the remembrance of it changes and the event cannot be accessed as an individual element anymore. In contrast, traumatic memories are those which are frozen in time, not subject to a previous contextualization or to subsequent experience, and are therefore reexperienced without change. The reality of the traumatic event "continues to elude the subject who lives in its grip and unwittingly undergoes its ceaseless repetitions and reenactments." Moreover, Van der Kolk and Ducey affirm that "a sudden and passively endured trauma is relived repeatedly, until a person learns to remember simultaneously the affect and cognition associated with the trauma through access to language."

In a traumatic context repetition can be an attempt to attack one's own fears, as in Cholly's rape of Pecola, but it can also be a sign of being caught in stasis, of not being able to move on and resolve the initial trauma. Pecola's compulsion to repeat begins after her rape. In her conversations with her imaginary friend, her obsessive but ineffectual questioning of herself and what happened with her father—"He just tried, see? He didn't do anything. You hear me?"—exhibits some of the repetition and dissociation common in the victims of such experience, and this coupled with her mother's denial— "She didn't even believe me when I told her"—cuts Pecola off from any reconcilable knowledge of what she endured. Pecola takes her other "voice" (a split-off part of herself) to task for continuing to question her about what happened with Cholly, expressing a desperate need to be believed, to understand, and yet to forget and deny as well. Her response is very similar to that of many trauma victims, who, as Robert Jay Lifton has observed, feel compelled both to confront and to avoid any traumatic experience.

Pecola's desire for blue eyes becomes obsessive after her rape, and her conviction that she has been given them by Soaphead Church (the man who promises her a miracle) indicates a complete psychic disintegration. Her own negative reflection in others' eyes had been the continual source of her pain, and her main wish is that her reflection be desirable. The extent of Pecola's obsession and pathology at this stage is presented through hallucinations, through her resistance to blinking, and her delusional view that others envy her gift. "Look. I can look right at the sun. . ." she says, "I don't even have to blink. . . He did a really good job. Everybody's jealous. Every time I look at somebody, they look off." Her obsessive return to the mirror for reassurance that her "blue eyes" are the bluest and the nicest—"How many times a minute are you going to look?" her "friend" asks—also represents a textual repetition of the destructive power of judgment based solely on appearance and prejudice.

With this repeated theme and imagery Morrison underscores her critique of the way that an individual's entire being is reduced to and determined in a glance, just as she is deeply critical of insubstantial and superficial images that lead to the creation of false selves and which assign such power to the gazer. Pecola's belief that she has blue eyes represents her pitiable attempt to take power, for she is now the one who looks, but they more importantly symbolize the trauma of not being loved. She defends against her pain by reexperiencing others' gazes with what she believes is an acceptable, if not loveable, appearance. Ironically, this delusion makes her more of an outcast because her madness spooks everyone, including her mother. In our last glimpse of Pecola, her wandering in a regressive animal-like state is punctuated by useless, repetitive movements:

> The damage done was total. She spent her days, her tendril, sap-green days, walking up and down, up and down, her head jerking to the beat of a drummer so distant only she could hear. Elbows bent, hands on shoulders, she flailed her arms like a bird in an eternal, grotesquely futile effort to fly. Beating the air, a winged but grounded bird, intent on the blue void it could not reach—could not even see—but which filled the valleys of the mind.

Duras' beggar acts in an even more repetitive fashion, particularly after the loss of her first child. The successive abandonment of her children is but one scenario connected with her own abandonment. In order to survive and obtain food she must prostitute herself to other fishermen, forcing her to reenact the original loveless encounter which led to her pregnancy and rejection. Her somnambulistic, interminable walking also exhibits reenactive and dissociative responses to trauma. In wandering, she is obeying her mother's early commands to leave. As she is about to leave the first child behind, she feels that the word for her home village, "Battambang," will protect her—a word she will repeat, the only word remaining to her, signifying a desire to return home to her mother and to the past.

This unproductive traumatic activity is also subtly linked by both Morrison and Duras to metaphors of nature or fecundity gone awry. Pecola, just become a biological woman at age eleven, cannot sustain her father's unwanted seed. In *The Vice-Consul*, like the cloyingly sweet custard apple, children are obscenely abundant beyond what can be sustained and are consequently wasted (just as in another of Duras's novels set in Indochina, *The Sea Wall*, the dead bodies of children are said to make the land fertile). Each girl (Pecola and the beggar) carries a child (or children in the beggar's case) that is lost or left behind, and these losses create dissociation and deterioration from which they never recover. In the beggar girl's rejection of her first, and subsequent infants, Duras represents in "the abandonment of a child the scandalous limit of dispossession: the limit of misery, of un-awareness, of madness." When babies do not survive, the future is cut off; so the loss of these children is a powerful symbol of an ultimate loss of the future. As the narrator of *The Bluest Eye* says, "I felt a need for someone to want the black baby [Pecola's] to live—just to counteract the universal love of white baby dolls. . ."

The most severe traumatic loss of the beggar girl's life was having to give up her first child, a girl. Although she knew that she would never be able to find work with a child in tow, she had heard that whites will sometimes take in children. Accordingly, she pursued a French woman and begged her to take her ill, starving child, which the mother did—as Duras's own mother once did. While the French foster-mother consults with a doctor and cries over the obviously doomed infant, the baby's girl-mother observes "It no longer concerns me. It is the business of other women now. You [the baby] in addition to myself, an impossible association, yet how hard it was to separate us." And then to dramatize this dissociation, the narrative shifts to the third person:

> The doctor approaches the newly-washed infant, and gives it an injection. the child gives a feeble cry. . . .Unconsciously, she mimics the grimace on the child's crumpled face. For the rest of her life she will feel, between her shoulders, the pressure of the child's weight, her exact weight now. Alive or dead, the

child will never exceed that weight. The girl leaves the spot from which she has been watching. She turns her back, now bare of its burden, on the window. She leaves.

Speaking for and about her, Duras's narrator predicts that the girl will in turn abandon all her other children after this one, that she will put them aside, miss them briefly and forget them. This detachment from them can be explained as a way of coping with the loss of the first child; in order to keep that original pain at bay, she shuts down effectively and separates herself from them both physically and emotionally. In doing so she also repeats her own traumatic separation from her mother.

When individuals are exposed to trauma, i.e., a frightening event outside of ordinary human experience, they experience "speechless terror." Traumatic memory, psychoanalyst Judith Herman explains, is "wordless and static" and initially iconic or visual; it also manifests itself in "behavioral reenactments, nightmares [or] flashbacks" because traumatic experience "cannot be easily translated into the symbolic language necessary for linguistic retrieval." Traumatic experience creates a "loss of voice . . . of knowledge, of awareness, of truth, of the capacity to feel . . . and to speak." In order to help the individual to reexperience the past full and affectively, it is therefore necessary for the therapist to encourage the victim to construct a completed narrative of the event, including "a full and vivid description of the traumatic imagery." Duras and Morrison are "textual" therapists who attempt to recover traumatic experience from the silence and repression that attends it.

In both novels there is an attempt for victims virtually silenced by the process of trauma. First, this takes the form of trying to articulate the victims' own words, suggesting their traumatized condition through the narratively dissociative yet emotionally overdetermined quality of these words. For example, the only word left to the beggar, the name of her hometown, "Battambang," is repeatedly invoked to emphasize her desire to return home (though there is some indication that she would no longer recognize it), and to symbolize the safe place of childhood. Even though this is the place of her mother's rejection of her, she longs to speak in her own language (she has strayed, symbolically, out of her own country). The narrator informs us that she speaks to her absent mother now that she no longer has the child to hear her, but she remains silenced in effect because her word(s) remain incomprehensible to others.

Julia Kristeva asserts that in Duras's texts the sense of loss or void is presented as "unused affects and in a discourse emptied of meaning," but that her texts also speak a "discourse of blunted pain," which represents "the trace of an absence." That is, all that is left for these dispossessed individuals is a profound sense of absence of self or of significant others. Kristeva does not directly link Duras's characterization and discourse to traumatic reactions, but I would argue that these "traces" also correspond to the left-over emotions and the inarticulateness common to victims of trauma, and that if such emptiness is in keeping with Duras's general philosophy, it is also important to acknowledge that this philosophical conception is born in a context of trauma and takes the form of a psychological critique of oppression.

Pecola similarly seeks comfort in words. In part she seeks understanding of what her father has done to her, but her conflicted dialogue with a split-off persona of herself also illustrates how much she has been isolated and how her pain and need to speak are ignored by her community and even her family. To characterize this self-splitting, Morrison utilizes an interchange of roman type and italics: "How come you don't talk to anybody? I talk to you. . . . I just wondered. You don't talk to anybody. You don't go to school. And nobody talks to you. How do you know nobody talks to me? They don't. When you're in the house with me, even Mrs. Breedlove doesn't say anything to you. Ever. Sometimes I wonder if she even sees you." Hence, both writers are faced with two important issues when speaking for these protagonists: first, there is the necessity of communicating their experience so that it will be known; second, there is the question of how this can be done when the characters are cut off from linguistic connections or from dialogue with others. They address this dilemma by creating other voices to compensate for the gaps.

Outsider narrators are employed by both writers to supplement the victims' voices and to construct the "completed narration" that is essential for their stories to be fully told and for the therapeutic function of such telling to occur. By demonstrating the limitations of their narrators, however, both writers also acknowledge the problem of the further oppression that might result from the attempt to give voices to oppressed victims. Morrison tells Pecola's story in part through an omniscient narrator and primarily through the sympathetic eyes of Claudia, who has been Pecola's friend and who realizes the harm done to Pecola by the community, including herself in that complicity: "She seemed to fold into herself, like a pleated wing. Her pain antagonized me"; "We tried to see her without looking at her . . . because we had failed her." Not only is Claudia sympathetic toward Pecola, but she is also self-conscious and self-critical about her own complicity. In this way, through her narrative we are doubly exposed to the dynamics and effects of racism. Similarly, if Claudia is an insider in the way she experiences some of the same pain as Pecola, she is also an outsider and privileged in the sense that having been loved, she possesses the strength to have her own desires. Outsider and insider at the same time, she is sympathetically aware of the need to recognize her community's role and their own defeat in Pecola's disintegration.

Duras's use of a male narrator to tell the story of an abused girl is equally effective in drawing attention to the suspect position of speaking for (i.e., defining) an other. Peter Morgan tries to understand the tragedy of Calcutta through the narration of the beggar's story, and his hope is that "wisdom may start to grow out of bitter experience." In his narrative appropriation of others' suffering, however, Morgan indulges in what Eric Santner would call "narrative fetishism," i.e., "the construction and deployment of a narrative consciously or unconsciously designed to expunge the traces of the trauma or loss that called that narrative into being in the first place." As Duras portrays him, Morgan, like most of the other colonists, keeps himself remote from the horrors of deprivation surrounding him by creating a narrative about a dispossessed beggar woman whom he sees in Calcutta. Only by focusing in on one case of destitution in a fictional form can he approach the woman's condition from a safe distance: "I am drunk with the sufferings of India. Aren't we all, more or less? It's impossible to talk about such suffering unless one has made it as much a part of oneself as breathing. That woman stirs my imagination. I note down my thoughts about her." The identification with suffering that Morgan claims for himself is actually more true of the Vice-Consul (whom Morgan studiously avoids) and Anne Marie Stretter, who are both immediately and emotionally affected by India, and almost driven mad by it. Thus Morgan's approach reveals the fear, denial and repression characteristic of the colonists' position, and though he uses his own memory and others' accounts to "explain the madness of the beggar woman of Calcutta," he remains out of touch with the sources and contexts of her madness.

Morgan's attempt to identify with this woman and with India through language is also problematic because she has no available language with which to express herself and her sufferings. Up to a point Morgan is aware of this problem: "How to put into words the things she never said? . . . How to describe the things that she does not know she has seen, the experiences that she does not know she has had? How to reconstruct the forgotten years?" Duras displays here an awareness of possible appropriation and the simultaneous need to understand that occasions any narrative. We should also notice the way that Duras ultimately removes the beggar from the control of the colonial viewer of her story. That is, though Morgan's narrative serves to establish the story's context and the voices of the colonists, Duras follows the beggar further than he does and allows her to surpass the definition and containment of Morgan's narrative when she is described toward the end of the novel by an unidentified neutral narrator. The beggar here emerges in an almost triumphant madness, as if in panoply; she ceases here to be the one who helps another (Morgan) to understand himself and becomes someone whose presence demands recognition in and of itself. By bringing her into contact with the obsessively rational Englishman Rossett, Duras forces a colonist to confront directly the awful reality of the beggar— i.e., one of their colonized subjects—and he is horrified by the encounter.

In *The Vice-Consul* the beggar becomes an externalized symbol of oppression and of the sufferings Duras witnessed during her childhood in Indochina; she becomes what Madeleine Borgomano has called the "generating cell" of Duras's work. In her more autobiographical novels (*The Sea Wall, The Lover,* and *The North China Lover*) the beggar is deeply mourned and internalized into the workings of the narrator's identity and Duras's relation to her family. According to Maria DeBattista, she "comes to symbolize for Duras the negative interpenetration of figure and world, indeed represents . . . the possibility of representing the sufferings of the world, the brutalities of colonialism . . . and it is here, and here only, that literature stops and writing becomes sacred—here where it rejoins the work as a transgressive text insistent on its sins but penitent for its self-absorption. In many of Duras's texts the characters are caught in madness and pain without social context and these works would seem to reinforce Kristeva's argument that in Duras's work political life becomes unreal, that "madness represents a space of antisocial, apolitical, and paradoxically, free individuation." Certainly, in many of her texts traumatic events are measured in the context of individualized human pain; to focus on the victims' pain, however, does not remove the influence of the world, but rather emphasizes the human consequences of its machinations. In *The Vice-Consul* however, and later works such as *The Lover* and *The North China Lover*, the contexts of colonized India and Indochina are specified, and it is precisely through Duras's rendering of the effects on individuals of such contexts that we can measure the traumatic impact of world events and practices. The "generating cell" that fuels her need to write is part of a real childhood memory—of her mother buying a dying infant from a beggar woman: "The act has remained with me in an opaqueness from which I will never emerge . . . the event recurs to me as a problem to resolve with the only means that I have, that is, writing . . . I have tried to put it in literature . . . and I have not succeeded." Much of Duras's writing has been an attempt to understand this woman's act, an event which has continued to haunt her, and which cannot be separated in her mind from the larger context of destitution and colonialism in the Third World.

Morrison's work also shows a strong awareness that victims of trauma are mentally imprisoned and isolated by their traumatic experience, and she makes it very clear that disturbed relationships reflect and interconnect with a broader social context. Focusing on traumatized characters who return to unresolved memories, she suggests that our ability to change the nature of our attachments to others depends on whether we evaluate the past and examine our behaviors and relations in it. What is especially needed from all black writers, she says, is "the clear identification of what the enemy forces are, not this person or that person and so on, but the acknowledgment of a way of life dreamed up for us by some other people who are at the moment in power, and knowing the ways in which it can be subverted." Thus the message that underlies her focus on traumatized victims is not merely that they are oppressed, but that correcting the situation cannot be done by solitary individuals who are psychologically and even physically immobilized. This is why Morrison emphasizes communal or collective knowledge, solidarity, refusal and resistance: "If my work is to be functional to the group then it must bear witness and identify that which is useful from the past . . . it must make it possible to prepare for the present and live it out, and it must do that not by avoiding problems and contradictions but by examining them." In a world where the social, racial and political exercise of power creates destruction of the human psyche so that it cannot oppose domination, Morrison's emphatic message is that the traumatized responses of individuals must not be relegated to the domestic sphere but should instead be seen as a clear signal that destructive forces are at work. For Morrison, the act of narration can be one means in the process of collecting and sharing knowledge heretofore held by "discredited people," a means of resisting the urge to see collective victimization only as individualized.

There is a tendency for both of those involved and the outsiders to want to forget or cover up real traumas. As Judith Herman explains, to become aware of extreme abuses leads us "into realms of the unthinkable and . . . forces us to face human vulnerability and our capacity for evil, forces us to bear witness to horrible events"; to become aware also sometimes requires that one take sides between victims and perpetrators, especially where the perpetrators promote forgetting and defend themselves through secrecy, silence, denial and undermining of victims' accusations. Duras and Morrison want their readers to confront the unthinkable, to be able to demystify what is denied or rationalized, to help readers unfold those "unspeakable things unspoken" that Morrison refers to in discussing the exclusion of African Americans from American literary and cultural history. Morrison has said: "My writing expects, demands participatory reading . . . it's about involving the reader. The reader supplies the emotions." Duras similarly will not let go of the injustices she witnessed in her youth in Indochina, incorporating them into her writing as much as possible, and she goes even further than Morrison in describing her engaged readers' connection to her texts as "a private relationship between the book and the reader. They weep and grieve together."

What can be the writer's rights and goals in describing such misery? Can such abjection be understood? Morrison and Duras are very sensitive to how the social construction of individuals and the internalization of inferior status can be formidable and brutal. They suggest that oppression and resulting psychic vulnerability will be perpetuated unless memories are collectively articulated and shared, and this I posit is where the greatest value of their work lies: in helping readers to empathize with and share the victim's experience from the victim's point of view, and in insisting through their portrayal of narrators that we must all explore our own role in this victimization, whether our guilt take the form of direct responsibility or complicity. Through their depiction of the larger social contexts of trauma, Morrison and Duras urge their readers to remember and evaluate the wrongs of the past. They recognize what Shoshana Felman calls the importance of testifying about what has been forgotten or repressed: "To testify is thus not merely to narrate but to commit oneself, and to commit the narrative, to others: to take responsibility—in speech—for history or for the truth of an occurrence, for something which, by definition, goes beyond the personal, in having general (nonpersonal) validity and consequences." Both writers acknowledge that the inarticulate victims of abuse can be spoken for only inadequately, can be understood only partially, and yet that they need such interpretation from outside because they cannot do it alone. In giving each of their characters the opportunity to speak or to act in his or her own right, however briefly, Duras and Morrison give us a sense of the victim's limited ability to communicate and act, and his or her need to find empathetic ears.

JAMES A. WREN

M'Dear's Deductive Methodology

"A threnody of nostalgia about pain," Toni Morrison's *The Bluest Eye* builds upon "the memories of illnesses" in a world populated by characters who "licked their lips and clucked their tongues in fond remembrance of pains they had endured—childbirth, rheumatism, croup, sprains, backaches, piles." The one illness sufficiently elaborated upon, however, ends not with forbearance but in death.

In the spring when Cholly was fourteen years old "Aunt Jimmy . . . went to a camp meeting that took place after a rainstorm, and the damp wood of the benches was bad for her. Four or five days afterward, she felt poorly. . . ." When the advice from her neighbors proved ineffective in treating her malaise, M'Dear was brought in. A woman who "loomed taller than the preacher who accompanied her" and "seemed to need her hickory stick not for support but for communication," she is venerated as "a competent midwife and decisive diagnostician." Supported as much by a deductive methodology based upon observance and verification as by her walking stick, it is her skills that set her apart from those neighbors whose lives are governed by "prolific, if contradictory" superstitions.

When she arrives, M'Dear quickly sets about deducing a medical history of her patient by making full use of all available clues. The acute onset of illness, "the foul odor of an old woman's stools," and the delirium as

From *The Explicator* 55, no. 3 (Spring 1997). © 1997 Helen Dwight Reid Educational Foundation. Reprinted with permission of the Helen Dwight Reid Education Foundation. Published by Heldref Publications.

"Miss Alice, her closest friend, read the Bible to her," in addition to an easily recognizable source of infection (for example, a contaminated water supply following a flood) and the expected seasonality for enteric diseases, immediately implicate a gastroenteritis, an umbrella term including dysentery and other diarrheal diseases. A number of pathogens are possible causes (Salmonella, Shigellosis, Campylobacter, or Vibrio cholera), but to make a good differential diagnosis, M'Dear must examine her patient first.

She begins by searching for any external signs of disease (for instance, ulcerations, rash, or tenderness); she runs "her left . . .[hand]. . . over Aunt Jimmy's body." Finding none, she places the backs of her long fingers "on the patient's cheek, then place[s] her palm on the forehead." Finding no fever, she can quickly rule out Salmonella infections in general. That the patient is prostrate and stuporous suggests typhoid fever, but M'Dear is able to eliminate this possibility because Aunt Jimmy lacks intermittent fever and rose-colored spots on the skin.

To rule out either parasitic infestation as an underlying source of infection or possible dehydration, M'Dear runs "her fingers through the sick woman's hair, lightly scratching the scalp then looking at what the fingernails revealed." She immediately lifts "Aunt Jimmy's hand and look[s] closely at it—fingernails, back skin, the flesh of the palm she pressed with three fingertips." That M'Dear specifically examines for impairments in the elasticity of the skin and for the presence of cyanosis (a characteristic "blueing" of the skin and nail beds) hints that she had found evidence of dehydration, but because cyanosis may suggest concomitant respiratory illness—severe asthma, bronchitis, pneumonia, or tuberculosis—she "put[s] her ear on Aunt Jimmy's chest." From there, she moves quickly "to the stomach to listen."

Lacking the necessary equipment to conduct a microscopic examination, M'Dear then considers the only other evidence available: "at [her] request, the women pulled the slop jar from under the bed to show the stools." The absence of blood or mucus, together with an absence of fever, excludes Shigellosis and Campylobacter. Consistent with the evidence that M'Dear has uncovered, the remaining possibility, Vibrio cholera, can on occasion be found in the Gulf Coast states during pandemics. Occurring during the warm months of the year, primary symptoms usually appear within five days and include watery diarrhea with no blood in the stool, a drop in body temperature, and cyanosis. After considering all of the evidence, M'Dear orders Cholly to "bury the slop jar and everything in it." Her concern readily suggests that she suspects cholera.

Nor does M'Dear's explanation to Aunt Jimmy, "You done caught cold in your womb," suggest a different diagnosis. In fact, by labeling the illness as "feminine" and therefore "personal," she shrewdly gives the neighbors something to gossip about, but more to the point, her naming prevents them from speaking openly about it, and hence she avoids widespread panic. But perhaps most telling of the nature of her diagnosis is her prescription, "drink pot liquor and nothing else." Thus, "that evening the women brought bowls of pot liquor from black-eyed peas, from mustards, from cabbage, from kale, from collards, from turnips, from beets, from green beans. Even the juice from a boiling hog jowl." Her insistence upon rehydration with fluid and electrolytes, arising from her rational understanding that the elderly are far less able to tolerate the loss of bodily fluids, is wholly consistent with the treatment of cholera.

Her advice obviously proves effective, for "two evenings later Aunt Jimmy had gained much strength." Unfortunately, however, "on a wet Saturday night before Aunt Jimmy felt strong enough to get out of bed, Essie Foster brought her a peach cobbler." Ignoring the warning of her physician, "the old lady ate a piece, and the next morning when Cholly went to empty the slop jar, she was dead."

I suggest that the importance of M'Dear's diagnosis to the larger concerns of the novel as a whole, however, lies not in her having named a disease but in having demonstrated the methodology by which she does so. Put differently, her approach to illness represents a radical departure from traditional attitudes, as well as a rationale by which we as diagnosticians may confront a horribly contagious, often pathological, at times maddening concern for physical beauty. Already provided with a good differential diagnosis, it is our challenge as readers to write the appropriate prescription for a cure.

LEESTER THOMAS

When Home Fails to Nurture the Self: The Tragedy of Being Homeless at Home

Numerous lyrics, speeches, quips, plaques, and other similar parapher-
nalia extol the virtues of home. Moreover, perusal of any reputable dictionary
confirms that home denotes a positive place—a place of sheltering
or protection from external forces that might inflict illimitable dangers or
nuisances. The term home may be used to refer to a physical place, such as
a dwelling, a community, geographical region, or better yet, a country itself,
as in one's homeland: take America, for example. The same term may refer
to people that inhabit a place—one's kin or family, with attendant positive
associations of warmth, comfort, acceptance, nurturing, and of course,
charity, as in love. Finally, the security of the physical home and the familial
home usually contributes to the development of a wholesome individual who
loves, accepts, and feels at peace—at home—with self. But what happens to
the psyche of the individual who is shown no charity in the larger environment nor at home? What happens to that psyche—to the self—when home
becomes a frightening, soulessly cruel abode and being inside is as traumatic
as being put outdoors? Toni Morrison addresses this very subject for African
Americans in her novel *The Bluest Eye*.

As Morrison has stated, the initial purpose of the novel as an art form
was to tell people something they didn't know, especially how to behave in
this [nineteenth-century England] new world, how to distinguish between

From *The Western Journal of Black Studies* 21, no. 1 (Spring 1997). © 1997 Washington State
University Press.

the good guys and the bad guys. At first, the emphasis was on moral development, but as the genre developed, more writers began to use it as a forum to
discuss contemporary social concerns as well as to provide moral instruction
and entertainment. And today, despite the myriad theoretical/literary/critical
traditions that have been applied in developing this art form, it remains a forum
for writers of different cultures, philosophies, and creeds to subtly or vehe-
mently express their heartfelt convictions or protest injustices and ideologies.

Morrison believes the novel is needed by African Americans now in a
way that it was not needed before because we no longer have access to stories
that heretofore had been handed down by ancestral storytellers that provided
healing. She states that the novel may be one of the most useful tools in
helping African Americans to understand new information and its ramifications. But in her novels she also shows how valuable the novel can be in
helping African Americans to understand and interpret old news that they
apparently never understood or took seriously. Such news might be called
timeless. In *The Bluest Eye* she treats one of these timeless subjects, or, as
Bernard Bell says, vintage wine in new bottles. He praises Morrison for
distill[ing] history and fact with the poetic freedom and Gothic vision of
modernist and postmodernist writers in this novel.

Like the black postmodernists, Morrison is concerned with fiction that
focuses on the truths of the perversity of American racism and the paradoxes
of Afro-American double-consciousness. Using fable, myth, and rituals, she
reveals the privation wrought upon African Americans due to the larger
society, white racist America; the compounded effects of racial divisiveness of
class and caste willfully accepted and perpetuated among African Americans
themselves who subscribe to the Euro-centric notions of superiority and
values; the contagious effects of self-hatred and loathing within the nuclear
family itself; and the annihilating effects of self-inflicted hatred upon the self
when the aforementioned wounds have been applied. Using the postmodernist tradition, she strips away the idols of whiteness and of Blackness that
have prevented Blacks in the United States from knowing themselves and
gives them their own true mythical, remembered words to live by.

Discussion

Much has been written about the tragic life of the Breedlove family in *The
Bluest Eye*, and Pecola's search for self and place in particular. In sum, Lorain,
Ohio, the setting of the novel, is a world of grotesques—individuals whose
psyches have been deformed by their efforts to assume false identities, their
failures to achieve meaningful identities, or simply their inability to retain

and communicate love. Specifically, the novel is about a little girl who longs to have blue eyes because everyone that she has encountered during her brief life has consciously or unconsciously upheld the ideals of white skin, long blonde hair, and blue eyes as the epitome of beauty and goodness. She believes that she is ugly because those around her at school, on the playground, in the city, in the community, and her family at home believe she is. What's more tragic, the family believe that they are ugly! In fact:

> No one could have convinced them that they were not relentlessly and aggressively ugly . . . The eyes, the small eyes set closely together under narrow foreheads. The low, irregular hairlines, which seemed even more irregular in contrast to the straight, heavy eyebrows which nearly met. Keen but crooked noses, with insolent nostrils. The had high cheekbones, and their ears turned forward. Shapely lips which called attention not to themselves but to the rest of the face. You looked at them and wondered why they were so ugly; you looked closely and could not find the source. Then you realized that it came from conviction—their conviction. It was as though some mysterious all-knowing master had given each one a cloak of ugliness to wear, and they had each accepted it without question. The master had said, You are ugly people, . . . And they took the ugliness in their hands, threw it as a mantle over them, and went about the world with it. Dealing with it each according to his way.

Bitter. Hostile. Cold. Dysfunctional. This is Pecola's introduction to life. This is what prompts her to pray for blue eyes that would make not only her family but the world, as she knows it, accept and love her. But the only love she experiences—other than the compassion that the MacTeer girls show her at intervals during the novel—is the paradoxically false but true, fleeting yet enduring fatalistic love of her father, Cholly Breedlove, who rapes and impregnates her. Having suffered a multitude of indignities and finally the miscarriage of her child, she goes insane, believing at last that she had blue eyes. Morrison contrasts the life of the Breedloves with the idyllic life of the white middle-class society with its economic stability and ideals of beauty and happiness by referencing the grade school primer which for years, prior to visual technology, was the earliest introduction of the African American child to the status quo. However, she also juxtaposes the Breedlove family—particularly Pecola—with another poor Black family of the same caste and class, the MacTeer family—specifically Claudia, the narrator—but in the MacTeer family there is genuine love and acceptance of self, clearly demonstrating the part that nurturing in the home can play in charting one's survival or success despite opposition of the larger society.

In the novel, as most critics have pointed out, nature is the dominant metaphor and structural element for plot development. The action goes from Fall through Summer, charting the gradual dissolution of the modicum of self-esteem Pecola felt and the false hope of gaining a better self to loss of self-realization—sanity—altogether. Of the various nature images presented in the novel, the marigold seeds seem to be the most symbolic representation of Pecola's tragedy, of Pecola herself. She becomes the seed that the earth—her world—would not accept, and, like the seed, which the earth refuses to root, Pecola cannot find her self, her place, in Lorain or its likeness. The profoundness of this seed imagery is inescapable and thus is reiterated or discussed in almost all commentary on the novel's theme about the quest for self or place. Yet, there is another metaphor that Morrison dramatically uses to illuminate the injurious effects that denying one the inalienable right to find the self to find a place in her society—has on the psyche. That metaphor is the concept of being put outdoors—being homeless or, more emphatically, being homeless at home.

Outdoors: The Meaning of Such Wretchedness

This concept of outdoors is explained through the voice and understanding of a child, Claudia, who offers such an honest point of view and thus such a poignant one. In the first major division of *The Bluest Eye*, the chapter entitled Autumn, Pecola—called a case: a girl who had no place to go—comes to stay with the MacTeer family because her father, that old Dog Breedlove had burned up his house, gone upside his wife's head, and everybody, as a result, was outdoors. Then, Morrison has Claudia expound the sorrowfulness of having no homeplace and the sinfulness of one responsible for another not having one of the most integral human needs met, for Claudia states:

> Outdoors, we knew, was the real terror of life. The threat of being outdoors surfaced frequently in those days. Every possibility of excess was curtailed with it. If somebody used too much coal, he could end up outdoors. People could gamble themselves outdoors, drink themselves outdoors. Sometimes others put their sons outdoors, and when that happened, regardless of what the son had done, all sympathy was with him. He was outdoors, and his own flesh had done it. To be put outdoors by a landlord was

one thing—unfortunate, but an aspect of life over which you had no control, since you could not control your income. But to be slack enough to put oneself outdoors, or heartless enough to put one's kin outdoors—that was criminal. There is a difference between being put out and being put outdoors. If you are put out, you go somewhere else; if you are outdoors, there is no place to go.

Explicitly and implicitly, Morrison makes an indictment against anyone or anything that denies one the right to have a place in society. To be outside is to be without a home—without a birthplace; without a cultural/racial identity; without family bonding; and finally, without self-esteem and, consequently, self-realization. There is nothing to be gained when one's potential for wholesome living—wholesome being and becoming—is destroyed. The victim lives a life of terror as Pecola does, forever hunched, crouched, like a trapped animal, wishing she could disappear, until the day she does just that.

The First Eviction: Rejection of Self by Mainstream Society

Writing as a realist, Morrison could not possibly write a story set in the 40s involving blacks without somehow depicting the racism that abounded in the larger environment and was the ultimate cause of Pecola's low self-esteem and search for beauty. Everything in the greater society reminded her that she was on the outside—that she did not belong or rather that she did not exist. The white store clerk does not acknowledge that she is a person when she enters his store because he does not look at her, for how can a fifty-two year old white immigrant storekeeper with the taste of potatoes and beer in his mouth, his mind honed on the doe-eyed Virgin Mary, his sensibilities blunted by a permanent awareness of loss, see a little black girl, and when he does, she senses in his eyes a kind of distaste because of her presence, a distaste made more evident when he speaks to her in a phlegmy and impatient voice. This is the kind of humiliation that reinforces her heartfelt belief that she is ugly and thus has no place in her environment. Added to this kind of encounter are the billboards along the streets that are graced with images of beauty—white beauty—constantly reminding her of her shortcomings.

In addition to presenting examples of overt racism, one of Morrison's harshest indictments of white ideals as standards for blacks to emulate is subtly and yet provocatively contested through structural references to the Dick and Jane grade school primer. Here the author incorporates myth with realism to contrast the American idea of the ideal family life and that of the Breedloves and the MacTeer families and to point out the lethal effects that constant exposure of this toxic romanticized image has on the psyche of young black children, Pecola in particular, and the larger black culture. Seven chapters in the novel are introduced with this or a similar scrambled mythical reference to middle-class American family life:

> Here is the house. It is green and white. It has a red door. It is very pretty. Here is the family. Mother, Father, Dick, and Jane live in the green-and-white house. They are very happy. See Jane. She has a red dress. She wants to play . . . Mother is very nice. Mother will you play with Jane? . . . See Father. He is big and strong. Father, will you play with Jane? Father is smiling . . . See the dog. Bowwow goes the dog.

As Barbara Christian states, The primer confronts the grossness of standardized bland concepts projected as desirable, the norm. She adds further:

> But young children are led to believe that others are happy because they are pretty, are not too noisy, or are living an orderly life, whatever line of demarcation or difference they can perceive as marking their own existence. The more confusing, different, poverty-ridden or depressed that a child's life is, the more she will yearn for the norm the dominant society says provides beauty and happiness.

Pecola is that confused, different, poverty-ridden and depressed child who yearns for the norm, which to her is blue eyes. Because of this repeated image of the perfect home presented in the primer, she is led to believe that this is the reality to which she must escape from her nightmarish existence in a loveless and lifeless storefront home, inhabited by people who have forgotten how or never really understood the need to play. She does not understand that her family lives in that storefront because of ideas that people whom the primer supposedly captions have about the place of poor black people or that the sofa purchased new, but split-across-back before delivery could not be exchanged by her parents who therefore had to pay the $4.80 a month regardless; she did not know that since they were forced to pay for merchandise that started off split, no good, and humiliating—[they] couldn't take any joy in owning it. And the joylessness stank, pervading everything. And just as important, she could not be expected to know that the story in the primer is myth, clearly destroyed by Mrs. Breedlove's assessment of the first white family for whom she works—a family of slender means and nervous, pretentious ways, nasty white folks, not one of [whom] knew so much as how to wipe their behinds, but more important, unhappy people in a pretty house like that and all the money they could hold on to but people who could not enjoy one another. The disgust and distaste that she sees lurking in the eyes of all white people whom she meets, their reverberating phlegmy voices made her feel that she was an intruder in the larger society, and the mythical images of their beauty and perfect world confirmed that she did not belong, that she was in fact on the outside—outdoors.

The larger society, here, may be compared to the landlord that Claudia refers to in her discourse on the terror of being outdoors. "To have been put outdoors—rejected—by the white society in general was one thing—unfortunate, but an aspect of life over which [blacks] had no control, since [they] could not control their economic destiny and thus had to live in inferior dwellings and since they could not change the cold, prejudiced hearts of bigots who sought to make their [blacks] lives uncomfortable, but to be slack enough to put oneself outdoors, or heartless enough to put one's own kin outdoors—that was criminal." Yet, Morrison charges, such is the case when blacks subscribe to the white mythical ideals of beauty and place in accepting their own racial kindred. Again, Pecola is victim, rejected by blacks in her class and outside it.

The Second Eviction: Rejection of Self
by the Black Community

The masses of black society had accepted the mythical standard of beauty that a blue-eyed doll given for Christmas was every black girl's dream, for adults, older girls, shops, magazines, newspapers, window signs—all the world had agreed that a blue-eyed, yellow-haired, pink-skinned doll was what every girl child treasured, and, consequently, that affection for white dolls was transferred to white girls or black girls like Maureen, who more closely resembled them. Thus, Pecola was cast aside—ignored by her black school teacher who failed to assign someone else to share her desk while all other students had seat partners; taunted by little black boys—boys black like her, who momentarily purge themselves of their contempt for their own blackness by conducting the ritualistic bullying game of referencing skin color and/or insulting one's parents—encircling her and chanting in tribal unison: Black e mo Black e mo Ya daddy sleeps nekked. She literally is encircled momentarily, only to be put outside again, physically and emotionally, reminded that she is not wanted.

Yet perhaps the hardest attack on self-mutilation by race comes in the narration of Pecola's meeting with Geraldine, a sugar-brown Mobile girl, college-educated, clean, controlled, cold colored woman who did not allow her son to play with niggers. Claudia mocks this kind of unfeeling creature who, despite her smarts, was as naive as Pecola in accepting white middle-class American myths of beauty, order, and happiness. In seeking to emulate whites, Geraldine spurned anything remotely suggestive of black-ness and all that the larger society had attached to it, for unlike the Breedloves, the MacTeers, and other black families who moved about the hem of life, struggling . . . [to] hang on, or to creep singly up into the major folds of the garment, she fallaciously believed that she owned the garment. Therefore, her outburst upon finding Pecola in her house is not surprising: Get out . . . You nasty little black bitch. Get out of my house. Pecola reminds her of all that she disdains for members of her own race that fall out of her caste.

Poor, black, and unkempt, Pecola gets a glimpse of the idyllic world that the primer has described, and in a black home at that, but her eviction from the premises must cause her to subconsciously ponder whether she will ever claim such ownership or whether she even deserves it, at least not as she is. Literally and figuratively, once again she is placed outdoors. Except for the prostitutes and Frieda and Claudia, most of the black people she encounters make her feel unwanted, homeless. While Frieda and Claudia make a concerted effort to keep her from feeling outdoors after their parents take her in as a case, their kindness is not enough to bolster her esteem.

Morrison shouts to the world the secret shared by many African Americans: knowledge of the prejudice and contempt that lie within the hearts of some blacks for other blacks and knowledge of the devastating effects that such hatred has on the psyche of blacks who are subjected to it. How can one become whole when he himself helps chisel away at his very being? How does one allow others to come into his home and dictate life for the residents there? These are the questions Morrison wants blacks to answer as she exposes their behavior and feelings toward one another. Through the mouth of a babe, Morrison says it is a miscarriage of justice to put oneself . . . one's own kin outdoors, and in the black community as perhaps no where else kin goes far beyond bloodline; for there, everyone is Cousin So-and-So, Amy boy, Amy man, or Amy people. She wants to prick the conscience and consciousness of blacks to remind them of the democ-racy within the black community that exists in few other cultures: a place where for years, everyone—the prostitutes, the Soapheads, the mentally disturbed, the property owners and the non-propertied, the young and the old, the black necks and the sugar-browns—have found safety, nurturing, and acceptance when it could not be found elsewhere.

The Final Eviction Notice: Rejection of the Self
by the Biological Family

The more acceptance and harmony within the race itself, the closer one comes to becoming whole; there is no need to seek acceptance within the larger society. Home (the culture itself) becomes the proverbial home, sweet home, a place that has no rival. But if there is no acceptance in the nuclear or familial home—the external home of the individual after leaving the womb—the chances of one becoming whole are greatly reduced, and such is the case with Pecola. Morrison attacks both the myth and legend about the relationship between one and his or her biological family. One commonly held myth of almost all cultures is that human beings (as do some other mammals) instinctively protect, accept, and nurture their offspring. And legend declares that black people more so than people of many other cultures have always been very protective and caring of their offspring. However, in the Breedlove family there is little warmth and love exhibited toward the children. Morrison ironically uses the term Breedlove to show the family's shortcoming and to instill in her audience the purpose of the family: to breed love, hence fulfilling and inculcating the mandate that charity begins at home. Yet the kindness shown to Pecola by her mother for the most part begins and ends with her daughter's tenure in the womb. Mrs. Breedlove confesses:

> I used to talk to it whilst it can be still in the womb. Like good friends we was. You know. I be hanging was and I knowed lifting weren't good for it. I'd say to it holt on now I gone hang up these few rags, don't get froggy; it be over soon. It wouldn't leap or nothing . . .On up til the end I felted good about that baby.

The friendship that blossomed in the womb became blighted when upon Pecola's birth, the mother noted she was ugly. Head full of hair, but Lord she was ugly as was the Breedlove family, and this contempt for the ugliness of Pecola and the mother's overall hatred of her family's ugliness and dissatisfaction with her marriage and poverty trickled down to Pecola. This factor notwithstanding, Mrs. Breedlove's repressed artistic longing for beauty, order, and power/acceptance finally found expression in her work as a maid for a white family, who represent in physical attributes what the silver screen had endorsed, and her acceptance of these ideals led her to reject and neglect her family: physically and verbally abusing Pecola, even when she is in pain, spit[ting] out words. . . like rotten pieces of apple, while comforting the little pink-and-yellow girl with words of honey. Into her son she beat a loud desire to run away, and into her daughter she beat a fear of growing up, fear of other people, fear of life. Mrs. Breedlove violates one of the more sacred and primal mores: She, in neglecting her own flesh and in breeding fear and uncertainly, pushes her children aside—outdoors. And the father's hatred and vile treatment assures that outdoors is where they will remain.

While Mrs. Breedlove slowly destroyed Pecola's spirit, Cholly ruined her. He had put his whole family outdoors earlier, having burned down their physical home and stirred the wrath of the community, catapult[ing] himself beyond the reaches of human consideration, having joined the animals and thus was considered by other blacks as an old dog, a snake, a ratty nigger. But he commits the ultimate crime when he, in a drunken state, sins against his own flesh—rapes and impregnates Pecola. Guilt, impotence, and—strangely—tenderness motivated him to rape his daughter, because he feels that his body is all he has to offer her. But the effects on Pecola have no redemptive value. The fear that Mrs. Breedlove had embedded in her multi-plied by the fear that bullies had aroused in her multiplied triply now by the fearfulness of not knowing how to respond to this foreign—physical and emotional—show of emotion from her father terrorizes her, causing her to faint—to step outside of self temporarily—and finally to step out of reality completely.

In narrating this fable, Morrison wants readers to be doubly aware of the sweeping double-edgedness of racism and sexism. While she criticizes the parents for destroying their daughter's self-worth, she also shows the catalysts which triggered their own warped sense of self and led to their deni-gration of the family. That is, Mrs. Breedlove's response to Pecola stems from her own repulsion with her physical makeup—her lack of beauty according to white America's standards—as well as with her childhood belief that her twisted foot made her different, the loss of front teeth, unrealistic dreams of a perfectly ordered world, and repressed romantic ideals, and ostracism by other blacks that had the same insecurities about their blackness as she, but who felt a smidgen of superiority because they were more adept at urban living than she. She could not escape the idealism of the dominant society which economically deprived her of realizing a better life nor the judgment and competition imposed by her own community—which in spite of its own common denominator of blackness—with its color consciousness and its caste system which delegated her and hers to an inferior or otherwise invisible existence; thus despaired of gaining a better life, she had nothing to look forward to but the sparring matches between her and Cholly. Unable to challenge the dominant white male society which denied her humanity—a society which, in fact, compared her and all black women to horses when they gave birth because she evidently like others did not hoop and holler during the birthing process—and unable to herself synthesize that very knowledge and make analogies between differences in giving birth to inherent physical but no less unappealing individual and cultural differences, she finds the only measure of self-reliance she can through her religion and through her work, even at the expense of alienating her own flesh. She must create a new world that excludes her daughter, for Pecola reminds her of all that she detests about herself.

Cholly, unfortunately but predictably, has become a product of his environment. Having been abandoned by his mother and father, raised by a great aunt who did the best that she could but died just as Cholly became of age, and emotionally raped by the white men who stumbled upon him during his first initiation into manhood (his first sexual relationship) and insisted that he perform as they watched, Cholly is now emotionally impotent. The anger and shame he felt because of the white man's control over him is now manifested in his relationships with all women, consequently his adaptation of a cavalier philosophy about life. Not having known the love of parents, Cholly does not know how to act like a parent. Though not physically unattractive, his gratification of his appetites and his violent ways make him so. He fights with his wife because she was one of the few things abhorrent to him that he could touch and therefore hurt. He poured out on her the sum of all his inarticulate fury and aborted desires. Hating her, he could leave himself intact.

Evicted: Alone with the Mutilated Self— the Only Salvageable Possession

Ironically, this rape takes place in the spring, the mythic time for a young love and mating, planning and planting, rebirth and growth. Cholly found his manhood and lost it during the spring, and he steals his daughter's childhood away from her during the same season. A child is conceived but does not grow to full term because it was conceived in abomination. And, finally, it is during this mythic season of rebirth, that a part of Pecola—the childless-mother-child—dies, but not until she goes to Soaphead Church, the mulatto community spiritualist to grant her blue eyes! Morrison juxtaposes nature with the life of the Breedloves, showing the incongruities of each. Just as ideals about the season can be distortions, so are the ideals that African Americans have accepted from white Americans about values and objectives.

Morrison illustrates that it is too late for the fabled Breedlove family who had wholeheartedly accepted ideas of the majority about their self-worth and place in society. But she wants other blacks to be appalled by the treatment of these parents (and others like them) who reject their offspring even though they share the same dwelling; those who ignore their young, ingest them with self-hatred and fear of self, and thus create an environment where there is no warmth—despite the coal stove—no warmth because a blackmama responds eagerly, in a honeyed-tone, when the little pink girl calls her by a nickname but is so formal and formidable at home that the flesh of her own flesh call her Mrs. Breedlove. But then, if there is more truth than myth in the notion that home is where the heart is, the storefront that she inhabits with her family is not home for Mrs. Breedlove, and she, considering her family only as afterthoughts, makes no effort to make it a home. Consequently, Pecola has no memories, at least not positive ones. For her the familial home, like the racial community, like the larger society of Lorain, was a frightening and soulessly cruel place.

Summary and Analysis

Could Pecola have helped herself? In a world where individuality is valued maybe she could have. In a world that never championed ideals of physical beauty probably [one of] the most destructive ideas in the history of human thought—she would not have had the problem with self esteem and identity in the first place. Perhaps if she had been more aggressive, like Claudia and Frieda, she would have survived the indifference shown her. Or better yet, had she been as angry as Bigger Thomas, she would have annihilated some of those who made her feel like an outsider and, if nothing else, would have assuaged some of her pain. But she did not. She could not. She wanted love too dearly. She wanted in—acceptance. She yearned to find peace—to be at home—with self.

Like many, Pecola began her search for self by looking at herself; hours she sat looking in the mirror, trying to discover the secret of the ugliness, the ugliness that made her ignored or despised at school, by teachers and classmates alike. But in looking, she, perhaps oblivious to her own self, looked for reflections of Shirley Temple, Mary Jane, Maureen Peal—high-yellow dream child—or even sugar-brown Geraldine. And, of course, she did not find any; they were not supposed to be there. Had she taken a look at herself through her own eyes, instead of through the eyes of others, she would have seen her own beauty. However, not seeing mythical beauty, she resolved that if her eyes, those eyes that held the pictures, and knew the sights—if those eyes of hers were different, that is to say beautiful, she herself would be different; thus, she began to pray for blue eyes, which would be the panacea for all her and her family's ills, for if she looked different, beautiful, maybe Cholly would be different, and Mrs. Breedlove too. She prayed for blue eyes and ate

Mary Janes in hopes of eat[ing] the eyes, eat[ing] Mary Jane. Lov[ing] Mary Jane. Be[ing] Mary Jane. If she had blue eyes, someone would finally love her. When she had asked Frieda and Claudia . . . how do you get somebody to love you?, they had not answered; however, her classmates, her teacher, her mother, and the larger society—the world around her—seemingly shouted in unison, with blue eyes!

Unquestionably, had she applied the same intuitive knowledge about the dandelion and cracks in the sidewalks in her community to herself—her beauty—she would have made strides toward her quest for self. The dandelions, which people said were weeds, were pretty to her. The cracks on the sidewalk, while unnoticed or considered an eyesore by others, were valued by her. Morrison writes, They were the codes and touchstones of the world, capable of translation and possession. Pecola owned both the dandelions and the cracks, and owning them made her a part of the world and the world a part of her. If she had been taught to value her own instincts, she may have paused long enough and looked soulfully inward long enough and then outward at herself to recognize the beauty in her that she instinctively noticed in the dandelion. She would have recognized that she, just as the cracks in the sidewalk, was precious and had purpose, but most importantly, she would have realized that she alone owned herself. But she would have had to spend some time in thought, accepting this perception—this insight—for what it was, the truth that had been distorted by the larger society and ignored by far too many of her kindred who, like Pecola, had acquiesced without questioning, too anxious too assimilate. She would have had to spend time in thought unlearning, what her brief lifetime had taught her so that she would not have abandoned her ideas— her pride in self—upon encountering racial and cultural bigotry, as she angrily abandoned her ideas about the beauty and worth of the dandelions and cracks immediately upon encountering the bigoted store clerk. Lacking knowledge of self-worth, she thus continued to pray for the miracle of blue eyes, despairing at last of mediating with god and going to a spiritualist to mediate for her.

Pecola's quest for self began at home with her looking at self, but then like her brother Sammy, her quest took her away from home—outdoors—in a manner of speaking, as well. She had to go outside to find a self that she could live with, but outside was not a physical journey. Her journey had begun gradually. She prayed to disappear when her parents fought:

Please make me disappear. She squeezed her eyes shut. Little parts of her body faded away. Now slowly, now with a rush. Slowly again. Her fingers went, one by one; then her arms disappeared all the way to the elbow. Her feet now. Yes, that was good . . . Then her chest, her neck.

And she was almost successful, except for the eyes, which were always left, thus the prayer to make them disappear and have new blue ones, the bluest eyes in their place. And she was forever tucking in her neck; hunching her shoulders; fold[ing] into herself, like a pleated wing; crouching (as though) from an unrelieved blow. One day she goes so far into herself, in an attempt to find a better self that can withstand the stares, the laughter, the gossip, the rejection, and shame that somehow seemed to have been her inheritance alone, that she does not return. Unable to stop the unrelieved blows, her psyche cracks, letting a new and anesthetized psyche emerge to the fore—a fractured yet resilient psyche able to withstand the nuisances and illimitable and normally insufferable hazards that living outdoors brings. The real Pecola dies, dies because she could not survive knowing she does not have blue eyes; dies because she now knows that she has always been and always would be outdoors as long as her family, race, and the larger society subscribed to the same ideals that mutilated her psyche.

Conclusion

Using Claudia MacTeer's family as a foil, Morrison shows what can happen to an individual who comes from the same socio-economic background of Pecola, and one that, to a certain extent, is fascinated with white baby dolls and Shirley Temple, but one who has better self-esteem because that self was fed with Love, thick and dark as laga syrup. Using poetry and the postmodernist tradition, she dramatically reveals what happens to individuals whose personhood and beauty are negated summarily by the society in which they live. Using the novel as a medium, Morrison hammers away at the pretensions of the black community in hopes of restor[ing] the mythos and ethos that will clarify the meaning of the journey of African-Americans in the United States. Or as Ruby Dee in her review of *The Bluest Eye* wrote:

> the novelist digs up for viewing secret thoughts, terrible yearnings little understood frustrations common to many of us . . . gnawings we keep pushed back into the subconscious, unadmitted, [which] must be worked on, ferreted up and out so we can breathe deeply, say loud and truly believe Black is beautiful.

Then, and only then, Morrison asserts, will African Americans realize the true attributes of home—their own home. A place of refuge from the outdoors. A nurturing environment, in fact, from where one dare not turn away one's own flesh.

JOHN N. DUVALL

Naming the Invisible Authority:
Toni Morrison's Covert Letter to Ralph Ellison

And all those people were me. I was Pecola, Claudia. . . . I was everybody.

Soaphead Church and his letter to God have occasioned a variety of critical responses. A fact generally overlooked in the commentary on *The Bluest Eye*, even in articles specifically on narration, is that Soaphead, because of his letter, is a narrator too. His narration is coterminous with his act of authorship. Since authorship is what Morrison herself stakes a claim to in her first novel, I want to argue that Church stands as a significant early figure in Toni Morrison's attempt to fashion a usable radicalized authorial identity. Growing up in the working-class town of Lorain, Ohio, where there were no black neighborhoods, Morrison's youth and adolescence were largely free of race consciousness. "I never absorbed racism," Morrison says in a 1992 interview. "I never took it in. That's why I wrote *The Bluest Eye*, to find out how it felt." Morrison's various accounts of her relation to her first novel invite speculation on how this fiction figures in a process of racial self-discovery that is indistinguishable from the act of writing.

Taken as an instance of self-fashioning, Church's letter to God reveals itself as a metafictional gesture that encodes Morrison's own ambitions and anxieties regarding her authorial identity. Church's urge to address God's

From *Studies in American Fiction* 25, no. 2 (Autumn 1997). © 1997 Northeastern University.

transcendent spiritual authority symbolically represents Morrison's desire to address and contest the cultural authority of Ralph Ellison. Church's letter, in fact, provides further evidence of the way the central plot situation of *The Bluest Eye*—Pecola Breedlove's rape by her father—rewrites the Jim Trueblood episode of *Invisible Man*, a connection suggestively articulated by Michael Awkward.

To argue that Soaphead Church should be read as an instance of self-fashioning might seem to overlook perversely the more obvious authorial figuration, Claudia MacTeer, who rather straightforwardly seems a portrait of the artist as a young woman. Like Morrison, Claudia is in 1942 a ten-year-old girl living in Lorain, Ohio. Morrison's thinly disguised autobiographical impulse becomes even more apparent when one examines her character's name. Morrison was born "Chloe," and "MacTeer" is a family name. Beginning the novel speaking from the child's perspective, Claudia/Chloe nevertheless concludes the novel speaking from an older and wiser adult perspective. From this adult perspective, she speaks a theory of radical implication, one that refuses to blame Cholly entirely for Pecola's fate and sees rather the entire community's role in what befalls Pecola. Nor does Claudia excuse herself in her communal/self-critique:

> we were not strong, only aggressive; we were not free, merely licensed; we were not compassionate, we were polite; not good, but well behaved. We courted death in order to call ourselves brave, and hid like thieves from life. We substituted good grammar for intellect; we switched habits to simulate maturity; we rearranged lies and called it truth, seeing in the new pattern of an old idea the Revelation and the Word.

This moment of self-critique by one author-figure leads back to Soaphead Church in two ways. First, there is his letter's content. Church makes his living through false revelation by marketing himself as the medium of God's Word, but his letter contains a strong element of self-critique even as it overtly criticizes God for flaws in his design.

Second, and perhaps more significant, a rhetorical pattern in Church's letter directly echoes the rhetorical strategy Claudia/Chloe deploys at the end of the novel. Speaking of Caribbean genealogy and its relation to the white ruling class, Church maintains:

> In retaining the identity of our race, we held fast to those characteristics most gratifying to sustain and least troublesome to maintain. Consequently we were not royal but snobbish, not

aristocratic but class-conscious; we believed authority was cruelty to our inferiors, and education was being at school. We mistook violence for passion, indolence for leisure, and thought reckless-ness was freedom.

In this rhetorical doubling, the metonymic chain of displaced author-figures becomes clearer. Church, by repeating the content and form of the novel's communal critique, approximately substitutes for the adult Claudia who in turn approximately substitutes for Morrison. This chain of substitutions suggests that there are some issues constellated around the cultural authority of names and naming as they relate to identity that Morrison perhaps can only address through the deeper cover of Church. As we shall see, the changes that transform Elihue Whitcomb into Soaphead Church obversely reflect Chloe Wofford's construction of Toni Morrison as her authorial identity.

One might reasonably object that Church could not be an authorial self-representation because Morrison, as a midwestern woman, is nothing like Church, a West Indian man. Moreover, Morrison has explicitly distanced herself from the ideological blindness of Church, even as she claims to have needed a character like him to provide Pecola her revelation; she sees him as someone who

> would be wholly convinced that if black people were more like white people they would be better off. And I tried to explain that in terms of his own Western Indian background—a kind of English, colonial, Victorian thing drilled into his head which he could not escape.

But by analogy, neither is the respectable Nathaniel Hawthorne overtly like his tortured artist figures, such as Roger Chillingsworth, who delve into the human heart. "Ethan Brand" is perhaps the best example of Hawthorne's authorial anxiety. Ethan's life-long search for the unpardonable sin constructs him as that unpardonable sinner—precisely because of his consciously willed artistic detachment from other people in order to study human motives. Again, Ethan is not like Hawthorne, yet the character surely figures the author's sense of the implications of authorship. In the self-exiled Soaphead Church, Morrison also seems to intuit the problematic that Hawthorne repeatedly represents in his artist figures—the eccentricity, marginality, and even the misanthropy of those who pursue their art.

In Soaphead Church, then, Morrison, who has stated that "the impetus for writing *The Bluest Eye*" was to construct a fiction about a group of people "never taken seriously by anybody—all those peripheral little girls," has created a character who is equally, albeit pervertedly, serious about peripheral little girls. In conversation with Robert Stepto, Morrison recollects that she needed someone who could give Pecola blue eyes—"that kind of figure who dealt with fortune-telling, dream-telling, so on." And indeed The *Bluest Eye* identifies Soaphead's own construction of self as a "Reader, Advisor, and Interpreter of Dreams," a calling "that brought him freedom and satisfaction" because it affords the misanthropic Church with "numerous opportunities to witness human stupidity without sharing it or being compromised by it." Church's satisfaction with the nature of his chosen work begins to create a series of parallels to the conditions Morrison deems necessary for writing. Morrison has said that although the writing of her first novel followed a period of depression, "the words 'lonely, depressed, melancholy'" do not describe her state of mind while working; rather, she says, writing comes during "an unbusy state, when I am more aware of myself than of others." Church deliberately creates the "unbusy state," which Morrison identifies as the precondition to artistic creation, by removing himself to the monastic existence of the back-room apartment he rents. In fact, Church's solitude suggests Morrison's own isolation while writing her first novel. She tells Kathy Neustadt that what may have been conducive to writing was the absence of any social contact: "I didn't have any friends and didn't make any, didn't want any because I was on my way somewhere else."

The solitary act of writing constructs authorial identity, as Morrison's comment to Gloria Naylor indicates; writing *The Bluest Eye*, "I fell in love with myself. I reclaimed myself and the world—a real revelation. I named it. I described it. I listed it. I identified it." As Morrison describes it here, *The Bluest Eye* serves as a writing of self for self and suggests a trope for authorship as old as the novel—the author as God of the fictional world—though with a twist. Morrison's description of the ex nihilo construction of identity through language would make her the metaphorical equal of God or of any other writer who similarly appropriated the role of self-creation and self-revelation through the word. If Morrison experiences writing *The Bluest Eye* as a revelation, then special consideration ought to be given to Church, who—after witnessing what he takes to be Pecola's moment of revelation—turns to the act of writing. Again, Morrison claims to have needed a character like Church who could provide Pecola her revelation, even though that revelation is fraudulent.

It is, therefore, in his role as dream teller and reader that Church's identity most clearly figures Morrison's own, if we credit another of her accounts of the composition of her first novel: "I was writing for some clear, single person—I would say myself, because I was quite content to be the only reader. . . . I am not being facetious when I say I wrote *The Bluest Eye* in order to read it. And I think that is what makes the difference, because I could look at it as a reader, really as a reader, and not as my own work." This emphasis on herself as audience for her novel collapses the space between reader and writer, consumer and producer. For Church to be a reader of dreams means necessarily that he tells others what their dreams mean. In this regard, Morrison herself is a dream-teller, for in constructing the climactic moment of her narrative, she deploys the symbolic logic of the dream work; her plot's climax is not one moment but two moments that speak together.

The letter to God occurs immediately after the novel's central moment of symbolic doubling, one with clear psychoanalytic implications. In Cholly's rape of Pecola, Morrison explicitly invokes the psychoanalytic notion of repressed memory. Pecola passes out and does not recognize what has happened to her. Her descent into madness occurs only when she unwittingly particpates in Church's plan to kill old dog, Bob, by giving the animal poisoned meat. The death of the dog presents to Pecola something akin to a symbolic dreamscape that represents the rape through a distorted lens that blurs the clarity of victim and victimizer. Although itself a victim of a plot, dog Bob becomes a symbolic substitute for Cholly, who from the outset is troped as "old Dog Breedlove"; the dog's spasmodic death symbolically repeats Cholly's orgasm. Prior to raping his daughter, the drunken Cholly approaches her "crawling on all fours" and, like the dog, which eats the meat prior to his spasm, Pecola is fully conscious of what is happening to the dog:

> Choking, stumbling, he moved like a broken toy around the yard. The girl's mouth was open, a little petal of tongue showing. She made a wild, pointless gesture with one hand and then covered her mouth with both hands. She was trying not to vomit. The dog fell again, a spasm jerking his body. Then he was quiet. The girl's hands covering her mouth, she backed away a few feet, then turned, ran out of the yard and down the sidewalk.

It is only Pecola's dawning equation of her father's act with the dog's death that can explain her nausea, since the dog's death, according to Church's deception, is the sign that God will grant her blue eyes. Otherwise, one would expect Pecola to rejoice at the sign telling her she will receive the gift she has so wished for. Pecola's subsequent belief that she now indeed has blue eyes therefore represents another form of repression, the way her unconscious forecloses the recognition that begins to happen in old dog Bob's death.

Church's letter, then, completes while complicating the repetition by revealing the intimate details of his molestation of little girls, details that suggest a kinship between himself and Cholly. But the sympathy in the portrayal of Church perhaps results from his symbolic kinship to Morrison. Church, however arrogant and unbalanced in the act of writing, has made a minimal movement from consciousness to self-consciousness; witnessing Pecola's felt revelation serves as Church's own revelatory moment inasmuch as it takes him from a position of nonimplication (his belief that his life allows him to be a witness to "human stupidity without sharing it or being compromised by it" to one that recognizes his implication. In his self-reflexive letter is the beginning of self-critique, a situation that parallels the revelation Morrison claims writing her first novel provided her. Significantly, Church's identity as a writer—the one capable of self-critique—emerges in the moment of his production and is not prior to his act of writing.

Here Michael Awkward's reading of *The Bluest Eye* as a rewriting of the Jim Trueblood episode of *Invisible Man* helps prepare the ground for understanding Church's letter to God as Morrison's letter to Ellison. For Awkward, Morrison's plot serves as feminist revision of Ellison's representation of Trueblood's violation of his daughter. Ellison's portrayal is problematic, as Awkward notes, for the way it silences the women and constantly makes the father-daughter incest a voyeuristic site for tile male gaze. What I would add to Awkward's argument regarding Morrison's rewriting of incestuous rape is the presence of another silenced female character who, although very minor in Ellison's novel, underscores the metafictional nature of Morrison's revision of Ellison: the midwife who Jim Trueblood fears will abort the fetuses of his daughter and wife and whom he threatens to kill if she comes near his house. Her name is Aunt Cloe. *The Bluest Eye*, then also functions as an act of literary criticism in which Cloe/Chloe finally does abort Ellison's masculinist presumption in representing the father's violation of the daughter as the father's problem exclusively.

Church's letter is crucial because it reveals that not only has Morrison rewritten Ellison's novel, she also has commented covertly on her revision in a way that is nevertheless unmistakably signaled, so that the criticism of God becomes simultaneously a criticism of Ellison. The opening paragraph makes Church's and, indirectly, Morrison's intent clear: "The Purpose of this letter is to familiarize you with facts which either have escaped your notice, or which you have chosen to ignore." It is precisely the violated daughter's perspective about which Morrison (through Church) is speaking, a fact made clear later in the letter: "Tell me, Lord, how could you leave a lass so long so lone that she could find her way to me? How could you? I weep for you, Lord. And it is because I weep for You that I had to do your work for You."

Here Morrison suggests why it was necessary for her to revise Ellison. It is as if Matty Lou Trueblood had wandered lost for nearly twenty years only to be transformed into Pecola Breedlove:

> Do you know what she came for? blue eyes. New, blue eyes, she said. . . . She must have asked you for them for a very long time, and you hadn't replied . . . . She came to me for them. She had one of my cards. (Card enclosed.) By the way, I added the Micah—Elihue Micah Whitcomb. But I am called Soaphead Church. I cannot remember how or why I got the name. What make one name more a person than another? Is the name the real thing, then? And the person only what his name says? Is that why to the simplest and friendliest of questions: "What is your name?" put to you by Moses, You would not say, and said instead "I am who I am." Like Popeye? I Yam What I Yam? Afraid you were, weren't you, to give out your name? Afraid they would know the name and then know you? Then they wouldn't fear you? It's quite all right. Don't be vexed. I mean no offense. I understand.

This dense passage does a number of things. First and foremost it makes clear the Morrison had read and is recasting *Invisible Man*, a fact that leads to the relation of Church's God and Morrison's Ellison. But the passage also self-reflexively turns the question of names and identity back on Morrison as she now claims authorship in her first novel.

In framing her questions regarding the relation of one's name to one's identity, Morrison's passage alludes specifically to a key moment of identification in Chapter 13 of *Invisible Man*. Prior to his speech to the crowd at the eviction of the old couple, the young man has a moment of self-reflection occasioned when he buys a yam from a street vendor. While eating the yam, anger rises in him about the discomfort that surrounds his attempts to enjoy aspects of African-American culture: "This is all very wild and childish, I thought, but to hell with being ashamed of what you liked. No more of that for me. I am what I am!" When the invisible man orders two more yams, the old African-American vendor says, "I can see you one of these old-fashioned yam eaters," to which the protagonist replies, "They're my birthmark. I yam what I yam."

This moment in *Invisible Man* to which Morrison alludes resonates with one of Morrison's recurring thematics—the dilemma of characters caught in the conflict between a desire to assimilate the values of the white middle class and the voices that urge them to acknowledge a black racial identity. Immediately prior to seeing the street vendor selling yams, the invisible man notices a window advertisement for skin-lightening cream. This instance of the overdetermined cultural messages that value white over black is of course precisely Morrison's subject matter in *The Bluest Eye*, a fiction that interrogates why even the black community prefers the light-skinned Maureen Peal to the dark-skinned Pecola Breedlove. Having recognized Morrison's address to Ellison in Church's letter to God, one can now hear the end of the letter resonate in a new way:

> I did what You did not, could not, would not do—I looked at that ugly little black girl, and I loved her. I played You. And it was a very good show! . . . Now you are jealous. You are jealous of me. You see? I, too, have created. Not aboriginally, like you, but creation is a heady wine, more for the taster than the brewer.

Church's observation that the work of creation is more for the consumer than the producer recalls Morrison's claim that in writing her first novel she was "quite content to be the only reader." Church then signs his name—Elihue Micah Whitcomb—choosing his birth name rather than the name he is known by in the community. This seems a particularly pertinent detail given what Morrison said in 1992 about her true identity: "I am really Chloe Anthony Wofford. That's who I am. I have been writing under this other person's name. I write some things now as Chloe Wofford, private things. I regret having called myself Toni Morrison when I published my first novel, *The Bluest Eye*." But is Morrison really Chloe Anthony Wofford? The answer to this question is hinted at by Soaphead Church's admission that he is not actually Elihue Micah Whitcomb, since the middle name is his invention.

Morrison's relation to her own name encompasses the apparent anxiety Ellison's protagonist manifest by remaining unnamed. The reason Church/Morrison can sympathize—indeed almost condescend to God/Ellison—is that Morrison takes an alternative yet parallel path to the invisible man's in order to create a foundation for an authorizing voice: she is not the unnamed (Ellison's protagonist) but rather the self-named. Morrison's act of self-fashioning is figured in Church's presentation of his card to God (again, the one who, like Ellison's protagonist, prefers to remain unnamed). In this moment of presentation, Church confides, "By the way, I added the Micah—Elihue Micah Whitcomb." In order to understand the issue of identity at stake in this detail of the invented middle name, it is necessary to consider the transformation of Chloe Wofford into Toni Morrison. While "Soaphead Church" manifests a communal act of naming that reclaims his African-Americanness from his white, ruling-class-inspired name (Elihue Whitcomb), Morrison's individual act of self-naming seems to move in the opposite direction.

Wofford becomes Morrison when she marries Jamaican architect Harold Morrison in 1958, but more interesting is Morrison's decision to become known as "Toni." In a conversation with Colette Dowling in 1979, Morrison claims to have made the change in college "because the people at Howard seemed to have difficulty pronouncing" Chloe. What makes Morrison's coded reference to her own name change in Soaphead Church's letter so striking is the way her fiction repeatedly examines the struggles of African Americans to forge an authentic identity for themselves. Often she ties this quest for identity to African-American names and the act of naming. Responding to Thomas LeClair's question about the significance of naming in *Song of Solomon*, Morrison says that for African Americans "the best thing you can do is take another name which is yours because it reflects something about you or your own choice." In *Song of Solomon*, Guitar Banes, responding to Milkman's complaint that he does not like his name, says, "Let me tell you somethin, baby. Niggers get their names the way they get everything else— the best way they can." It is difficult not to hear in Milkman's complaint about his name Morrison's relation to her own name.

Morrison denies "Chloe" and chooses "Toni," but why? It is hard, perhaps, to register why such a change might have been useful, especially since recently "Chloe" has gained a certain cachet, as evidenced by the white female characters who bear this name in two recent television dramas, *ER* and *Malibu Shores*. But in the 1950s, to a bright young black woman with career aspirations, "Chloe" strongly signaled a form of radicalized identity from which Morrison may have wished to distance herself. Quite simply, this name often signals a particularly hated form of racial oppression and servility in the agrarian South. In her undergraduate and graduate literary studies, Morrison certainly could find unflattering Chloes in American literature beside the one in Ellison's novel. For example, in Harriet Beecher Stowe's *Uncle Tom's Cabin* (1852), Uncle Tom's wife, the prized cook of the Shelby family who loves her master's son better than her own children, is named Aunt Chloe. Taken together, both Stowe's and Ellison's Aunt Chloes partic- ipate in a racial stereotype that signifies in a fashion parallel to Aunt Jemima. Whatever the exact motivation for Morrison's decision to become Toni, one thing is clear: the matter of identity was not a given for Toni Morrison, because she rejects her given name.

One might object that I am placing too much emphasis on this name change. After all, the published biographical information on Morrison agrees that her full name was Chloe Anthony Wofford, so that the adoption of

"Toni" as a substitute for "Chloe" still honors her given name, if somewhat obliquely. Morrison's middle name, however, was not Anthony; the birth certificate indicates her full name as Chloe Ardelia Wofford, revealing that Ramah and George Wofford named their daughter for her maternal grandmother, Ardelia Willis. While the origin of "Toni" is now obscure, the example of Milkman Dead illustrates that names in the African-American community do not come exclusively from birth certificates. Moreover, the naming of Milkman's grandfather, the original Macon Dead, through a gesture of casual racism by a drunken Union soldier, is but one example in Morrison's fiction that should remind the reader not to place too much faith in legal documents. But Morrison's name change seems fundamentally different than those suggested by Milkman and Macon Dead because in her case there is no apparent need to subvert a white authority to name, since "Ardelia" comes from her parents.

Why, then, has Morrison constructed "Anthony" as the fictional origin of "Toni"? Perhaps by 1979 (when she tells Dowling that "Toni" is derived from "Anthony") Morrison was uncomfortable with a first name that might be perceived as masking familial identity. Perhaps, though, one might read the fictional Anthony/Toni as a gesture of authorial self-fashioning, akin to Willa Cather's use of "William" in certain instances or to William Faulkner's insertion of the "u" in his family name. What Morrison seems to have done is to have created an authorial identity that can only be true insofar as it is fictional, as tile examples from *Tar Baby* and *Song of Solomon* suggest. Both possibilities—an uneasiness over disguised identity and an authorial self-fashioning—converge in her claim to be "really Chloe Anthony Wofford." In a sense, however, only by denying Chloe (as well as Ardelia) as her public name can Morrison become Chloe in her private discursive creation of herself as novelist. What the symbolic logic of Soaphead Church's letter reveals, then, is the way Morrison—who claims not to have experienced racism prior to writing *The Bluest Eye*—uses her novel to respond to doubts, whether her own or those of others, about her authenticity.

In the course of her illustrious career as an author, Morrison has come to represent to many an unassailable authenticity. My essay in no way wishes to gainsay the cultural authority Morrison has achieved but rather to argue against a presumption that this authentic identity was a fait accompli before she ever put pen to page. Again, the question of identity was not a given for Toni Morrison, because she rejects her given name. Soaphead Church's letter to God, with its oblique reference to the necessity of an authorial self fashioning distinct from that generated by a birth name, encodes many of the issues of identity that Morrison clearly struggled with, not just in *The Bluest Eye*, but later also in *Song of Solomon* and *Tar Baby*, where naming and authentic racial identity are central. At the same time, her covert address to Ralph Ellison indicates the scope of her writerly aspiration, which even with her first novel seems to be to supplant Ellison as a cultural authority on the African-American experience. Church's letter, as well as his perversion, serves a Morrison's metafictional reminder to herself that the author can never escape implication in what she critiques.

Chronology

1931   Toni Morrison born Chloe Anthony Wofford on February 18 in Lorain, Ohio, the second child of George Wofford and Ramah Willis Wofford.

1953   Graduates with B.A. in English from Howard University; changes name to Toni during years at Howard.

1955   Receives M.A. in English from Cornell University for thesis on the theme of suicide in William Faulkner and Virginia Woolf.

1955–57   Instructor in English at Texas Southern University.

1957–64   Instructor in English at Howard University.

1958   Marries Harold Morrison, a Jamaican architect.

1964   Divorces Morrison and returns with her two sons to Lorain.

1965   Becomes editor for a textbook subsidiary of Random House in Syracuse, New York.

1970   Morrison's first novel, *The Bluest Eye* published; takes editorial position at Random House in New York, eventually becoming a senior editor.

1971–73   Associate Professor of English at the State University of New York at Purchase.

1974   *Sula* published and an edition of Middleton Harris's *The Black Book*.

1975   *Sula* nominated for National Book Award.

1976–77   Visiting Lecturer at Yale University.

1977   *Song of Solomon* published; receives the National Book Critics Circle Award and the American Academy and Institute of Arts and Letters Award.

1981   *Tar Baby* published.

1984–89   Schweitzer Professor of the Humanities at the State University of New York at Albany.

1986   Receives the New York State Governor's Art Award.

1986–88   Visiting Lecturer at Bard College.

1987   *Beloved* published and is nominated for the National Book Award and the National Book Critics Award.

1988   *Beloved* awarded Pulitzer Prize in fiction and the Robert F. Kennedy Award.

Since 1989 Toni Morrison has been Robert F. Goheen Professor of the Humanities at Princeton University.

Contributors

HAROLD BLOOM is Sterling Professor of Humanities at Yale University and Professor of English at the New York University Graduate School. His works include *The Anxiety of Influence* (1973), *Agon: Toward a Theory of Revisionism* (1982), *The American Religion* (1992), *The Western Canon* (1994), and *Shakespeare: The Invention of the Human* (1998). Professor Bloom is a 1985 MacArthur Foundation Award recipient and served as the Charles Eliot Norton Professor of Poetry at Harvard University in 1987–88. He is the editor of more than 30 anthologies, and general editor of several series of literary criticism published by Chelsea House.

KEITH E. BYERMAN is author of *Fingering the Jagged Grain, John Edgar Wideman: A Study of the Short Fiction, Seizing the Word: History, Art, and Self in the Works of W.E.B. Du Bois,* and *Two Warring Ideals: The Dialectical Thought of W.E.B. Du Bois.*

MADONNE M. MINER is author of *Insatiable Appetites: Twentieth-Century American Women's Bestsellers.*

STEPHANIE A. DEMETRAKOPOULOS is Professor of English at Western Michigan University. She is author of *Listening to Our Bodies: The Rebirth of Feminine Wisdom* and articles on a variety of subjects in the fields of literature, women's history and consciousness, and Jungian psychology.

KARLA F. C. HOLLOWAY is Associate Professor of English, North Carolina State University. She is author of *The Character of the Word: The Texts of Zora Neale Hurston*, as well as journal articles on Black women and politics, and oral language structures. She is associate editor of *Obsidian II: Black Literature in Review*, and on the editorial board of *Linguistics and Education: An International Research Journal*.

SUSAN WILLIS is Associate Professor of English at Duke University. She is author of *Specifying: Black Women Writing the American Experience* and *A Primer for Everyday Life*.

MICHAEL AWKWARD is Associate Professor of English and Afro-American and African Studies at the University of Michigan, Ann Arbor. He is author of *Inspiring Influences: Tradition, Revision, and Afro-American Women's Novels* and editor of *New Essays on Their Eyes Were Watching God*.

DONALD B. GIBSON is Professor of English at Rutgers University, New Brunswick. His published works include the *Politics of Literary Expression: A Study of Major Black Writers* and *The Red Badge of Courage: Redefining the Hero*.

LINDA DITTMAR is editor, with Gene Michaud, of *From Hanoi to Hollywood: The Vietnam War in American Film* and, with Diane Carson and Janice R. Welsh, of *Multiple Voices in Feminist Film Criticism*.

SHELLEY WONG has taught in the Asian American Studies Program at the University of California, Berkeley. Her essays have appeared in *Sagetrieb*, *Mainstream*, *Line*, and *Telos*.

DOREATHA DRUMMOND MBALIA is author of *Heritage: African American Readings for Writing* and *John Edgar Wideman: Reclaiming the African Personality*.

LINDEN PEACH is author of *Angela Carter*, *English as a Creative Art*, *The Prose Writing of Dylan Thomas*, and *British Influence on the Birth of American Literature*.

JAN FURMAN is editor of *Slavery in the Clover Bottoms: John McCline's Narrative of his Life During Slavery and the Civil War*.

LAURIE VICKROY is Assistant Professor of English at Bradley University. Her essays have appeared in *Modern Language Studies*, *Obsidian*, and *The Journal of Durassian Studies*.

Bibliography

Awkward, Michael. *Inspiriting Influences: Tradition, Revision, and Afro-American Women's Novels.* New York: Columbia University Press, 1989. 81–88.

Clark, Norris. "Flying Back: Toni Morrison's *The Bluest Eye, Sula,* and *Song of Solomon, Minority Voices* 4 (Fall 1980): 51–63.

Dickerson, Vanessa D. "The Naked Father in Toni Morrison's *The Bluest Eye,*" *Refiguring the Father: New Feminist Readings of Patriarchy.* Eds., Patricia Yaeger and Beth Kowaleski-Wallace. Carbondale: University of Illinois Press, 1989. 108–27.

Flick, Thomas H. "Toni Morrison's 'Allegory of the Cave': Movies, Consumption, and Platonic Realism in *The Bluest Eye,*" *The Journal of the Midwest Modern Language Association* (Spring 1989): 110–22.

Harris, Trudier. "Reconnecting Fragments: Afro-American Folk Tradition in *The Bluest Eye,*" *Critical Essays on Toni Morrison.* Ed., Nellie Y. McKay. Boston: G.K. Hall, 1988. 68–76.

Hovet, Grace Ann, and Barbara Lounsberry. "Flying as Symbol and Legend in Toni Morrison's *The Bluest Eye, Sula,* and *Song of Solomon,*" *CLA Journal* 27:2 (December 1983): 119–40.

Klottman, Phyllis R. "Dick-and-Jane and the Shirley Temple Sensibility in *The Bluest Eye*," *Black American Literature Forum* 13 (September 1979): 123–25.

Lott, Nicole Gelon. "Ownership and the Loss of Communal Ties in Toni Morrison's *The Bluest Eye*. http://www.mcnair.berkeley.edu/96journal/lott.html

Ogunyemi, Chikwenye O. "Order and Disorder in Toni Morrison's *The Bluest Eye*," *Critique* 19:1 (1977): 112–20.

Portales, Marco. "Toni Morrison's *The Bluest Eye*: Shirley Temple and Cholly," *The Centennial Review* 30 (Fall 1986): 496–506.

Rosenberg, Ruth. "Seeds in Hard Ground: Black Girlhood in *The Bluest Eye*," *Black American Literature Forum* 21 (Winter 1987): 435–45.

Sargent, Robert. "A Way of Ordering Experience: A Study of Toni Morrison's *The Bluest Eye* and *Sula*," *Faith of a (Woman) Writer*, eds. Alice Kessler-Harris and William McBrien. Westport, CT: Greenwood Press, 1988. 229–36.

Somerville, Jane. "Idealized Beauty and the Denial of Love in Toni Morrison's *The Bluest Eye*," *The Bulletin of the West Virginia Association of College English Teachers* 9 (Spring 1986): 18–23.

Tignor, Eleanor Q. "Toni Morrison's Pecola: A Portrait in Pathos," *MAWA Review* 1 (Spring 1982): 24–27.

Weever, Jacqueline de. "The Inverted World of Toni Morrison's *The Bluest Eye* and *Sula*," *CLA Journal* 22:4 (June 1979): 402–14.

Acknowledgments

"Intense Behaviors: The Use of the Grotesque in *The Bluest Eye* and *Eva's Man*" by Keith E. Byerman from *CLA Journal* 24:4 (June 1982): 447–57. © 1982 College Language Association.

"Lady No Longer Sings the Blues: Rape, Madness, and Silence in *The Bluest Eye*" by Madonne M. Miner from *Conjuring: Black Women, Fiction, and Literary Tradition*. Eds., Marjorie Pryse and Hortense J. Spillers. © 1985 Indiana University Press.

"Bleak Beginnings: *The Bluest Eye*" by Stephanie A. Demetrakopoulos from *New Dimensions of Spirituality: A Biracial and Bicultural Reading of the Novels of Toni Morrison*. © 1987 by Karla F. C. Holloway and Stephanie A. Demetrakopoulos.

"The Language and Music of Survival" by Karla F. C. Holloway from *New Dimensions of Spirituality: A Biracial and Bicultural Reading of the Novels of Toni Morrison*. © 1987 by Karla F. C. Holloway and Stephanie A. Demetrakopoulos.

"Eruptions of Funk: Historicizing Toni Morrison" by Susan Willis from *Specifying: Black Women Writing the American Experience* by Susan Wills. Reprinted in *Toni Morrison: Critical Perspectives Past and Present*, eds. Henry Louis Gates, Jr. and K. A. Appiah. © 1987 Board of Regents of the University of Wisconsin System.

"'The Evil of Fulfillment': Scapegoating and Narration in *The Bluest Eye*" by Michael Awkward from *Inspiriting Influence: Tradition, Revision, and Afro-American Women's Novels* by Michael Awkward. Reprinted in *Toni Morrison: Critical Perspectives Past and Present*, eds. Henry Louis Gates, Jr. and K. A. Appiah. © 1989 by Michael Awkward.

"Text and Countertext in *The Bluest Eye*" by Donald B. Gibson from *Toni Morrison: Critical Perspectives Past and Present*, eds. Henry Louis Gates, Jr. and K. A. Appiah. © 1990 by Donald B. Gibson.

" 'Will the Circle Be Unbroken?' The Politics of Form in *The Bluest Eye*" by Linda Dittmar from *Novel: A Forum on Fiction* 23:2 (Winter 1990): 137–54. © 1990 Novel Corp.

"Transgression as Poesis in *The Bluest Eye*" by Shelley Wong from *Callaloo* 13:3 (Summer 1990): 471–81. © 1990 John Hopkins University Press.

"*The Bluest Eye*: The Need for Racial Approbation" by Doreatha Drummond Mbalia from *Toni Morrison's Developing Class Consciousness* by Doreatha Drummond Mbalia. © 1991 by Associated University Presses, Inc.

"Afterword to the 1994 Edition of *The Bluest Eye*" by Toni Morrison. (Plume, Penguin Books) © 1993 by Toni Morrison.

"*The Bluest Eye*" by Linden Peach from *Modern Novelists: Toni Morrison* by Linden Peach. © 1995 by Linden Peach.

"Black Girlhood and Black Womanhood: *The Bluest Eye* and *Sula*" by Jan Furman from *Toni Morrison's Fiction* by Jan Furman. © 1996 by the University of South Carolina Press.

"The Politics of Abuse: The Traumatized Child in Toni Morrison's *The Bluest Eye* and Marguerite Duras' *The Vice-Consul* by Laurie Vickroy from *Mosaic* 29:2 (June 1996): 91–110. © 1996 Mosaic.

"M'Dear's Deductive Methodology" by James A. Wren from *The Explicator* 55:3 (Spring 1997): 172–6. © 1997 Helen Dwight Reid Educational Foundation.

"When Home Fails to Nurture the Self: The Tragedy of Being Homeless at Home" by Leester Thomas from *The Western Journal of Black Studies* 21:1 (Spring 1997): 51–59. © 1997 Washington State University Press.

"Naming Invisible Authority: Toni Morrison's Covert Letter to Ralph Ellison" by John N. Duvall from *Studies in American Fiction* 25:2 (Autumn 1997): 241–54. © 1997 Northeastern University.

Index